Dangerous
Water

Other Books
by Ron Powers

Newscasters: the News Business as Show Business

Face Value (a Novel)

Toot-Toot-Tootsie, Good-Bye (a Novel)

SuperTube: The Rise of Television Sports

White Town Drowsing: Journeys to Hannibal

Far from Home: Life and Loss in Two American Towns

*The Beast, the Eunuch and the Glass-Eyed Child:
Television in the 80's*

The Cruel Radiance: Notes of a Prosewriter in a Visual Age

Dangerous Water

A Biography of the Boy Who Became Mark Twain

RON POWERS

DA CAPO PRESS

Cataloging-in-Publication data for this book is available from the Library of Congress.

First Da Capo Press edition 2001
ISBN 0–306–81086–7

Published by Da Capo Press
A Member of the Perseus Books Group
http://www.dacapopress.com

Da Capo Press books are available at special discounts for bulk purchases in the U.S. by
corporations, institutions, and other organizations. For more information, please contact
the Special Markets Department at the Perseus Books Group, 11 Cambridge Center,
Cambridge, MA 02142, or call (617) 252-5298.

1 2 3 4 5 6 7 8 9 10—05 04 03 02 01

CONTENTS

ACKNOWLEDGMENTS

I extend my thanks to Donald Fehr of Basic Books for championing this book and steering it to publication; to Charles Flowers for his scrupulous, instructive editorial reading of the manuscript; to David Robinson for his rigorous copyediting; and to Henry Sweets, curator of the Mark Twain Museum in Hannibal, for playing Bixby to my Cub Pilot and guiding me along the troublesome river of historic accuracy. Any remaining scrapes against snags (although, Sawyerlike, I would like to lay them off to some Sid) are my own fault.

For stimulating and exhortive conversation about Samuel L. Clemens, I am grateful to David McCullough and to Professors Stephen Donadio and Jay Parini of Middlebury College.

Jim Hornfischer provided superb representation at a critical time. To Geri Thoma, who worked tirelessly and ably on my behalf, I offer many thanks and much esteem.

I am grateful to Patricia LaPointe of the Memphis Public Library for her cooperation in providing newspaper accounts of the wreck of the *Pennsylvania* on the Mississippi River on June 13, 1858, and its aftermath, and to the St. Louis *Post-Dispatch* for supplying copies of reporter Robertus Love's coverage of Mark Twain's final visit to Hannibal in May 1902.

And once again I warmly thank my wife, Honoree Fleming, Ph.D., for helping me believe that this idea was worth the journey—and for forgiving Sam for what he wrote about the microbes.

One

"I was young and foolish then;
now I am old and foolisher."

On October 15, 1900, in the twilit moments of the shifting century he had dissected in his books and embodied in his life, Mark Twain reemerged as from a long, dark dream into the welcoming uproar of his native America.

He had been abroad in auto-exile, save for brief visits, for nearly ten years. It had been the most public of privations, this self-inflicted banishment of his. The newspapers had chronicled his plunge from literary eminence into bankruptcy; Europe had welcomed him and his family as interesting fugitives, fallen literary royalty of an obverse kind. Then the western world had watched him mount an obsessive journey around it, lecturing in Ceylon and South Africa and other exotic lands to earn his way out of his $100,000 debt. Recovering in Guildford, England, at the end of that year-long ordeal, he had suffered a thunderclap of nearly unendurable grief, a bereavement that would leave him stunned and crazy in the night for the remainder of his life.

For a man predisposed to brood on the unstable borders between apparent reality and the cataclysmic demimonde of dreams, the past decade must have seemed at times like a sleep-induced psychosis; indeed Twain, the childhood sleepwalker, had written compulsively in those years on the theme of dreams as storm-tossed voyages that engulfed and drowned the dreamer. But now he had awakened into a kind of dawn, his ship in the harbor, his dreamvoyage over at last. The welcoming shock of American light bade fair to bathe him for the remainder of his days. Unless of course the light was beckoning him into the refuge of some new oblivion.

There was nothing to do but move toward it. And so on this gusty October Monday, Twain at sixty-four made his way down the crowded gangplank of the *Minnehaha*, off the Atlantic seas from London, docked in New York harbor.

The world was quietly shifting from one order of consciousness to the next. Sigmund Freud's *The Interpretation of Dreams* had been published that year. (No record exists that the dream-obsessed Twain read that work, but Freud was aware of Twain, and regarded his work as the leading example of the "highest" form of humor.) Albert Einstein graduated from Polytechnic Institute of Zürich, Switzerland— his great theory, completed fifteen years in the future, would give scientific weight to Twain's metaphysical anarchies. Queen Victoria neared her demise—her era had constrained Mark Twain's sexual candor but not his gleeful truant wit.

Twain, who had confessed in his notebook that the twentieth century was a stranger to him (he was to be, in ways he would not live to appreciate, among its most profound prophets), was walking down the gangplank toward it.

"Twain" of course was the necessary artifice, the carefully manufactured persona that the wary man inside kept wrapped ever more tightly about him in public; soon it was to bloom full and white as the new century's first pop-cultural icon. The horde on the pier recognized the image at once, and the outcry was worshipful and noisy. All the press were there, his old jackleg calling. They'd taunted him with their sarcasms before; had him destitute, even reported him dead just three years earlier ("an exaggeration," he'd replied famously); but now they were here to yell out questions and jot dutiful notes. The next day they would tell the nation that "Mark Twain Comes Home," and would call him "the bravest author in all literature" and "the Hero as Man of Letters," and compare him to Walter Scott,[1] a writer he detested, but the fellows meant it kindly; let it go. He put a ruddy smile on his face for the straw-hat reporters and "showed off" a little bit and soon had them laughing and fawning (for they, as Twain himself might have written it, were "showing off" too).

A master mesmerizer of lecture-hall audiences, Twain treated the newsmen to a vintage performance. His gray-blue eagle eyes glinting, he struck a pose of careless élan that seemed magically to banish the darkness of his recent past. No trace of pathos or grief or humiliation tarnished his playful indulgence.

"Never looked better, was in splendid humor," the *New York Times* assured its readers the following day. "As soon as the author had finished with the salutations of his friends, he was surrounded by a large number of newspaper men and asked for a story of what he had been doing during all the nine years of his absence from his native land."

Genially, as his wife and two surviving daughters looked on, Twain obliged.

"Now, that is a long story, but I suppose I must give you something, even if it is in a condensed form," he drawled.[2] And he began to delight the reporters, this small narrow-shouldered man with the famous tangled eyebrows and heraldic mustache, with fine summonings of Frankfort and the Riviera and Aix-les-Bains.

"Most of 1892 I spent at Florence, where I rented a home. While there I wrote *Joan of Arc* and finished up *Pudd'nhead Wilson*. For the next two years I was in France. I can't speak French yet . . . "

Expansively, in the wash of laughter, he continued to embroider the contours of a fabulous idyll.

"In the spring of 1895 I came to the United States for a brief stay, crossing the continent from New York to San Francisco, lecturing every night. In October of that year I sailed from Vancouver for Sydney, where I lectured, or, more properly speaking, gave readings from my works to the English-speaking people. I also visited Tasmania and New Zealand . . . "

He conjured India for them: Bombay and Calcutta. He told them of his arrival at Delagoa Bay, South Africa, in April 1896. He limned Kimberly, of the fabulous diamond mines (the source of an old private obsession of Clemens's), and Johannesburg and Cape Town, and of his daring contacts with some principals of the Boer War.

"I met Oom Paul,*" he casually disclosed, and told them the great Transvaal patriot conformed to his popular image—"that beard, frock coat, pipe, and everything else. The picture is a true likeness." Indifferent to the transient squabbles that divide mankind, he had visited Paul's imperialist enemies, the famous

---

*Stephanus Johannes Paulus Kruger, the South African leader of the earlier Boer rebellion against the British in 1880; in 1900 the fiercely nationalist president of the Transvaal Republic.

Jameson raiders,* in their jail. "I told them of the advantages of being in jail. 'This jail is as good as any other,' I said, 'and besides, being in jail has its advantages. A lot of great men have been in jail. If Bunyan had not been put in jail, he would never have written *Pilgrim's Progress*. Then the jail is responsible for *Don Quixote*. So you see being in jail is not so bad, after all.' Finally I told them that they ought to remember that many great men go through life without ever having been in a jail."

All this time, Twain told the reporters, his family had been with him. After their adventures in Cape Town they had taken a steamer for Southampton. "On arriving in England we went to Guildford, where I took a furnished house, remaining two months, after which for ten months our home was in London. All this time I was lecturing, reading, or working hard in other ways, writing magazine stories and doing other literary work."

There followed some further badinage: He was "absolutely unable" to speak of his plans; he was, "as near as I can find out, an anti-imperialist"; he was a political Mugwump and didn't know whom he intended to vote for, he'd have to look over the field; yet he'd remained a taxpaying citizen of the United States throughout his nine-year absence; and with those credentials he could run for President, couldn't he?—and if that were so, "why, then, I am a candidate for President!"

Grateful chuckles over this shaft of the famous Twainian foolery; and now one of the more awestruck newsmen made bold to invoke a topic of nearly celestial magnitude—Mark Twain's rumored autobiography "that is to be published 100 years hence."

---

*Participants in an abortive invasion, in December 1895, of Kruger's republic, led by Sir Leander Starr Jameson at the behest of the British empire-builder Cecil Rhodes.

A practiced pause from the great man for effect, and then: "It is true I am writing it."

"That's not a joke, is it?"

A setup for a set-piece witticism, and Twain grabbed it.

"No; I said it seriously; that's why they take it as a joke. You know, I never told the truth in my life that someone didn't say I was lying, while, on the other hand, I never told a lie that somebody didn't take it as fact."

Laughter all around; and then another questioner, apparently swept away in the lovestruck mood of the moment, cried out: "Well, it's not wrong, anyway, to tell a lie sometimes, is it?"

"That's right, exactly right!" Mark Twain exclaimed. "If you can disseminate facts by telling the truth, why that's the way to do it, and if you can't except by doing a little lying, well, that's all right, too isn't it? I do it."

With that the famous writer gave a pleasant nod to the genuflecting newsmen and, allowing himself to be swept up by an entourage of friends and family, strolled off, the *New York Times* reported, "to locate his baggage."[3]

He strolled, in fact, into an America that wanted to carry his baggage for him, and that would garland him with honors and banquets and worshipful attention for the remaining ten years of his life. Within weeks of his return, his slight, shuffling figure was drawing stares and salutations in theaters and restaurants and the swarm of Fifth Avenue; he was the first public celebrity in a new century destined to be saturated with them. He manipulated his visibility with the same shrewdness that he'd summoned to manipulate lecture-hall audiences as a kind of proto-rock star of the 1870s; a new wardrobe of six white broadcloth suits to match his white mane and mustache, and worn in all seasons and for virtually all occasions, offered the world's rotogravure sections a distinctive image. He loved white, but his true taste was more than half a century ahead of its time; its descriptive term, yet uninvented, was "psychedelic." "I would like to dress in a loose and flowing costume made all of silks and velvets," he remarked in 1906, "resplendent with all the stunning dyes of the rainbow, and so would every sane man I have ever known; but none of us dares to venture it."[4]

A publishing friend soon said of him: "I doubt if there is another man on earth whose name is more familiar." Common people, the folks who had bought his subscription books from door-to-door salesmen and who now bought the daily papers, felt at ease stopping him and chatting him up. Porters rushed to grab his bags when he traveled. At railroad stations the conductors solemnly held up express trains while Mark Twain relieved himself in the Gents room.

The old rivertown urchin strutted among the gods of his time. His friendships had already touched the giants of the nineteenth century— Ulysses S. Grant, Whitman, and Emerson among them. Now they expanded to embrace the coming titans of the twentieth. Two months after his return, Twain introduced the twenty-six-year-old Winston Churchill to his first American lecture audience at the Waldorf-Astoria. As the decade progressed he would dine at President Theodore Roosevelt's White House and hobnob with the future President Woodrow Wilson in Bermuda; he would gossip and drink with Andrew Carnegie; he would greet the Russian revolutionary Maxim Gorky with Jane Addams and Finley Peter Dunne; he would have Helen Keller to dinner.

By 1902 his fortune was fully restored: His income exceeded $100,000. In that year he made a triumphal final visit out west to Hannibal, Missouri, the Mississippi rivertown of his boyhood and the seedbed of his richest imaginings. He posed for photographs by the doorway of the little whiteframe house on Hill Street where the Clemenses had lived for a time, and thus consecrated it. A century later that same dwarfish house, propped upright with reinforcing dowels and framed in the background by a billboard advertising "Mark Twain Fried Chicken," stood as an official shrine to his memory.

Back East, his evenings were lit by banquet-hall chandeliers; oysters and champagne became his regular bill of fare. In 1905 he was toasted at a seventieth-birthday banquet at Delmonico's that included, among its guests, Willa Cather and Emily Post. ("If you find you can't make seventy by any but an uncomfortable road," he told the celebrants, "don't you go." It was received as a witticism.) Two years later at Oxford he received an honorary doctorate of letters and met King Edward VII. (The Queen scolded him to keep his hat on, for fear of him catching cold.) He also met Sir James Barrie, of *Peter Pan* fame, and George Bernard Shaw, who called him "by far the greatest American writer."

William Dean Howells, the editor of *The Atlantic* who was his lifelong friend and ardent reviewer, would exalt him as "the Lincoln of our literature," and gave him a nickname that another blazing icon of the culture would one day claim: "The King."

And yet this King was far from the serene "whited sepulchre" that he seemed to the world. Beneath his calculated outer wrappings, the small figure descending the *Minnehaha* gangplank was a Mysterious Stranger, alienated and dream-driven, and the glint in his eye was not public amusement but private fury. A great dark river raged out of control through the vast channels of his being, a river that roiled against the foundations of his past, his friendships, his art; against mankind, against fate, against the Christian God, and against the fat and grasping nation that even now rushed out dumbly to worship him.

A cultural treasure he might have been; but the Mark Twain reentering America at the opening of the twentieth century had hardened as well into a kind of cultural Antichrist. The manuscripts in his trunk, and the others yet unwritten in his head, would swell against and seek to drown the tinny pieties that his doting host culture held dear, or thought it did.

His performance with the welcoming reporters had established the watershed between his public and private selves. He hadn't lied to them exactly, but he had not disseminated all the facts by telling the truth, either. The pierside interview had amounted to a serenely promiscuous gilding, if not an outright revision, of inner reality. The decade and a half just concluded had been progressively disheartening for Samuel Clemens; the past ten years had all but wrecked his health and the most recent five had pushed him to the borders of insanity.

The press—the world—knew some of this, but by no means all. And in a way peculiar to Mark Twain's reputation available through his life and his works, the darker dimensions lay, and would remain lying, concealed in plain sight: available as evidence in his novels and essays and memoirs, but discounted somehow, against the blinding glosses of the man himself and the encircling custodians of his legacy.

Europe had been a refuge, a continent of sanctuary and cheap lodging where he had fled with his wife Olivia and his daughters Jean and Clara. (Elegant Susy, his eldest, most literary and most adored daughter, had stayed behind to pursue her education at Bryn Mawr.)

A catastrophic loss of fortune had driven him abroad; the fortune he had earned as author of celebrated travel books and founder of the Tom Sawyer/Huckleberry Finn mythos. He'd squandered that wealth by increments during the 1880s through irrational, addictive investments in publishing and in the demonically unworkable Paige typesetting machine. By 1889, Clemens's unrecovered payouts to the eccentric putterer James W. Paige—whose invention he'd imagined would make him a multimillionaire—had exceeded $150,000.

Tortured with rheumatism (his writing arm nearly useless) and frantic with financial anxiety, Clemens closed down his extravagant house in Hartford in the spring of 1891. He dismissed the servants and sold off many of the lavish furnishings accumulated over seventeen legendary years as the presiding genius of a storied literary/social enclave that included Charles Dudley Warner and Harriet Beecher Stowe. In June 1891 he and the family left America—first for Aix-les-Bains, France, and then on to Germany and Italy and a spacious but inexpensive villa in the hills above Florence.

There he had indeed written much of *Joan of Arc* and finished up *Pudd'nhead Wilson,* as he'd blandly informed the reporters, but the process had been at once more nakedly commercial and more heroic than he'd let on. In Aix-les-Bains, preoccupied with debt, he had labored through his arm pains, trying to generate cash through travel journalism, even switching to his left hand when the agony of motion grew unbearable. That winter an attack of influenza had left him with a permanently damaged lung. It would be yet more months before his inflamed joints allowed him to grasp a pen with his right hand. [5]

His output at Florence had been physically prodigious for a man approaching sixty and nursing an afflicted writing arm: nearly two thousand manuscript pages in something under six months. Artistically, it yawed wildly, in quality and intent, forking the polarities of his nature. *Personal Recollections of Joan of Arc,* stilted and unctuous, would rank among the quaintest of his novels; he wrote it out of an old clinging piety (toward women, if not God) and perhaps a sense of determinism—as a fifteen-year-old boy in Hannibal, he'd been brushed by a windblown page from a Joan of Arc history, and it had awakened his lifelong absorption in medieval life. He had modeled St. Joan's traits upon his prim daughter Susy, had read aloud from it sonorously at every opportunity, and had thought at first to have it published as an anonymous gift of cultural uplift.

Pudd'nhead Wilson, which would prove his last novel of any merit, unsheathed his colder, more modern vision. Begun as a playful piece of mixed-identity farce, it had matured into a flawed but unrelenting satire of man's flattened moral state and the instability of the human self.

"For the next two years I was in France," he'd told the reporters, and wisecracked, "I can't speak French yet . . . "

The little jest masked a season of ghastly anxiety. Speaking French was scarcely the point. Sam Clemens spent large draughts of that period sailing between Europe and America. He made eight crossings, begging loans and investments to salvage his failing publishing enterprise, Charles L. Webster & Co., and, of course, to feed the curse of the Paige typesetter.

In May 1894 Clemens slunk back across the Atlantic to his exiled family in humiliation. Magazine installments of *Pudd'nhead Wilson* were rekindling a national admiration for him as a literary light, but his finances had now slipped beyond his control. He arrived back in Paris a declared bankrupt, his slide into irretrievable poverty being averted by the guidance of an admiring captain of Standard Oil named Henry Huttleston Rogers. Still he hoped obsessively that Paige could somehow stanch the typesetter's breakdowns. When that hope collapsed for good early in 1895, Clemens could see nothing but failure in himself. Life was a dream from which he could not awaken.

"In the spring of 1895 I came to the United States for a brief stay, crossing the continent from New York to San Francisco, lecturing every night . . . "

No, not San Francisco. He'd ended up swinging well north of California, which he'd departed a generation before, and into British Columbia. "San Francisco" was a typically Twainian mistake of memory, or a mixing of memory and desire. He had wanted to include his old "heaven-on-the-half-shell" city of bygone newspapering days on this transcontinental barnstorm, but was talked out of it by his agent.

In every other respect, the remark was singular for its understatement: Mark Twain's lecturing sweep of the United States in the summer of 1895, just months after a near physical collapse, was the first leg of the protean round-the-world platform tour—Livy and Clara in tow—on which (combined with "Following the Equator," his literary accounting of it) he earned the money to pay back his creditors one hundred cents on the dollar. This was the odyssey that allowed him finally to regain financial and spiritual control of his life, and the world recognized it for the heroic gesture it was. As the Clemenses made ready to sail the Pacific from Victoria, B.C., one newspaper sent them off with this salute:

> At the age of sixty years Mark Twain manfully faces four [sic] years of the hardest labor to provide money, not for his comforts nor for a heritage to descendants, but to pay debts contracted by a firm of which he was a member . . .
>
> Without any appeal for sympathy or any suggestion of assistance, keeping away from pathos and avoiding pity,

this man of stern honor begins in his old age the same struggle as he once before made.[6]

Back in England in August 1896, in the house at Guildford where he was staying alone, Clemens received a cable telling him: "Susy was peacefully released to-day." Only twenty-four, she had died of meningitis back home, in the old family house at Hartford.

Neither Sam nor Olivia Clemens ever stopped suffering the ache of that loss. Sam tortured himself by grasping at artifacts of her; he read and reread the biography she had begun of him when she was thirteen. ("He has the mind of an author exactly," one passage had gone, "some of the simplest things he can't understand."[7]) An entry in his own great disheveled memoir, dictated shortly before his death, cried out: "It is one of the mysteries of nature that a man, all unprepared, can receive a thunder-stroke like that and live."[8]

This, then, was the accounting beneath the accounting; the essence of the dark twin concealed beneath the amiable lion of American letters who disembarked from the *Minnehaha* in New York harbor on October 15, 1900. Mark Twain, the figure in white, would reign over his mechanizing, urbanizing culture almost as a living statue through the new century's ambiguous first decade—a comforting symbol of the accelerating nation's virtue, its unbroken connection with its arcadian, small-town (in certain ways feudal) past. A self-"petrification," to use a favorite term of Twain's—one he employed only in the service of undeviating contempt.

Unobserved by the enveloping entourage of friends and family was the man entire—the dream-ridden, river-tossed world wanderer out of the old Interior, a purer product of America in his gorgeous flaws and terrible genius than most of his celebrants would ever want to consider. His flaws were to some extent the flaws of the nation: exploitative appetite, an irreducible nativism that endured despite his travels, an uncritical faith in technical progress and the perfectability of man's nature via the machine. As a writer he had seldom shown concern for the received aesthetic demands of his craft. Form inconvenienced him; bother form; a Twain book, especially a Twain novel, went drifting like a river, from change to change, until it ended. Likewise consistency of tone, or consistency of anything: He would be uproarious one minute, maudlin the next, turgidly "historical" the moment after that, and then the writerly voice might disappear utterly into a Cheshire smile of reportage. The characters in his novels could be shockingly cardboard, grown-up ones especially and grown-up females most especially of all. In this, too, he was distinctly American; form, the nuances of character and the edgy implications of gender were worse than precious; they were downright French.

But his genius was distinctly American as well, the raw, improvising genius of a rich new culture in eruption, and that genius lay partly in his way of either adjusting his flaws to accommodate reality, or else melding them into the service of his art. His self-liberation from high European style (except when he was lampooning it) gave him room to write U.S. English in as pristine and stripped-down a way as it had ever been written, especially when he was replicating speech; and this in turn made him the fountainhead of modern U.S. literature.

His most characteristic mode—humor in its many varieties—betrayed his American stamp more than anything else. Twain had lived long enough to have experienced New World humor in its still-forming, unconsecrated state, and in that state it was seldom merely funny; more often it was a densely accumulating series of myths and metaphors for rationalizing chaos. Men and women of the frontier had traded in humorous archetypes—a kind of diplomatic folk-language—in order to understand and safely negotiate the backwoods country's extreme religiosity, its uncontrollable violence, and the many deadly gradations between the two. More than one commentator remarked on Twain's preternatural deadpan; his lecture audiences were mesmerized into hysterics by it, and some people thought he actually never spoke or wrote in deliberate jest at all. "He was an American; that is, an unfathomably solemn man," ventured G.K. Chesterton,[9] who also found him "serious to the point of madness." Even his unfailing booster Howells cited "the profoundly serious, the almost tragical strain"[10] that was the fundamental tone of the Southwestern culture from which Twain sprang. Still, the man could get a laugh.

But now as Twain returned scarred and grieving to America, the locus of his humor had shifted to a place outside the limits of his own petrifying canon. "For several years I have been intending to stop writing for print as soon as I could afford it. At last I can afford it," he had written to Howells while still in England. And while he would not abandon "for print" entirely, he plunged now with avidity into his newly defined subject-matter. "It is under way now, & it *is* a luxury!" he informed Howells, "an intellectual drunk . . ."[11]

W. D. Howells knew "Clemens" (as he always insisted on calling him) for forty-six years. He probably knew Mark Twain better than any other human being, with the possible exception of Olivia. Among the most fundamental and unqualified pronouncements Howells would ever make was that his friend "had the soul of a boy." (Olivia would seem to have agreed—her pet name for her husband was "Youth.")

Now, it seemed, the aging boy's subject-matter, the substance of his intellectual drunk, was to be man; was to be mankind; was to be the loss of Mark Twain's pride and respect for mankind.

He wrote furiously now out of a hot dark private place, where men are trapped on monstrous voyages inside drops of rainwater; where angels mock the works of a conscienceless God (whose motto read, "Let no innocent person escape"); where mankind's "Moral Sense" is shown inferior to the base instincts of animals; where the human hope of free will is exposed as a sham and men are nothing more than self-deceiving machines; where a malign Source of All Etiquette can exterminate the house of Baasha for the crime of pissing against the wall. This new sulfurous strain of humor knew no limits of blasphemy whatsoever: it even imagined the game of baseball as a sport in which the batsman, "in the fullness of time," "did lay the Umpire dead," and then was himself annihilated by a beanball that cracked his skull.[12]

No more the self-kidding of his old California newspapering days, no more the indulgent manners-and-morals humor of the great set pieces in the travel books, no more the brilliant explosions of rendered vernacular, no more the containable naughtiness of his immortalizing boyhood novels. (It would still be some decades before the critics pried loose the more subversive visions embedded in those.) His endearing public writings were all behind him now. Ahead lay the full discharge of the pen warmed up in hell.

The world received a sampling of this heat six weeks after Twain's return, after he had settled himself and Livy into a townhouse on West Tenth Street—an area that would become famous among midcentury artists as Greenwich Village. On New Century's Eve, he unveiled what he called "A Salutation Speech from the Nineteenth Century to the

Twentieth taken down in shorthand by Mark Twain" in the December 31 edition of the *New York Herald*:

> I bring you the stately matron named Christendom, returning bedraggled, besmirched and dishonored from pirate raids in Kiao-Chow, Manchuria, South Africa, the Philippines, with her soul full of meanness, her pocket full of boodle and her mouth full of pious hypocrisies. Give her soap and a towel, but hide the looking-glass.

That was for practice. A month later, Twain shocked his public by unleashing all, concerning that subject, that was on his mind. He chose the February *North American Review,* an unassailably stately journal of opinion, for a corrosive assault against American highhandedness in the Far East. Modeled vaguely on Swift's "A Modest Proposal," and laced with ironic allusions to Biblical scripture, "To the Person Sitting in Darkness" mocked the false pieties that had attended the recent coercive demands by United States missionaries upon the Chinese following the Boxer rebellion.* The screed ended with nothing less than an early-century version of a flag-burning: his suggestion that the American flag be repainted black and its field of stars replaced by a skull and crossbones.

---

*The Rev. William Ament of the American Board of Foreign Missions had traveled to China and compelled indemnity payments from the defeated Boxer insurgents who had killed Chinese Christians in an uprising. The Boxers, who had rebelled against the influx of outsiders (particularly Christian missionaries), had been put down by an international expeditionary force. Twain considered the Boxers "China's traduced patriots" and condemned the rapaciousness of the conquering army and the missionaries.

For a while, the creamy banquets and the polemic bursts alternated in an uneasy tension. Luxury and radicalism coexisted—validating the insight of Howells, who called him a theoretical socialist and a practical aristocrat. After moving to a large rented house in fashionable Riverdale in the autumn of 1901, Mark Twain joined the Anti-Imperialist League, which was monitoring the Philippine situation. So did Howells; they both served as vice presidents. Twain threw in with the activist Society of Acorns and helped them turn public opinion against an enclave of rascals from the Tammany Hall machine. Writing to *Harper's Weekly* in 1905 in the voice of Satan, Twain excoriated the philanthropies of John D. Rockefeller as "conscience-money." (This was an especially ticklish stance, given that Rockefeller's Standard Oil colleague, Henry H. Rogers, had recently saved the author from the poorhouse. Perhaps that incongruity was on Twain's mind when an ingratiating friend remarked to him that the Rogers wealth was "tainted," and Twain snapped back: "Yes. 'Tain't yours, and 'tain't mine.")

Such polemical firebursts made a public stir, influencing the political thinking of the decade and creating, temporarily at least, an altered image of Americana's great white father. Yet neither the firebursts (the public ones, anyway) nor the new image was destined to endure. By the time Halley's Comet, which had hovered over his birth in 1835, came round again to reclaim him on April 21, 1910, the overheated old man had slipped back into the comfort of his nation's damp embrace. He died beloved and was laid to rest in one of his white suits—"humorist," aphorist, family patriarch, valiant traveler, enduring poet of American arcadia, American boyhood, unending American summer. Riding the comet into the next world, Mark Twain was still performing, still fooling the press. And still the cultural Antichrist underneath.

All of this might suggest that by the end of his life, Mark Twain had voyaged irretrievably far from the memories and the qualities of temperament that had infused his canonical works: *The Innocents Abroad, Roughing It, Life on the Mississippi,* and especially his signature "boys'" novels, *The Adventures of Tom Sawyer* and *Adventures of Huckleberry Finn.* It might suggest that Twain in the tortured final decade-and-a-half of his life had in some elemental sense ceased being Mark Twain at all, or at least had ceased being the Samuel Langhorne Clemens whose early life—his boyhood and youth in Hannibal, on the great river and in the far western territories—had given Twain his mythic stature and the canonical works their content.

This has remained, roughly, the assumption of many of his readers—and many more of his nonreaders—in the century since his death: that after a sunny, pastoral boyhood in Hannibal ("what began to seem the most memorable boyhood ever lived," in the phrasing of Justin Kaplan[13]), followed by an idyllic, dream-come-true adventure as a Mississippi River steamboat pilot and some prospecting and newspapering exploits in the West, Mark Twain settled in to an extended career as a fond memoirist and novelist, then grew old, grew unaccountably alienated and "bitter," and died. The popular-cultural consensus, especially among the many commercial marketers and theme-park packagers of his image, has been to focus on the sunlit tales and aphorisms of Twain the "humorist," and leave Twain the bewildering dark prophet to his convenient obscurity.

Twain's own inner circle collaborated in this smothering, sterilizing legacy. The chief perpetrators were Clara and his genuflective first biographer and literary executor, Albert Bigelow Paine. To a lesser extent, Twain was muted by his astute and worshipful, but fatally Victorian chum Howells.

Howells, plump and humid, is the least suitable object of blame; without Howells and his passionate effusions stretching across forty years, there might have been no Mark Twain—at least as a sustaining figure in American literature. It was Howells, among the "serious" critics, who had first paid attention to Twain in 1869, Howells who swept the rough-edged westerner into respectability among the New England literary elite. But it was also Howells who gave Twain a discrete nudge now and then regarding the limits of good taste, and it was Howells who in 1883 had sent Twain a strong signal about the suitability of his more searing childhood memories. "Don't let anyone see those passages,"[14] he implored his friend about a particularly morbid anecdote in the manuscript of Orion Clemens's autobiography—which went unpublished and eventually was lost.

Clara was the most vigilant suppressor of her father's unbridled imaginings. The middle of the three daughters, and not the favorite, she was the last to survive her father and influenced his legacy until her own death at eighty-eight in 1962. She had trained for a career in music, excelling at voice and the piano, but caring for her invalid mother, her aging icon of a father and her epileptic sister Jean had nearly broken her—she'd repaired to a sanitorium in 1904 after her mother's death. Recovering, she took on the role of managing her father's household and, more tellingly, his wholesome "humorist" image. (She'd found his taste in white suits vulgar.) After Twain's death, Clara hovered over the process of any book published about him, suppressing photos she didn't like (including some of her dad with members of his "Angelfish" club) and the entire contents of *Letters from the Earth* until after her own death.

Clara found a malleable ally in the fastidious Paine. A dapper, starch-collared Iowan, sometime photographer, and writer of children's books, Paine had attached himself to the old writer after having met him several times in the early 1900s, including the seventieth birthday fete at Delmonico's. In 1906 he boldly sought and immediately received Twain's permission to write his biography. From that time until the end, Paine virtually merged his identity with Twain's, indulging him at billiards, moving his own family into the author's house, even going so far as to retrace the author's voyage to the Holy Land that had resulted in *The Innocents Abroad.*

As Paine scrutinized his subject, Clara scrutinized Paine. She would make sure that this biographer betrayed no hint of her father's dark side. In the event, there was no serious conflict; the two of them were equally determined to enforce a sanitized, sentimental perception of Twain that had no place for satanic angels, hellacious dreamvoyages, degraded Moral Senses, or pissing against the wall.

Paine's three-volume, half-million-word study, *Mark Twain, a Biography: The Personal and Literary Life of Samuel Langhorne Clemens,* was published in 1912. Exhaustive and valuable in many ways, it fatally suppressed the brimstone. And Paine's damage to his subject's legacy extended well beyond his prim and proper biography. As literary executor, he maintained control of those unpublished papers for a crucial quarter-century after Twain's death. His selections of material for publication were invariably skewed by his and Clara's notions of propriety. More unforgivably still, Paine actually meddled in the work—abridging Twain's letters, even rewriting (and bowdlerizing) passages of "The Mysterious Stranger" (published in 1916) without disclosing his interventions.

But there was yet a final culprit in the expunging of Mark Twain's savage prophecies: Twain. He had always warred within himself over his outlaw impulses—the Connecticut literary gent contending with the western roughneck—and he'd always shown a docile streak in regard to the opinions of refined women, including Livy and the imposing Mrs. Fairbanks* of his first great literary adventure. And now, in his dotage and his loneliness, the old "whited sepulchre" had grown fond of all the public petting, the ribbons and the champagne and oysters that came his way. "My holiday will consist of writing two books," he had speculated to Howells in that letter from London of 1899—by "holiday," he meant the remainder of his life—"simply for the private pleasure of writing. One of them will not be published at all; the other written for the remote posterity of a hundred years hence."[15] (This last was the source of the newsman's awed question at New York harbor.) Much of the work he withheld from publication over the ensuing years was withheld out of a simple wish not to shock genteel society. There was more than a bit of Victorian in Mark Twain, too.

And thus it was that America in the last years of its greatest author's life and the first decades after his death never truly discovered Twain—certainly not in the full range of his disputatious philosophies, his anti-imperialist politics, his fiercely wounded religious dissent. Nor did the country discover the distinctly American obsessions and experiences that fueled these hidden reservoirs. To a significant extent, America has not discovered Twain since.

Had Mark Twain completed his unfinished manuscripts, and published the unpublished ones (the mediocre work along with the best), his reading public might not have been quite so eager to canonize

---

*Mark Twain had met Mary Mason Fairbanks aboard the *Quaker City*, bound for the Holy Land, in 1867. The older woman, wife of a Cleveland newspaper publisher, had cast a spell on the young journalist. He corresponded with her for years, and is believed to have modified some of his writing to satisfy her notions of decorum.

him—to "petrify" him. But it might have been more eager to read him freshly, critically, seriously, and with an eye toward the onrushing new century that always lay at the edges of the late work.

The perspective of nearly one hundred years—the "century hence" that the pierside reporter so reverently invoked—has only amplified the discordant profundity of Twain's final movement. And it has opened up a clearer vision of the author's long voyage outward from Arcadia into fallen Eden, and of his imaginative return.

This much, certainly, is clear: Twain had not ceased being Twain in those final years of his burning light and darkest shadow. The evidence of his own work and letters shows that the reverse was more likely the case: that in this epoch he reached continually back toward distant formative memory and toward the fictional archetypes he had created out of that memory. His "departures" into new themes and forms were not departures at all; rather, they were concentrated re-workings of his early impulses. These impulses in turn were deeply resonant with what happened to Clemens as a boy and as a young man.

In his long disheveled rummagings after his return from Europe and the brink of madness, Twain inventoried his past incessantly. He surrendered himself more abjectly to it than at any time in his adult life, save that period from about 1874 through 1883, when he'd first turned from travel books, business, and Connecticut gentility to that great stream of his youthful consciousness.

He remembered his dead siblings and revisited the guilt of transgressions against them unforgiven. He recalled old sweethearts, often with photographic clarity of the moments of final partings. His manuscript papers revealed, posthumously, that he had carried inside his head a remarkably detailed mythic version of his boyhood Hannibal,

populated with some 168 inhabitants. His factual recall of their exis-
tences, or most of them, could be verified by independent checking.*

He reinvoked Tom and Huck and Jim time and again, and thrust
them into new contexts, new tensions with the changing times he lived
in. As early as 1891 he imagined them as old men; he imagined Huck
returning to "St. Petersburg" at sixty, insane, searching pathetically for
his old friends and beholding Tom, wandering in at last, just like old
times, but now "both are desolate, life has been a failure, all that was
lovable, all that was beautiful is under mold. They die together."[16]

These images, and their resonance with the changing nation, were
permanently imprinted in the mind of the man who called himself
Mark Twain. Always, for him, there was the Emersonian town of his
origins. Always, for him, there was the godlike river. Always, for him,
and always renewing itself in equal measures of hope and perfidy,
there was the West.

---

*As Walter Blair did with the fragmentary notes called "Villagers of 1840–3,"
which Blair included in *Mark Twain's Hannibal, Huck & Tom* (Berkeley and Los An-
geles: University of California Press, 1969).

Two

"My parents removed to Missouri in the early thirties;
I do not remember just when, for I was not born then
and cared nothing for such things."

He was conceived heading west. Very likely, he was conceived aboard a westward-steaming riverboat.

His people had been moving west forever, it seemed; the old fugitive passage of fallen gentry—England to Virginia; then, a generation or so later, up over the Alleghenies and then across the Cumberlands and then God knew where, just following the Louisiana Purchase farther into the rattlesnake wilderness. Floating always in a tinted mist of magnificent dreams—as Twain was to say about a second cousin of his—and rarely destined to live them out.

His grandfather Samuel was a Virginian born in the year of the Boston Massacre; he was five when America declared itself independent of Britain in 1776. He married in 1797, and met with early misfortune, typical of the line. The tale of it (drenched in foreshadowings, abrupt death, and layered consequences) left its imprint on the boy. This Samuel B. Clemens had sold his Virginia farm in 1803, the year of Thomas Jefferson's big Purchase, and crossed the mountains into what would become West Virginia. He took with him his wife, a Quaker woman named Pamela, and the first four of their five children. John Marshall was the eldest, named in honor of the new nation's first Chief Justice. A later boy, who disappears from all accountings, was for some reason or another named Hannibal.

Samuel B. Clemens was a true son of the new republic. A yeoman farmer who wrote poetry, he believed in the life of public service and got himself named commissioner of revenue for Mason County when it was organized. He seems to have had the kind of faith in the embryonic nation that Tocqueville noticed as representative: "a lively faith in the perfectability of man"; in the land itself as "a land of wonders, in which everything is in constant motion and every change seems an improvement."[1] The "land of wonders" killed him, however. One morning in the autumn of 1805, he got up before dawn and headed over to a hillside spot where some people were raising a log cabin for a new settler. Samuel wedged himself behind a heavy log and started to push it uphill. Somehow he lost his footing on the morning dew. The log slipped backwards and battered him back downhill and crushed him to death against a tree stump. Samuel B. Clemens was thirty-five; John Marshall seven. When he told his own children the story of that day, he would always add that his father had not kissed him goodbye before he left the house, as he usually did. A paramount trait of John Marshall Clemens, his son Sam later recalled, was his helplessness at physical affection for his wife and children. The only time young Samuel Langhorne ever saw his father and mother kiss, he wrote, was at the deathbed of his brother Ben.

Mark Twain would inherit something of his grandfather's faith in the new nation, in wonders, perfectibility, something better tomorrow. But Tocqueville also observed that he knew of no country "where the love of money has taken stronger hold on the affections of men . . . "[2] And that would be the log that would come barreling down on upward-pushing Twain.

The dream of perfectability, and wonders, remained elusive for the surviving family members after Samuel's death. The widow Pamela hauled her five children on farther west, into Kentucky, where she married an old suitor named Simon Hancock in May 1809, three months after Lincoln was born. Simon fathered three more children with Pamela, provided for her other five, and was deeply touched by the experience of fatherhood. Touched for $884.38, by his own calculation. Years later he presented a bill to each of the children to cover his expenses bringing them up. John Marshall's read: "Support of Marshall Clemens three years at twenty dollars per year, $60.00."[3]

John Marshall's son Sam paid close and shrewd attention to all the nuances of the family's evolving history—those which he could sense for himself, and those he heard. The nuances of the family tales churned in his memory across the decades; his needful imagination shaped and reshaped them into an onflowing story.

More than half a century into his adulthood, in Switzerland in 1897, as he composed his "Villagers of 1840–3" sketches without recourse to notes or documentation, Mark Twain remembered a certain Hannibal character named Judge Carpenter. At once an intimidating and pathetic figure, he had married his wife Joanna in Kentucky back in 1823, and they'd had a number of children, but the union was hollow at its core: "She married him to spite young Dr. Ray, to whom she was engaged, and who wouldn't go to a neighboring town, 9 miles, in the short hours of the night, to bring her home from a ball."[4]

The family had "removed" a couple of times, finally settling in "St P" in 1838. There, something horrid had happened involving the small children; Twain described it, then added a sentence that alluded to another memory, unstated in the sketches as yet: "The case of memorable treachery."[5]

Twain recalled Judge Carpenter as stern, unsmiling, unaffectionate. "Had found out he had been married to spite another man. Silent, austere, of perfect probity and high principle; ungentle of manner toward his children . . . never punished them—a look was enough, and more than enough."[6]

This Judge Carpenter never managed to rise above hard times; in fact a double-crossing by a presumed friend pauperized him. As for religion, "It was remembered that he went to church—once; never again. . . . What his notions about religion were, no one knew."[7]

Carpenter's bad luck never turned. He was elected County Judge in 1849, "and at last saw great prosperity before him. But of course caught his death the first day he opened court. He went home with pneumonia, 12 miles, horseback, winter—and in a fortnight was dead."[8]

After a few more doleful lines describing the Judge's deathbed behavior, Twain scrawled a two-word sentence, evidently another memo to himself for further development: *The autopsy*.

Historians have verified that in "Villagers," Mark Twain's memory—which in these later years especially could be treacherous as well as fanciful—was uncannily acute. But in the case of Judge and Joanna Carpenter, no mystery applied. Their names were among the very few that Twain falsified in "Villagers," just as he had falsified Hannibal's name ("St P, for St. Petersburg") in their connection. In reality they were Judge John Marshall Clemens and his wife, Jane.

This is the last and the least adulterated of four identifiable appearances that John Marshall makes in his son's fiction. In the other three he has been recast—rehabilitated—to meet the requirements of the story.

He is the stereotypically noble Squire (later "Judge") Hawkins, backwoods gentleman, in *The Gilded Age*. In this stilted 1873 collaboration with Charles Dudley Warner, Twain's first effort at fiction, the Squire hauls his struggling family from Tennessee to Missouri in search of riches and dies nobly and conveniently halfway through the novel.

His best-known turn is as Judge Thatcher, Becky's father, in *The Adventures of Tom Sawyer,* published in 1876. In a famous set-piece scene of comic manners, he is "the fine, portly, middle-aged gentleman with iron-gray hair" who visits Tom's Sunday School class, his daughter in tow. In the euphoria of his first solo novel, the forty-year-old Twain plays his father mostly (and a bit heavily) for laughs, lampooning the inflated hick dignity a local judge commands by his office:

> The middle-aged man turned out to be a prodigious personage—no less a one than the county judge—altogether the most august creation these children had ever looked upon—and they wondered what kind of material he was made of—and they half wanted to hear him roar, and were half afraid he might, too . . . [9]

Marshall returns eighteen years later, as York Driscoll in *Pudd'nhead Wilson,* again a county judge, icily honorable, "very proud of his old Virginian ancestry."[10] In this incarnation, the Judge is marinated in the restrictive codes and chivalries of the Old South; he is also childless. "To be a gentleman—a gentleman without stain or blemish—was his only religion, and to it he was always faithful."[11] So faithful that near the novel's end he will fight a duel with pistols to avenge a subtle affront to his honor.

The real Judge was not portly and he never fought a duel. In most other respects John Marshall is drawn as his son remembered him. But just as Twain had spared the pierside reporters the more disturbing details of his European odyssey, he took care, in his early writings, to withhold the Judge's more pathetic dimensions. Piety and affectionate comedy formed his early stance—just as it was with the rivertown of his youth, whose labyrinthine depths it took him decades to fully confront.

Only with the passage of years did truer portraiture emerge. With each rendering, each unmasking of comic decoration and protective mercy, Twain reveals a new layer of reckoning with his enigmatic, unapproachable father—a kind of progressive grieving for a figure whose failures created the hard inevitability of his own success. So it was to be with Hannibal as well. By the very facts of his pinched and wandering and foreshortened existence, John Marshall Clemens shaped much of Mark Twain's Americanness—his early poverty, his later dread of it, the velocity of his flight, his constant and ever-increasing ache to return. Necessary ingredients, all, of the post-Civil War archetype that Howells once described as "the man who has risen."

With his father dead, John Marshall began supporting himself by the age of fourteen. He clerked in an iron foundry at Lynchburg, working nights, reading a little when he could. The bad health that would kill him in 1847 was incubated in this hothouse of sleepless labor and anxiety. The terror of poverty drove John Marshall. He'd had in effect no boyhood, nor any humor either, lacunae that would be compensated by his son. He paid off his debts, though: in 1821 he remitted to Simon Hancock the full $884.38 for Simon's raising of Pamela's children.[12]

He had been named for a great lawyer, and a career in the law was the dream Sam and Pamela had tinted for him. He was judge-haunted in a way; the family nourished a myth of noble blood, embodied in Gregory Clement, the London merchant-judge who in 1649 had signed the death-warrant of Charles I.* In Columbia, Kentucky, John found a law firm that would take him on as an apprentice. Eventually he earned a certificate that said he could practice in the Kentucky courts. By this time John Marshall Clemens was a tall, thin young man with a hard gray-eyed stare and short hair combed back tight against his skull. He was edgy and quick to anger, as his famous son would be—"shattered nerves" was the matter-of-fact diagnosis of one local historian[13]—but still, in that rough country, he kept a clean mouth. And in a frontier society of often intense belief, he harbored his doubts about a Christian God.

But he fancied himself a Virginian—that is, a gentleman, another motif he would pass along to his son—and he had a Virginian's bearing, and that self-imposed code of remorseless honesty, even though he would never make a single success in business in his life. John Marshall had inherited his father's progressive instincts; he liked to think in terms of roads and bridges and libraries cutting into all that western wilderness. He would soon purchase an amazing expanse of land in Tennessee amazingly cheap, that would come to be the mocking skull of phantom riches for him and his children. ("It is good to begin life poor; it is good to begin life rich," the aging Twain would write, "these are wholesome; but to begin it *prospectively* rich! The man who has

---

*No conclusive link between Gregory Clement and Samuel Clemens's line was ever established, but the run of fortune has a familiar ring: Gregory himself was beheaded and disemboweled in 1660, a victim of the Restoration.

not experienced it cannot imagine the curse of it."[14]) When the Whigs, that party of cautious booster-gentlemen, formed in 1824, John Marshall declared himself a Whig.

By that time he had a taken a wife. In May of 1823, in Adair County, Kentucky, he married—in effect—the incandescent other half of Mark Twain's famously divided personality.

Jane Lampton was in many ways the feminine version of the son who would in turn render her immortal as Aunt Polly, among several other fictional characters: She was small and red-haired, as Sam would be, with small feet and hands; yet she was a passionate dancer, and her son would be a dancer too. She spoke in the soft, almost mannered drawl that Sam would inherit and use to mesmerize his close-up listeners and his lecture-hall audiences—the drawl that could be mistaken for a drunken slur, and which he once lampooned as "my drawling infirmity of speech."[15] "Sammy's long talk," Jane herself came to call it.[16]

And Jane noticed things. And she had a fierce justice, the residue of her own Quaker heritage. And she was witty and inventive; she could tell a story. And she could carry a grudge. All Sam.

She married John Marshall at twenty, outlived him by forty-three years and bore him seven children without, apparently, taking a great deal of notice of him. Her detachment from him differs in its factual details, but not in its substance, from Twain's accounting in "Villagers." When the two were married in May of 1823—John was a volunteer in her uncle's fire company—Jane was still seething over the departure from Adair County of her true love, one Richard Barrett, who was studying to be a doctor and lived eighteen miles from the Lampton farm. One day in his absent manner he jotted a note to Jane's uncle asking him to drive Jane over there so he could propose to her; the uncle untactfully read the note out loud to Jane. The mortified girl declared she would not and could not go there; the suitor eventually muddled off elsewhere; and Jane Lampton Clemens loved him in absentia for the rest of her life.

The seven Clemens children, on the other hand, suggest that she and John shared the American frontier's blunt relish for conjugal sex. But nothing of this erotic intimacy survived beyond the bedroom door. In the household, John Marshall and Jane treated one another with a distanced, formal courtesy throughout their married life. Friends. Nothing warmer. Grief was the only kissing passion for them.

Mark Twain may have taken many character traits, and anti-traits, from his dark, fierce father. But from his mother he harvested all the ardencies of his genius. He absorbed her wit and her outspokenness (they sparred and bantered constantly through his boyhood), and he learned pity from her, and anger, and the fine-pitched phrasing that can come from anger ("When her pity and indignation was stirred . . . she was the most eloquent person I have heard speak"[17]) and he took on her voracious interest in the world, and everything and everybody in it. He also absorbed from her stories and attitudes a susceptibility to the gravitational pull of the past.

For all the pathos that would eventually accrue to her, Jane was a laughing, dancing, large-hearted woman, emotional and vaguely oc- cult. A storyteller, eloquent in her unschooled native speech; fierce in the face of oppressors, a champion of the dispossessed. Sam tricked her into defending Satan once by encouraging others to heap abuse on the fallen angel until Jane couldn't stand it anymore. She burst out that, well, yes, he was utterly wicked and abandoned, but had he been treated fairly? "Who prays for Satan?"[18] Sam loved that about her. "This Friend of Satan," he called her, admiringly.[19]

Like her husband, Jane Lampton came from a lineage of westering hopefuls with traditions of fallen nobility. Her people claimed blood relationship with the British Lambtons, Earls of Durham, and tried for many years to cash in on the wealth of the Lambton coal interests. These tenuous connections to exalted blood, insisted on by both sides of his scrabbling family, appealed to Twain's sense of irony; but they stirred him as well, and drew him to his repeated themes of claimants, and of royal authority gained and denied by switched identity.

Like her son, Jane clung to old memory, compulsively revisited the past, frequently erased the line between the real and the dream world. It is more accurate to say that Twain was like his charismatic mother in this regard; he was often swept up in his mother's dreams, and he invented versions of his past as richly fanciful as her own.

At eighty-two, living in Keokuk, Iowa, with her son Orion and his wife Mollie, Jane came across what she thought was evidence that Richard Barrett had reemerged from the distant past and was in the vicinity. She'd spotted his name, or what she took to be his name, in a newspaper: an announcement of a convention of old Mississippi Valley settlers being held in a nearby town. At once she demanded that Orion and Mollie take her there.

"My brother's wife was astonished; & represented to her the hardships & fatigues of such a trip," Twain wrote to William Dean Howells. (He had listened to a version of this story during a visit from his sister Pamela, who earlier had been at Keokuk.) But Orion and Mollie relented, he went on:

> They started; & all the way my mother was young again
> with excitement, eagerness, interest, anticipation. They
> reached the town & the hotel. My mother strode with the

same eagerness in her eye & her step, to the counter, & said:

"Is Dr. Barrett of St. Louis, here?"

"No. He was here, but he returned to St Louis this morning."

"Will he come again?"

"No."

My mother turned away, the fire all gone from her, & said, "Let us go home."[20]

In this passage, Mark Twain is not merely reporting an incident that he learned at third hand. (None of the dialogue was conveyed to him; he supplied that in his letter to Howells.) He is clearly living inside it, from Jane Clemens's point of view—acutely aware of mood, stride, language, and the compressed arc of fate, dramatized. It hardly matters, in the end, that none of it may have happened. The entire episode is in fact transcendently murky, an inspired commingling of Jane's addled grasp toward the past and Twain's nearly helpless empathy for it. Richard Barrett seems to have died in 1860.[21] A "Tri-State Old Settler's Association" reunion was indeed held in September 1885—but in Keokuk, not a town distant from there. And yet the fiction that Mark Twain constructed, no doubt half-believing it, from this shifting field of facts shows him in a moment of deeply characteristic truth: the truth of his mother's lifelong thrall to pathos and nostalgia; the truth of his own identification with that; and the mythic, or cathartic truth of the romantic dream dissolved.

In 1825 John Marshall took his bride from Kentucky south into Tennessee, and Orion, the eldest and dreamiest of the seven offspring, was born in July at Gainesboro. Two years later the family crossed the Cumberlands into Fentress County, where John Marshall was named Circuit Court Clerk of the county and sometimes acted as Attorney General—hence his lifelong honorific. Here Clemens bought up the deeds to the seventy thousand acres of Cumberland mountain yellow-pine land, probably for about $400 total. This was the "prospective wealth" that Twain would curse in his old age, the land presumed to be laced with coal and silver, with minerals, with something, anything that would convert to a Lambton-like fortune; the land that was always about to be sold, but never quite; the land that would leech hope out of two generations of Clemenses.

The immediate result was to make John land-poor and instill him with lifelong headaches. He opened a general store and put the family in a corner of it. Pamela was born here in September 1827; then Pleasants Hannibal, who died at three months; then, in May 1830, came Margaret.

The store languished; farmers tended to pay their tabs in whisky and bacon. John noticed that he was taking to the whisky, so in 1831 he swore off drink forever and moved again—this time to a backwoods site nine miles away, beside the confluence of three mountain streams, where he built a smaller cabin and tried again. He farmed; he opened another store and post-office; he sired another child—Benjamin, in 1832—and he watched some more years pass and some more hopes turn stale. The financial crash of 1834 eradicated all his credit, and so in 1835 he threw it all over again, and gathered up his family for one more great spasm of western thrust.[22]

Daniel Boone had blazed the Wilderness Trail west across the Appalachians half a century before, hacking through to the amorphous territories known as Kentucky and, finally, Missouri. A gush of settlers followed, but the vast land absorbed them, thinned them out over hundreds of thousands of square miles, and toughened them into lethal survivors, Indian-fighters: a tenuous membrane of self-improvising civilization. This membrane hummed with rumor and myth. The myth of riches predominated: endless riches in the endless West.

Several Lamptons had already breached Missouri by 1835. Jane's uncle Joshua had ventured out there ten years earlier, and her father Benjamin followed around 1830. He returned to Kentucky long enough to boast of seeing "the finest timber in the world." His vivacious son-in-law John Quarles was all ears; he packed up his family, including his wife Patsy—Jane's sister—and followed the old man on the long trek back to the far side of the Mississippi. They staked out a homestead and opened a general merchandise store in the hamlet of Florida, between the forks of the meandering Salt River. And like all newly settled pioneers in the west, they set the membrane humming with visions of a New Jerusalem.

It was almost certainly the effervescent letters written to John and Jane by Quarles that inspired John Marshall to make this longest and most irreversible of his many pilgrimages. In *The Gilded Age*, the novel's one sublime character, the insanely boosterish "Colonel" Beriah Sellers, lures Squire Hawkins westward from his Tennessee land in a dispatch frothing with promise:

> Come right along to Missouri! Don't wait and worry about a good price but sell out for whatever you can get, and come along, or you might be too late. . . . It's the grandest country—the loveliest land—the purest atmosphere—I can't describe it; no pen could do it justice. . . . Mum's the

word—don't whisper—keep yourself to yourself. You'll
see! Come!—rush!—hurry!—don't wait for anything![23]

Like the Hawkinses, the Clemenses came. In early April 1835 they
sold everything (except a young slave named Jennie and the seventy
thousand acres of Tennessee land). They heaped a two-horse
barouche with clothing and their three youngest children, placed
Orion astride one of the horses, and set off north to Louisville. There
they boarded a steamboat for the long passage west along the Ohio
river to its confluence with the Mississippi, then up that churning
brown god of a river, awaiting its prophet, to St. Louis, awash in
cholera. From there they traveled overland again, north to Florida,
Missouri. They arrived near the first of June. Halley's Comet glowed
in the night sky. By this time Mark Twain had joined them on the river.

Three

"Dr. Meredith . . . was our family physician
and saved my life several times. Still, he was
a good man and meant well. Let it go."

He was born the following November, on the thirtieth, two months premature, and named for his grandfather Sam. Called "Sammy" throughout his childhood, he was born into an atmosphere more dreamlike than real: an atmosphere of deep winter prairie, the hamlet a glowing nighttime ember in the center of that; the Clemens's two-room clapboard house a center of the ember; himself a frail bluish infant and then a sickly small boy; bound often to his bed and the allopathic care of Jane. No one expected him to live.

He spent his first years on that cusp, cabin-bound and dosed on castor oil laced with molasses, requesting pure-white dresses for his clothing as soon as he was old enough to form the wish in words; and with words his dreamy atmosphere deepened into an atmosphere of voices: family voices telling stories and always recounting the past; his mother Jane, the curator of family legends, going on and on in the chill Missouri night with tales of Indians wildly pursuing her grandmother, a woman also named Jane, and breaking into a cabin and killing Jane's brother, a man named John, and capturing his wife and children, and of terrible retribution by the settlers . . .

For all his famous lifelong repudiations of racial prejudice, Mark Twain would virtually never find a kind word about Indians. "Finally they crucified the girls against the wall opposite the parents," a far more typical passage would go, "and cut off their noses and their breasts. They also—but I will not go into that. There is a limit."[1]

There were the soft bluegrass voices of his grandparents and the hard-r'd Missouri twangs of the gossiping neighbor-women who brought clothing and advice; and the hesitant Clemens drawls of his siblings, Pamela and Margaret and responsible little Benjamin, who tried to look after the baby; and solemn Orion, hovering, at a loss, as he always would be. There was the loud glad voice of the merchant John Quarles, soon to start up a tremendous farm four miles outside town—big golden-haired John with his laughing stories of village idiots and stuttering slaves and of a certain Tennessee frog into whose mouth he'd once poured buckshot.[2]

And always, floating up from under into that atmosphere like tendrils of smoke from an exotic scented leaf, there were the haunting different-rythmed voices of the black slaves.

Florida, Missouri, was hardly the center of a slaveholding empire. A tiny village beside a winding inland stream surrounded by corn and tobacco farms, it boasted a town center—Mill Street crossing Main Street—a store or two, a log church, some log houses, a rail fence, about a hundred people; pigs, dogs, not much else.[3] Its founders, like all founders of all towns in the great American awakening, had dreamed a prosperous future: They would dredge the shallow Salt to its joining with the Mississippi, eighty-five miles east, to open up the traffic of steamboats and cargo barges. They would petition Congress for a railroad line. And the log church and cabins would swell into a glittering hub of commerce, a mid-continent metropolis. The small boy was listening, and replayed all this frenzy within *The Gilded Age*. In the voice of Col. Sellers: "The Salt Lick Pacific Extension is going to run through Stone's Landing! The Almighty never laid out a cleaner piece of level prairie for a city . . . "

The Almighty, as it turned out, harbored more whimsical plans. A century and a half later the remnants of Florida/Stone City lay flattened beneath a man-dammed recreational liquefaction, a venue for water-skiers labeled, by some latter-day Sellers, Mark Twain Lake. The hut in which Sam Clemens was born had been scooped up and stored on high ground, covered with an all-weather capsule and offered as a tourist attraction: Mark Twain's Cabin, the jewel of Mark Twain State Park.

Florida was small, poor, doomed. But not so desiccated that its white inhabitants could not keep a few slaves. Farm and household slavery in Missouri lacked the organized economic intensity of regimented plantation slavery in the Deep South. The system was totalitarian, but diffuse and small in scale. John Quarles might have been considered a large holder in the region; he kept about 30 human chattel on the 230-acre farm he opened up in 1839. These relaxed economic relations and close daily contact between whites and blacks insured a lower incidence of brutality, even a rough sort of intimacy between the races, if not outright enlightenment. This intimacy was particularly felt by the children.

While his father risked more of his scarce capital on land and tried again to make a go as a storekeeper partner of Quarles, the pale redhaired boy Sammy moved in that charged demimonde. Even after his parents left Florida for Hannibal, he'd keep coming back to his uncle's farm for summers until he was about twelve. "A heavenly place for a boy," he called it, and its contours burned a deep and permanent imprint in his memory. Nearly sixty years after he last saw it, Twain could visualize it with perfect clearness: "The farmhouse stood in the middle of a very large yard, and the yard was fenced on three sides with rails and on the rear side with high palings; against these stood the smokehouses; beyond the palings was the orchard . . . "[4]

Beyond the orchard were the Negro quarters and the tobacco fields, a floating dream-atmosphere. Black voices filled that atmosphere, filled his consciousness in fact from the time he gained the strength to walk outdoors. (Through his sickly infancy he'd been attended partly by the Clemens's slave girl Jennie.) The saturation of voices he heard out there in the hot pungent fields, and on the sagging wooden front porches of the "quarter" after suppertime in the long evenings, formed a lingering chorus in his mind.

With his brothers and sisters and cousins—Quarles's eight children—Sammy would sit listening to vivid personalities such as the bedridden bald-spotted Aunt Hannah, rumored to be a thousand years old, a confidante of Moses. She told them of witches. And to Uncle Dan'l, a bright generous man "whose sympathies were wide and warm and whose heart was honest and simple and knew no guile."[5] The great voice of Jim began to gather its tidal cadences in Uncle Dan'l's speech, and the great character of Jim its rolling notes of suffering and forbearance.

"It was on the farm that I got my strong liking for his race and my appreciation of certain of its fine qualities," he wrote as an old man, still the racial democrat, still oblivious of his deeper presumptions. "This feeling and this estimate have stood the test of sixty years and more and have suffered no impairment." [6]

The small boy had found his way into the fringes of a captive culture that was already two and a quarter centuries forming, and would endure about twenty more years until the Civil War liberated and dispersed it. Words were, of necessity, the formative protective tissue: the encoded words of stories and songs. The words of the black slaves were luscious, captivatingly off-center from the similar words of his parents and relatives; the hybrid language of West Africa and England and Haiti, of the Bible and the white American slavemaster, flowed into a vast drifting dreamlanguage that conjured images and half-concealed notions more enveloping than anything he heard among his own people, except perhaps from his mother Jane.

"I know the look of Uncle Dan'l's kitchen as it was on privileged nights when I was a child," he would write, "and I can see the white and black children grouped on the hearth, with the firelight playing on their faces and the shadows flickering upon the walls, clear back toward the cavernous gloom of the rear, and I can hear Uncle Dan'l telling the immortal tales . . . " [7]

Tales of talking animals and magical spells and ghosts come in the night to reclaim their golden arms. He also heard true stories, laments for distant wives and husbands and children separated at auction. He heard terror and grief reconstituted into the formalities of myth, and given hope in the promise of a hereafter. He heard King Jesus and he heard, no doubt, deeply metaphoric references to a more contemporary and perilous salvation, the underground railroad.

The boy listened—as would the young man, and the man, Twain: "I listened as one who receives a revelation."[8] As a grown-up writer he would render great washes of this language—sometimes as dialogue attributed to Jim, or Roxana in *Pudd'nhead Wilson;* at other times presented as transcript from memory: "I took down what he had to say, just as he said it—without altering a word or adding one."[9] In his mimetic absorption of language, especially black language, he was exercising a gift of recall analogous to the accomplishment he would later claim as a steamboat pilot: the minute memorization of thirteen hundred miles of Mississippi river, from St. Louis to New Orleans—and back again.

But the boy heard something besides language. He heard horror, and the special terror of the slave's estate. Its abysses, wrote one of his early scholars, were to have their share in his soul.[10] The special force of terror in *Huckleberry Finn*—the constant dread of Huck and Jim that saturated their consciousness downriver, the fear of capture, punishment, annihilation—has its roots in those slave-quarter stories of spells, retribution, the walking dead.

While the boy gathered strength in the cabin and later ventured into the slave demimonde, his unromantic father kept up his futile pursuit of the chimera of wealth.

Within weeks of his arrival in Florida, John Marshall had begun buying tracts of government land: first 120 acres east of town, then 80 acres near the eastern county line, then 40 acres to the north. In September he bought a homesite from a veteran of George Washington's army and hoped to build the family homestead there, a big enduring house that would anchor the family and end its constant drift.[11] Two years later, he seemed to have pulled it off: He was not only a substantial landowner, he was a leading citizen in the public life of the town— a squire. He sat on commissions: one that would raise the capital necessary to dredge the Salt and draw the steamboat trade, another to drum up support for a Florida & Paris Railroad—so many territorial hamlets of that time groaned under fanciful names: Herculaneum,

Palmyra, Hannibal. He even got involved in a visionary scheme to establish an academic citadel, the Florida Academy. (All of this would be scrupulously lampooned in *The Gilded Age.*) On November 6, 1837, he was sworn in as a judge of the Monroe County Court.[12]

And then it started to come apart again. The expansive John Quarles and the tight-lipped John Marshall Clemens were never destined to be compatible business partners, and by the beginning of 1838 Quarles had ended his involvement in the store and fled across the street to set up a new shop by himself. John Marshall turned to the law, and to his boosting of the town. He built a house on the homestead property—no rural mansion, but a couple of single-room cabins conjoined.[13] And he waited, figuratively and literally, for Florida's ship to come in.

The small boy heard something besides stories and superstitions and fables as he wandered the slave-quarters demimonde. He heard singing. Like slaves throughout the American South, the Florida, Missouri, slaves sang all the time, and there was urgency and deep significance to their singing. They chanted rhythmically while working in the fields; they crooned in the kitchen while cooking; they whooped up jubilees at weddings; and they sang with special focus and intensity in the night. This nighttime singing of the slaves had a particularly spellbinding pull about it, for it was often in this distilled and coded singing that the slaves spoke to one another of the things that mattered most, and that carried the greatest risks of overt expression. "When night crept out from the forest," Bernard DeVoto wrote, "the singing created something at once awful and sublime."[14] It was in this singing that they spoke of the separation and the distant deaths of loved ones; of visitations from the spirit world; of the hideous floggings they had heard of or endured (even mild John Marshall flogged Jennie once with a cowhide whip, having bound her hands with a bridle rein[15]); of surcease in the hereafter; and of their real attitudes, which were not always wide and warm, and of their true hearts, which were not always honest and simple and without guile. It was in this sweet subversive singing that the slaves spoke their sadnesses and sarcasms and contempt for their white masters; their lust for revenge; their generational hunger for release. Sweet old Aunt Hannah's friend Moses had led the Hebrew tribes out of bondage to the Promised Land. Canaan. Canada.

The spirituals that little Sam Clemens listened to were aesthetic hybrids, like the speech itself. By the 1830s they had evolved into finished forms after nearly a century of development: brilliant intuitive pastiches of the old West African folk rhythms overlaid with good Protestant melodic structure. The pentatonic scale, the hand-clapping, the call-and-response, the long lingering tones, the adaptations to available instruments, the patches of folk tunes picked up from the Irish pushing west or the French voyaging down from the northern forests—these were among the many and dissimilar scraps of found music that were distilled and shaped over the decades into the great literature of Southern black spirituals.

Radiating through the music, always—borne on the deceptively soothing waves of the melodies—was the deep disguised sedition of the verses. The white owners listened indulgently as their slaves crooned, "Steal Away to Jesus," and "Old Ship O'Zion," and "Swing Low, Sweet Chariot," and "Nobody Knows the Trouble I've Seen," and the lyrics of these and other anthems passed frictionlessly, over time, into the American archive, as beloved and misunderstood as, say, the boyhood classics of the "humorist" Mark Twain. For here, in even more distilled and codified form than in their speech, the slaves delivered the bad news and the hard warnings and the lamentations impermissible under the Proscriptive Laws.*

Ambiguity and double meaning threaded the verses whose ironies would only deepen in complexity with the long passage of time. (At the close of the twentieth century, black churches in Harlem, preserving those same spirituals and that same textured rhetoric in their litany, would find their sanctuaries jammed with coarse white tourists, come to witness the old sacred rituals as entertainment—dumb as ever to the deeper meanings.)

West Africa always lay as an alternative referent to heaven in the songs of return, such as "Better Day A-Comin'" and "Come Go With Me to My Father's House." "You Gonna Reap Just What You Sow" conveyed certain hooded warnings to the whip-wielding overseers. And the Biblical figure of Moses was far from a petrified scriptural name: in 1849, when Sammy was thirteen, a Moses-like black woman named Harriet Tubman would venture back into the South after her own escape and lead more than three hundred slaves to freedom via the underground railroad. "Steal Away to Jesus" was the coded cue for the venturesome to prepare quickly for flight along her route.

While the meaning of the hymns was typically elusive and deliberately diffuse, not so the imagery. Listening to the slaves singing, the boy was drawn into a universe of phantom shapes and terrible presences and natural elements gone amok. This symbolism drew on origins as diverse as those of the tunes themselves: African folk tales, Biblical metaphor, fantasies of ghosts and witches and skeletons gathering up their bones to

---

*Laws enacted by Southern states in 1831–32 to prohibit slaves from holding meetings, which the owners feared as the seedbeds of insurrection.

walk around. Evil was everywhere in the night, the Evil Eye, and spells and curses; the merest howling of a dog meant death approaching; and all the world's prayers and incantations and charms were necessary to hold evil at bay. The dark singers sang in the oil-lamp darkness, and the boy visualized blood in the skies, tremendous angels thundering down, flaming chariots, parted seas, drowning armies. Fire and water, fire and water out of kilter, fire and water bringing death.

Samuel Clemens never stopped hearing that language, that incantatory music; he never stopped seeing the images that the language and the music conjured. He had only to close his eyes and the language, the music were there, memory was there, his tremendous power of recall manifested. He picked up some skills on the guitar and the piano—possibly from his pious sister Pamela, who gave music lessons to earn household money—and at moments throughout his life he would close his eyes and, trancelike, sing those old songs in a softly resonant tenor voice. While courting his future wife Livy in Elmira, New York, he would hold the Langdon parlor in thrall with a medley of spirituals and jubilees. Playing host at Hartford to a houseful of visitors from Boston in 1874, he offered "Swing Low," and "Golden Slippers," and "Go Down, Moses." A houseguest wrote that he swayed gently as he stood; "his voice was low and soft, a whisper of wind in the trees; his eyes were closed, and he smiled strangely."[16] He would sing those hymns compulsively in Florence in 1904, on the night that Livy died.[17]

In those swaying, whispering, crooning moments, it would seem, Mark Twain was in the grip of a kind of self-mesmerization. Those around him at such times frequently reported the feeling that he had left the present and was visiting somewhere else, some previous time: his boyhood.

"The soul of a boy," Howells had said of him. DeVoto thought of him as "imprisoned in his boyhood."[18] And Howells, offering what seemed a narrowly literary analysis of Twain, in fact sounded the deep stream that connected the writer's every impulse to his reservoirs of recall.

"So far as I know," Howells wrote, "Mr. Clemens is the first writer to use in extended writing the fashion we all use in thinking. . . . You have noted the author's thoughts, but not his order of thinking; he has not attempted to trace the threads of association between the things that have followed on one another; his reason, not his logic, has convinced you . . . "

Many critics have made the point that Twain's works, including his very best works, were nearly always pastiche. The paradigm is oral. Structural design is rarely apparent; one event leads meanderingly to another; tributaries of ancillary plot or reminiscence or information flow in, and the narrative sweeps on beyond the frame of the story, infinite, like a long summer evening on a shanty porch, or a river. Such were the contours of the distilled stories and songs of his early childhood.

Jane Clemens bore Sammy a brother, Henry, on June 13, 1838. Thirty years later Twain would recall that "I used to remember my brother Henry walking into a fire outdoors when he was a week old." It was only a delusion, of course, a kind of prophetic dream.

A year later, in August, little Margaret died, of what was diagnosed vaguely as "a bilious fever." This was the first of the many family deaths that Twain would endure across his seventy-five years. At age three, he was already a chronic sleepwalker, and a few nights before his sister's death he sleepwalked into her bedroom and began tugging at the blanket that covered her suffering form. That sort of gesture had a name in nineteenth-century rural America; called "plucking at the coverlet," it was a reflex that the dying were believed to perform. Since Sammy had been the one plucking the coverlet, his mother decided afterward that the boy had second sight.[19]

On November 13, 1839, John Marshall Clemens once more erased his status quo with a wildly hopeful land deal. When his boosterism and farmer attempts began to fail once again, he sold his best properties around Florida to a speculator named Ira Stout for about $3000. In the same exchange, he bought from Stout a quarter of a city block in the river town of Hannibal, some forty miles to the east, for $7000, and paid the sum in full. (A week later he unloaded another large land parcel to Stout for $2000.) Once more John and Jane packed up and headed off for better times. Sunk in his preoccupation, John Marshall prepared to chuck the reins and drive the family wagon off, oblivious of the fact that his eldest son, fourteen-year-old Orion, was not aboard. Orion never forgot it—nor did Sam, who, many years later, recalled the near-abandonment as having happened to *him*.

Nonetheless, in deep November the Clemens entourage—John, Jane, Orion, Pamela, Benjamin, little Sammy, the baby Henry, together with the slave girl Jennie—made it intact from the doomed village to the awakening rivertown. Now little Sam Clemens entered the theater of his most enduring dreams and delights and terrors and sorrows. He entered the place that he would transform with words into the crucible of American literature: Hannibal.

Four

"After all these years I can picture that old time
to myself now, just as it was then: the white town
drowsing in the sunshine of a summer's morning;
the streets empty or pretty nearly so . . .

A t Hannibal the family took up residence in the Virginia
House, a putative "hotel" whose stately name belied its
humble woodframe structure and scarcity of guests. The Virginia
House stood in the quarter block of John's new property holdings,
about a block from the Mississippi and virtually at the foot of a steep
bluff. This was a different order of landscape from the sleepy Salt and
the rounded but low-lying prairie—a setting of compacted visual
drama for a small child. The family's new property was bounded by
Hill Street, sloping eastward toward the river, and Main, which ran
north and south, beside the flow.

John Marshall had bought the House and some other wooden
buildings from Ira Stout with just about all of his remaining savings
and collateral. He hoped to bring in revenue from transient guests, and
also from yet another grocery and dry-goods store he had planned.
This would tide the family over until the chimerical Tennessee Land
bonanza, John's own Louisiana Purchase, kicked in.

But once again, the Virginian's vision had overshot his judgment. His hotel was half a decade early. It would fail shortly before the great transient surge westward through town generated by the Gold Rush. (Ironies abounded in John Marshall's doomed business schemes, here as in Florida. The most successful hotel in Hannibal's history would open a few blocks to the south sixty-six years in the future. Four stories high, fronting an entire city block, boasting seventy rooms and made of elegant pressed brick and granite, it owed much of its cache to its name: the Mark Twain.)

John Marshall's luck in Hannibal was not all bad: As soon as he arrived in the village he got drafted into a militia group to help fight a war against the Territory of Iowa over a border dispute. But before he had a chance to get himself shot, the confrontation was settled peacefully.

That was pretty much the extent of John Marshall's good luck. His most prosperous days were behind him—probably in Florida. Ahead lay failure, bankruptcy, an early death.

Sammy turned five shortly after the move. He would remain frail and sickly for the next three years. Among his symptoms were convulsions. His high-strung mother, steeped in backwoods ailments and their remedies, had her own diagnosis for these seizures. She attributed them to "worms." She once told Dr. Meredith, the family doctor, that she had come upon her little boy as he literally gagged on worms. She could see them in his mouth and had poured salt down his throat to destroy the parasites—a potentially lethal action in itself.

Tapeworms, attaching to unprotected meat such as pork and then flourishing in the digestive tract of the pork-eater, were a genuine concern on the frontier. Hannibal was on its way to becoming a "porkopolis" by 1840, with ten thousand pigs a year running through town en route to the slaughterhouses at Bear Creek.[1] One common effect of tapeworms was the slow starvation of the host; little Sammy was underweight throughout his childhood. So Jane Clemens had good reason for her concern.

Less credible was Jane's lurid image of the visible vermin. At least one biographer[2] has suggested that Sam might have stuffed his mouth with earthworms to draw a reaction from his mother; his dedication to practical jokes, sometimes bordering on the morbid, was a lifelong passion, and Jane was always a richly rewarding victim.

Perhaps more likely, the excitable Jane Clemens had convinced herself that she saw the wriggling life in her son's mouth. Hallucination, and the tendency to confuse fantasy with memory, were tendencies shared by mother and son. Brooding by himself through his sickly years, he became a curious mixture of fitful energy and quiet contemplation. Sammy's nights were frequently disturbed by sleepwalking and apocalyptic dreams, while his days were filled by agitating his mother, handing her bats and garter snakes; at the table, he compulsively stole sugar, getting his knuckles rapped, almost seeming to enjoy the cat-and-mouse.

His restless playfulness could turn mean. He fed Pervy Davis's Pain-Killer to a family cat to watch it "perform under its influence." He slipped several hundred wasps one night into the bedclothes of the bashful boarder Jim Wolf. "He was talking as usual but I couldn't answer, because by anticipation I was suffocating with laughter, and although I gagged myself with a hatful of the sheet, I was on the point of exploding all the time."[3]

He took outlandish risks with his safety, as he would all through his youth and young manhood (when he toyed with a pistol duel in Nevada, then prowled an active volcano floor and tried a primitive form of surfing in Hawaii). At Hannibal he leapt about on cracking ice floes on the Mississippi and nearly drowned several times in Bear Creek—seven by his own count. ("People who are born to be hanged are safe in the water," he recalled his mother drawling.[4]) He was smoking by age seven, but that was less a risk than a social obligation among his peers. Visiting the country schoolhouse near his uncle John Quarles's farm that summer, he encountered a strapping sunbonneted girl of fifteen who announced to her friends, scandalized: "Here is a boy seven years old who can't chaw tobacco." He never did learn. Smoking was as close as he could come to respectability.

The boy kept wild heaps of things in his pockets: knives, marbles, fishhooks, string, bats, teeth, toads. He used these objects to get an edge on his friends and relatives, and throughout his life he would be interested in people's pockets and to what degree they kept their hands in or out. He developed a perverse taste for bad poetry, "showing off," disfigurements, adult sham of all kinds. His stonemason/Sunday School teacher's thumb, bent like a parrot's beak by a missed hammer stroke, diverted him a good deal more than the Scripture.

He memorized kitsch-art and sentimental household furnishings: "His oil-cloth window-curtains had noble pictures on them of castles such as had never been seen anywhere in the world but on window-curtains."[5] Style drew his eye; the nuances of style revealed character to him, like spoken language: "This fellow had money, too, and hair-oil. . . . He wore a leather belt and used no suspenders." He thought that a long cloak was about the most dramatic thing a man or a boy could wear. ("Worn with a swagger," he stipulated in "Villagers.") The red merino sash adorning the Cadets of Temperance in Hannibal was enough to make him give up smoking (for a while). He was beguiled and a little saddened by the quaint dress of his father's two or three close friends and their eighteenth-century high stocks, pigtails, knee-breeches, buckle-shoes.

Much about his father beguiled and saddened him. "My father was a justice of the peace," he would write, "and I supposed he possessed the power of life and death over all men and could hang anybody that offended him." The boy would continually be disabused of this familiar, hopeful supposition. Of all the children—Pamela excepted, perhaps—Sammy was the most acutely tuned to the family currents; and his father's anxiety at failure, suppressed under an arctic detachment that gave way to eruptions of temper, grew progressively more oppressive to him.

Although Jane Clemens may occasionally have been hysterical, she was at least accessible. "My father and I were always on the most distant terms when I was a boy," Twain would recall. "A sort of armed neutrality, so to speak."[6] Gaunt John cut an almost Biblical figure in the household: grim, aloof, obsessively principled. Less biblically, he was preoccupied with money worries. He seldom struck his children (he was less gentle with slaves), but in his reprimands he could be terrifying. His admonishing stare could chill their blood. He never joked. Only the thought of the Tennessee land, and the fortune it would inevitably bestow on the family, seemed to save him from black despondency.

At Hannibal, having tethered himself to a questionable landlording venture, the scholarly and unworldly Virginian embarked on the last and most fatal in his lifelong series of financial blunders: He splurged on about two thousand dollars' worth of foodstuffs and durable goods from a number of St. Louis wholesalers. He bought this merchandise on credit. Moving the goods would be Orion's job: Orion, distracted and dazed at fifteen as he would be distracted and dazed through his long sad wondering life, was to be the grocery store's clerk.

Finally, the elder Clemens began, uncharacteristically, to borrow from relatives: $250 from his distant cousin James Clemens Jr., a prosperous lawyer in St. Louis; $747.13 from James A. H. Lampton, Jane's younger brother who had remained in Florida. While Jane and the children amassed housecats—nineteen by 1845—and began to take stock of their new surroundings, the patriarch guided them swiftly and unerringly toward bankruptcy.

As his health slowly improved, the boy's attentions would be rescued from the growing household tensions by the infinite intrigue of his new habitat. What he beheld and experienced there, in light and in darkness, enlarged him, and his shaping of it into story would enlarge the nation's discovery of itself.

It is difficult now to imagine fully how that might have been so. It is difficult, at the close of a century enmeshed in the saturations of globally transmitted information, to conceive an isolated, unelectrified American hamlet of the 1840s as anything but culturally benumbed and benumbing: barren of enrichment from art, entertainment, the pageantries of a thousand miles' remove. A medieval wilderness whose inhabitants forged brutish subsistence lives.

This cloture of empathetic imagination took hold quite early, in fact, and it diminished Mark Twain's legitimacy with the American (if not the global) public for at least three decades following his death. Most influential among the opinion-makers who held that Twain's literary genius was compromised by his arid place of origin was Van Wyck Brooks. Here is how Brooks, infatuated by the newly fashionable theories of Sigmund Freud, imagined the Missouri frontier of Sam Clemens's youth:

A desert of human sand!—the barrenest spot in all Christendom, surely, for the seed of genius to fall in. . . . Essentially, [frontier] America was not happy: it was a dark jumble of decayed faiths, of unconfessed class distinctions, of inarticulate misery . . . it was a nation that had no folk-music, no folk-art, no folk-poetry, or next to none, to express it, to console it. It was a horde-life, a herd-life, an epoch without sun or stars, the twilight of a human spirit that had nothing upon which to feed but the living waters of Camden and the dried manna of Concord.[7]

Seldom has a recognized scholar been more drastically self-deluded, and with more destructive consequences, about the crucial resonance between an artist and the artist's formative habitat. It was not simply that the emerging American culture did indeed reach Hannibal in the early nineteenth century. It is also that the terrain itself was almost uncannily organized to stimulate the furies of a personality such as Clemens's.

Remove the artifacts of civilization from the old glacial ground beside the Mississippi—reverse two centuries of the accreting town: mall, subdivision, automobile, picture-show, trainyards, restaurant, hospital, school, library, store, cemetery, brothel, saloon, levee, church, distillery, printing-shop, house, street, surveyor's stake, plat, campfire. What remains is still an embrasure of layered place perhaps unequaled on the continent in its intense compacted variety. An extension of the childhood soul, at once Edenic and Satanic, Hannibal was "a heavenly place for a boy," and a hellish one as well.

Begin with the river, for that is why and where the town began. The Mississippi was a gigantic interruption in that landlocked midcontinental prairie, a fabulous anomaly, an *event,* motion in the midst of stasis. The river was insistent not only by its preemptive effect on the eye, but by its pull upon the other senses as well: its deep abiding scent, a compost of all its natural cargo, the treetrunks and leaves and algae and earth and feces and decaying animals and people, of the fish- and turtle-life below the surface—a scent briny and stale and intoxicating, beckoning; a little heavier than air. And its sound: sharp and dramatic in winter, with ice floes colliding and breaking up like tectonic plates; subtler in the warm months, but there; the washes of its current-ripples against the shore; *there;* a murmurescent conversation, the words just beyond discerning, a vast quiet voice in the night. And its touch: the thrilling chill and flowing pressure of its skin against the extended hand or foot; the dark promise of that touch to sweep one under and away.

Rivers are among mankind's oldest, most irreducible symbols: the river of life, the river of time, the river of memory, the river of immortality, the river of oblivion. The river as story, as dream, as journey, as stream of consciousness. Riverrun. The river as sacred (Alph); as death (Lethe); as the passage between the two (Styx); as deliverer (Jordan). The river as a strong brown god. *Sometimes we'd have that whole river to ourselves for the longest time,* said Huck, looking at the sky all speckled with stars and living with Jim the myth of Adam; later on downstream the two would nearly be ploughed under and have to dive for it, into Hades. The boy and the river understood one another right away.

The land on the western edge of the river was a hollow of floodplain where the town would form; the plain framed by high wooded limestone bluffs to the north and to the south, overlooking the great flow; the high ground tapering off westward, cupping the floodplain, embracing it. The northern bluff, more than 200 feet high, would come to be known as Holliday's Hill and later, after Twain's own fictionalized name for it, Cardiff Hill. The southern bluff, crowned by a jutting tooth of limestone 230 feet above the river, would be called Lover's Leap. Bear Creek was a smaller, more peaceful river winding beneath this southern ridge, between thick stands of trees, to join with the big one. All the valleys and hillsides were dense with oak and walnut and sycamore and elm and hickory, the trunks twined in bittersweet and trumpet vine; the ground floor a tangle of blackberry and gooseberry and mint and burdock and Spanish needle; the open fields teeming with dandelion and columbine and bloodroot and toothwort and wild ginger. Chiggers in the summer, digging at the skin. The bordering heights, and lesser ridges between them, assured that life in the floodplain would move in vertical as well as horizontal patterns. For a child, this meant a life of climbing and concealment and descent, by day and by night and in all the seasons, amidst natural growth and formations as specific and numinous as the rooms of a cathedral.

And it meant terror as well, terror and guilt. Restless ghosts and spell-casting witches and mortal predators could prowl those deep naves of Missouri forest—hard lone butchers and murderous gangs. Vast boulders adhered to the framing bluffs, boulders large enough to gather tremendous force if dislodged and pushed downhill toward the river. The boy and a comrade did that once, dislodged a boulder on the northernmost bluff, and it nearly killed a man. The black prairie night could unleash ferocious thunderstorms, the rains sweeping along in pelting sheets; everything glaring out white and blinding for a quivering instant, then solid darkness shutting down again and a splitting peal of thunder close behind. These storms could sound like the destruction of the world, and in fact to a dreamy boy were manifestly punitive in intent, charged with celestial interest, the lightning stretching his unrepentant friends all dead in their beds.

And finally, three miles downriver from the floodplain, another powerful extension of the childhood soul: the cave.

Two cave systems, actually, though once a common labyrinth in geologic history. (The larger cave, separated from the first by a membrane of earth, and extending four and a half miles under the bluff, lay unsuspected as a lurking spirit until fifteen years after Twain's death.) Their limestone joints had been created while the land was lifting up from beneath the water table; as the hill rose slowly through the millennia, the water drained out, eroding the joints into narrow avenues and crevices, some of them sixty feet high—intersecting dry mazes uncharacteristic of caves in the region, which tended to be low-lying and muddy. A layer of shale, forming on the hillside, further insulated the passages from the porous topsoil; what little water got through dripped gradually, taking calcium from the limestone with it to form stalactites and stalagmites, making a vast fanged orifice beneath the hill, choked with bats (the limestone itself the residue of the skeletons of marine invertebrates—the old riverlife grew the teeth of the cave).

The smaller system, two miles of "crooked aisles that ran into each other and out again and led nowhere," would be made world-famous by the boy and fed his romantic fantasies. He courted girls at picnics and played out chivalric fantasies by its mouth. At sixteen, he made a charming connection between this subterranean mass and a hive of human settlement. "It has innumerable passages," he wrote, "which are not unlike the streets of a large city."[8]

But the cave also evoked his most morbid terrors: It was an abyss, able to suck one under as the river could; able to punish horribly, like the nighttime landscape. It contained a corpse, after all: the remains of a fourteen-year-old girl, the daughter of a ghoulish St. Louis surgeon, who placed her remains in a glass cylinder filled with alcohol, then enclosed in a copper one that was suspended from a rail. "It was said that loafers and rowdies used to drag it up by the hair and look at the dead face," Twain would write.[9] He populated it with a fictive corpse of his own: Injun Joe's.

"No man 'knew' the cave," Twain would write in *The Adventures of Tom Sawyer.* "That was an impossible thing." He imagined his alter ego Tom leading Becky Thatcher deep into nightmare in the cave in that book, a stolen flirtation's consequence: lost and pursued by the terrible doomed Injun. After he had aged and grown sick of chivalry, he moved the cave to England and made it the site of another alter ego's exploits. Hank Morgan, the Connecticut Yankee, set up his perimeter of mechanized weaponry in front of the cave—electric fences and Gatling guns—and with that nineteenth-century firepower, a foretaste of the twentieth's, wasted twenty-five thousand medieval knights.*

The vast river, the embrasure of hills, the rich and varied vegetation, the great pageants of weather and the brilliant changing seasons, and the deep ambiguous cave: these were the compacted features of the elemental world that surrounded the little flood plain to which John Marshall Clemens removed his family in the late autumn of 1839.

The town of Hannibal had taken root there just twenty years earlier. In a sense it had been born of convulsion and apocalyptic stroke. On December 1, 1811, a titanic earthquake, the most violent in recorded North American history, erupted near the village of New Madrid, in the

---

*A Connecticut Yankee in King Arthur's Court (New York: Oxford University Press, 1996).

southern Missouri Territory. It rippled a million square miles beyond its epicenter; its shocks reached Washington, D.C., and briefly reversed the Ohio's and the Mississippi's flows. In the quake's aftermath, the federal Congress authorized land certificates, good for anywhere in the Territory, for survivors whose homes had been destroyed. Speculators began to buy up the certificates and plan entire towns. One such entrepreneur, Moses D. Bates, enlisted a partner, Thompson Bird, to stake out lots on what was then an obscure trading post on the Mississippi beside Bear Creek. (He foresaw it as a stop for the steamboat line he planned.) By 1819, a few families had made the keelboat voyage upriver and started a fragile community on the bartered land.

The naming of Hannibal is lost in obscurity. Settlers of that time had a taste for reference to antiquity, and Hannibal was the name of the black Carthaginian hero of the Punic Wars. An oral black legend, which Mark Twain never indicated having heard, might have intrigued the old admirer of Uncle Dan'l: The town drew its name from an African slave. This former ocean pilot had been taken into slavery personally by Thomas Jefferson and then sent west to join the Lewis and Clark expedition of 1804. He was called York, but insisted that his authentic name was Hannibal. Guarding the expedition's campsite at the confluence of the Mississippi and Bear Creek, the slave cried out, to members of the expedition returning from their inland foragings, "This is Hannibal! This is Hannibal!"

By 1830, the town remained little more than a primitive settlement of thirty people. Nine years later, the Clemenses rolled in on a new tide of settlers, and the population rose to a thousand in the year of their arrival. A "white town drowsing," Twain recalled it; but through Sam's boyhood the village grew denser and livelier, and richer in human character, with each passing season.

He would witness Hannibal's efflorescence even as he witnessed his family's stagnation, catastrophe, and decline. A delicious, textured hive was shaping itself around him, a right-angled municipality rising up from the desultory shacks and mud streets. Hammers rang against nails, saws bit into boards, mule-drawn wagons carried teams of workers to the sites where the skeletons of new buildings stood. Crews labored with heavy stones at the river's edge, where steamboat whistles sounded more and more frequently. The town formed, adding its soul-extensions to those of the Mississippi River, the embracing hills, the deep ambiguous cave.

Sammy would watch as sawmills went up to make lumber from the forests and from logs floated down the Mississippi from Wisconsin. He would see the construction of slaughterhouses and factories built to process hemp and tobacco. He would see a few homes built of brick and rimmed with trim lawns and picket fences. More typical were the long wooden add-on shacks, garnished with weeds and hollyhocks, where dirt-poor extended families lived, or several families.

By 1844, the infrastructure of a permanent town was in place. Hannibal claimed four general stores (not including John's failed one), three sawmills, two planing mills, two hotels, three saloons, two churches, two schools, a tobacco factory, a hemp factory, a tanyard, and a distillery.[10] Circuses came there, and minstrel shows; there were parades and great speeches on Independence Day. The parades flowed down the wide expanse of Market Street, later renamed Broadway, which tilted downhill toward the levee. All the town, by that time, had focused itself toward the river.

The Mississippi was already a crowded thoroughfare when the Clemenses reached town, the eccentric shapes of keelboats and rafts and scows and Broadhorn arks dotting the river. Steamboats were rare at first—a packet a week in 1830—but soon at least three boats a day were stopping at Hannibal. The town fathers reinforced the land between First Street and the river, and laid a stone wharf to smooth the loading and unloading.

What all this meant to the boy Sam Clemens was that the town, virtually before his eyes, was achieving a hivelike density whose features would resonate with, and compliment, the elemental embrasure of hills, the majesty of the river, the ambiguous enchantments of the cave. With each new house or store or craftsman's shop that the grown men finished for their purposes, a new layer of a parallel childhood universe would emerge: an alley, a rooftop, a livestock pen, a forbidden back yard. This parallel universe held its own terrors—the American frontier was saturated with violence, and Hannibal was no exception—and that was essential, too, for a boy's imagination.

Adults and children had little to do directly with one another, outside the family circle, in frontier towns such as Hannibal. The two societies moved in the same plane of space, but mutually oblivious. This meant among other things that the society of childhood was intensely self-aware and self-regulating, with its own traditions, initiation rites, hierarchies, and secrets. It meant that a bright, sociable, high-strung boy, dreamstruck with stories and legends and needing to break free, could rise quickly through the ranks of the *ur*-society of children in a frontier town. As the boy Samuel Clemens quickly did.

Five

"... everything in a dream is more deep and strong and sharp and real than is ever its pale imitation in the unreal life which is ours when we go about awake. ... When we die we shall slough off this cheap intellect, perhaps, and go abroad into Dreamland clothed in our real selves, and aggrandized and enriched by the command over the mysterious mental magician who is here not our slave, but only our guest."

Emerging from his sickliness, he now began to live the gigantic childhood that would inform America's mythic consciousness of "childhood." (That this particular childhood was specifically white, and masculine, and of the nation's rural "Interior," and partly invented, were delimitations that failed, for nearly a century, to modify that myth.)

Judged through the prisms of his literature and his sweeping, refocusing memory, Sammy Clemens's life in Hannibal can take on a Homeric luster, the inevitability of a comet. He became his own tall tale. Everything the boy did, or saw, or heard, or ate, or touched, or thought, or dreamed, seemed magically connected to some universal.

At least that is how his legions of grateful bourgeois readers would choose to view it: the radiance of his boyhood casting new light on deep, fine principles of plain American culture that until then had been unnoticed by the culture itself. His most appreciated gift to his countrymen would be that of the laughing childhood they never had. (His somewhat less-appreciated gift to American children would be the onus of living up to it.)

Archetype followed his footprints like seawater in sand. The drab locale of his fitful education became The School House; his nighttime escapades, Midnight. His summers became Enjoying the Vacation; his household truculence, Aunt Polly Beguiled; his Sunday mornings slouching in the pew, At Church; his bursts of energy, Showing Off; his forays toward little girls, A Flirtation (followed by A Sudden Frost); his small triumphs, the work of A Hero.

The sunlit parts of his childhood cast deep shadows, of course, and in those shadows lay the dark artifacts that would torment and compel him to his masterpieces. These, the grateful readers were less inclined to acknowledge having noticed, although the dark artifacts were never completely obscured from the world's view.

But what was it, exactly, that he did? That he saw, heard, ate, touched, thought, dreamed? What was this life like, this succession of miracles, this daily wash of outlandish adventure and intrigue? The full answer of course is irrecoverable. Twain's literature and memoirs are nothing if not rich in suggestion; but even these, if they could be sorted out and superimposed on an actual timeline of his youth, would cover only a few days, or weeks, of a chronology that covered ten critical years. Giant dioramas were a fad in that energetic era just before the Civil War—monster canvases that stretched on for three miles and depicted, say, the entire Mississippi on a scale of 1:400. The surviving scenes of Mark Twain's childhood, as exquisitely detailed as he painted those for us, would stretch intermittently but for a few yards across such a canvas, most of which would be blank.

Our tendency has been to consecrate, selectively, what little we do know of that childhood (and, by extension, our national claim to innocence). We have largely assumed what the aging Twain often wanted to assume, and wanted us to assume along with him: that a celestial light appareled his Hannibal days, giving them the glory and the freshness of a dream. "St. Petersburg,"* he called the town, an allusion to the Pearly Gates. His summers on the Quarles farm were "heavenly." Few who grew up in such enchanted enclaves can doubt he meant it. "The loveliness of prairie and forest suffuses American literature," wrote Bernard DeVoto, while it was still possible to write such things, "to make our most authentic theme."[1]

The danger of such consecration has been sentimentality, and the danger of sentimentality is that it reduces Mark Twain's achievement. There is a terrible immensity to the day-to-day life of a child. Attitudes or behavior that adults encapsulate as merely "cute," or otherwise decorative, might have for a child the weight of dignity or shame, revelation or confusion, fulfillment or failure. All senses are open; small events can be charged with lifelong significance. Children constantly tell themselves stories to give order to the sensory barrage; lightning at night is God's judgment on sin. Sammy Clemens seems to have imposed a story line onto his childhood even as he was living it—his alter ego, Tom Sawyer, always consults a tale or legend for guidance in behavior.

---

*He occasionally added a final "h."

His adult, literary self never surrendered those stories. More importantly, he never trivialized them. The Mark Twain of Tom, Huck, Pudd'nhead, and the memory passages of *Life on the Mississippi*—this Twain was not simply a gifted descriptive writer or a winning anecdotalist. He managed to recover the inner dignity and gravity and terror of childhood; the child's investiture of the numinous upon each day; the endless ricochet between heaven and hell. This heroic intensity of childhood rarely lasts in memory, but ends up lost with adolescence and its narcissistic demands. For some reason, perhaps intertwined with trauma, Twain never let it go. He imported it into adulthood and the adult's capacity to frame epiphany with words. "He was the average adolescent-minded American," wrote one midcentury critic, "rooter at ball games, political banquets, exhibitions of pseudo-heroic claptrap. He was that man plus genius."[2]

But as to the particulars of that boyhood which he left us:

"In [Hannibal], when I was a boy everybody was poor but didn't know it; and everybody was comfortable and did know it," he would write,[3] and for a while, for him, it must have been true. The early 1840s, when he was not yet ten, were anxious enough financially for his father, but that anxiety had not yet soaked into Sammy. There was sugar in the sugar bowl, a bed to sleep in (though he shared it for a time with Henry), some change for donations to the schoolmasters and the Sunday collection plate; there was wherewithal for Pamela's piano and guitar; there was denim for jeans and muslin for vast-collared shirts; there was a little cash for castor oil and Perry Davis's Pain Killer and John Marshall's constant pills; there were pennies for circuses and vaudeville shows; and that, to a boy in the prewar, pre-industrial frontier South was world enough.

". . . Yet you perceived that the aristocratic taint was there," he added quietly. Already he could sense that certain social and class lines had been drawn, and he could decipher the reason: "the town's population had come from slave states and still had the institution of slavery with them in their new home."[4] The Clemenses kept that institution in their own household, in the person of Jennie among others who came and went—that is, were bought and sold. Humanitarian Jane, who "would not have allowed a rat to be restrained of its liberty," seemed airily unconscious of the institution's rebuke to her ideals. But then most seemed so—certainly John Marshall. Among those who did feel differently were the Clemens children; two of them, at least. Orion would soon become an outspoken Abolitionist. As for Sammy, the infinite contradictions of slavery were already forming his rich ironic sense. (In *Adventures of Huckleberry Finn,* Mark Twain would insert this subtle mockery of white racism: "We blowed out a cylinder-head," Huck tells Aunt Sally on the Phelps farm. "Good gracious! Anybody hurt?" "No'm. Killed a nigger." "Well, it's lucky, because sometimes people do get hurt . . . "[5])

Sammy was not the darling of the household. Nor was Benjamin, nor Orion (sent off to the printer's trade in St. Louis by 1842 in any event), nor even Pamela, although she alone could penetrate through to John Marshall's gentleness. The honor belonged to Henry, the youngest, and it may partly explain the origins of Mark Twain's virtuosity with humor. Competing for attention within the family against an adored sibling, children often play the antic. "My mother had a good deal of trouble with me but I think she enjoyed it," he would write. "She had none at all with my brother Henry, who was two years younger than I, and I think that the unbroken monotony of his goodness and truthfulness and obedience would have been a burden to her but for the relief and variety which I furnished in the other direction."[6]

Serious, seraphic, curly-haired like Sammy, Henry could exasperate by that goodness of his. Sammy's feelings toward him were complex. There was that dreamy, "remarkable" memory he had of the child walking through fire a week after his birth. ("It was still more remarkable that I should cling to the delusion for thirty years that I *did* remember it—for of course it never happened; he would not have been able to walk at that age."[7]) There was the time he dropped a melon on his little brother's head from an upper-story window; the time he bombarded Henry with black clods from the garden, "which he warded off with his tin bucket the best he could."[8] Yet Twain's recall of his little brother was beatific: "I never knew Henry to do a vicious thing toward me or toward anyone else—but he frequently did righteous ones that cost me as heavily."[9]

Most famously, he nailed Sammy once for playing hooky to go swimming by pointing out to Jane that he had re-sewed the collar of his shirt together with a different-colored thread than she had used. This incident made it to chapter one of *Tom Sawyer*, with Henry in the role of Tom's "half-brother," Sid. "But Sid was not Henry," Twain wrote, under the burden of heavy memory. "Henry was a very much finer and better boy than Sid ever was."[10]

Henry's precious status within the family must have intensified in May of 1842 when John and Jane suffered their second loss of a child. Benjamin, not yet ten, came down with an unexplained illness and died within a week. Jane took it hard. She fell into a moaning fit. She summoned the other children to the deathbed and made each in turn kneel beside the boy's body and place a hand on its cheek. For Sammy, at least, this was a nightmare, an experience oddly laced with guilt. He never forgot it. Nor did he forget the other, vaguely analogous intimacy in that morbid tableau: the kiss between Jane and John Marshall—the only kiss Sam Clemens ever witnessed between the two.

Jane's insistence on the cheek-touching ritual left its impression. Half a century later, Mark Twain still believed himself somehow responsible for Ben's death—that he'd had a hand in it, so to speak. A note he'd written read: "Dead brother Ben. My treachery to him." And in "Villagers," his gallery of Hannibal personalities, he had added, cryptically, "The case of memorable treachery." Similarly, Twain would blame himself for the death of his first child, Langdon, in 1872, although the sickly baby's illness was diagnosed as diphtheria. Other family deaths would haunt his conscience as well.

Within a year of Benjamin's death, the soulful Jane Clemens decided to join a church. Pamela, Sam, and Henry followed her. John Marshall went once with them, then remained aloof. Jane's denominational choice could hardly have been better calculated to feed Sammy's appetite for guilt. She became a Presbyterian.

Presbyterians amplified the currents of brooding, theological mysticism that flowed on the American frontier. Deriving from the chilly Puritanism of the sixteenth-century ascetics John Calvin of France and John Knox of Scotland, this church in Twain's boyhood still sought to develop a model society based on strict discipline and a Moral Sense enforced by the terror of an eternal Hell. The red-haired boy sat in the Sunday pew, his straw hat on his lap, and swiped at flies and pinchbugs and listened to endless sermons depicting God the Avenger, who loomed over a world of fallen men. Man's fall in fact was "predestinated" by John Knox's God—a "sarcasm" that bitterly amused Twain as he churned out his *Letters from the Earth* in the year before he died. The hired choir sang and the boy heard warnings of "heresy" applied to any hope that man can play a part in his own salvation, warnings that surely fed into his old-age conviction that "Man's proudest possession—his mind—is a mere machine: an automatic machine."[11]

The boy counted bonnets furtively and heard bursts of the same feverish apocalyptic imagery—evil everywhere, fire and water out of kilter, fire and water bringing death—that had burned into his dreams through the spirituals and the tales of the slaves on his uncle's farm. The terror was separate and equal, though: the "Old-School" theology of southern Presbyterians in the 1840s had no comfort to offer black people in bondage.

If Sammy Clemens heard tell of God's bounty, forgiveness, and love in Reverend Joshua Tucker's sermons, the impact of it escaped him. God affronted, God implacable, God the punisher was what sunk in. Nor was the Almighty's aim all that good. "I was educated, I was trained, I was a Presbyterian and I knew how these things are done," he would write. "I knew that in Biblical times if a man committed a sin the extermination of the whole surrounding nation—cattle and all—was likely to happen. I knew that Providence was not particular about the rest, so that He got somebody connected with the one He was after."[12] And as for the question of guilt, whether one chose to be guilty or not: "Presbyterianism without infant damnation would be like the dog on the train that couldn't be identified because it had lost its tag."[13]

Fortunately the boy had access to gaudier entertainments. The nascent American culture was edging, across long distances, into Hannibal in the 1840s. Bright-painted circus wagons lumbered into town in those prewar summers, and minstrel shows spilled in, and traveling actors, and mesmerizers, and self-anointed healers and patriotic frauds and humbugs and liars of all kinds. Wedding-cake showboats sounded their calliopes along the Mississippi. Stories, myths, archetypes moved overland and by water, like a constant pulse, in the talk of settlers, peddlers, con men, and visitors from the East.

All these were carriers of the fast-forming American aesthetic in all its sublime vulgarity, aggression, and excess. Just sixty years had elapsed since the Treaty of Paris, the breaking of Europe's umbilical. America was improvising itself as a distinct entity, trying out its own voice as unbeholden to the received truths and the hardened class systems of the Old World. Lowdown, wild, grittily optimistic against the chaos and bloody violence of this great formation, the traveling shows and impresarios left a residue of excitement far out of proportion to their uneven talents. Sammy Clemens was watching and listening. The literary language he eventually improvised—plain people, talking—took part of its unprecedented energy from the shows that came to town.

He could not have been more than seven or eight when he saw his first minstrel show in the early 1840s—an antebellum mix of song, strutting, and racial stereotyping that continued to be performed in Hannibal through the 1950s. Good Presbyterians did not attend these spectacles, but Sammy did; his Heaven-for-climate/Hell-for-society stance was already firm. Perched resolutely amidst the "worldlings," he drank it all in. And he remembered it all his life. As an old man, he could still call up the stunning gaslit brilliance of the minstrels with their coal-black hands and faces, and their clothing—"a loud and extravagant burlesque of the clothing worn by the plantation slave of the time."[14] Here the old man—and perhaps the boy as well—made a subtle and compassionate distinction:

> . . . not that the rags of the poor slave were burlesqued, for
> that would not have been possible; burlesque could have

added nothing in the way of extravagance to the sorrowful accumulation of rags and patches which constituted his costume; it was the form and color of his dress that was burlesqued.[15]

The boy noted, and the writer remembered, the standing collars that hid half the minstrel's head, his coat of curtain calico, his clumsy shoes five or six sizes too large for him. He remembered "Banjo" and "Bones," the prime jokers who sat at either end of the row of minstrels. He remembered, without commenting on it, the visual mockeries of their negritude: their lips thickened and painted so as to resemble slices in a watermelon. And he remembered the dainty middleman, his features undoctored, himself "clothed in the faultless costume of white society." He remembered how the middleman used "a stilted, courtly, artificial and painfully grammatical form of speech," and he recognized that negroes were not the only ones being sent up by the merry minstrels. The stilted, courtly speech was a subtle parody of the villagers' notions of what talk sounded like in "high and citified society."[16] That "painfully grammatical" was a neat distinction. His grasp of language and its uses as weaponry was already forming.

Somewhat later in his boyhood, probably as an early teen, Sammy was on hand for the arrival of the "mesmerizer." This was another sort of act that continued to link mid–nineteenth- and mid–twentieth-century Hannibal: The hairslicked hypnotist in his shiny black tuxedo gliding about the stage, conjuring transparently hoked-up bits of foolishness from grinning local boys who'd been bribed and rehearsed in advance. Sammy, eager to show off, volunteered as a "subject," but he was a little slow on the uptake: He sat on the volunteers' bench for three nights and struggled to "get sleepy" while gazing at the charlatan's "magic disk," and watching a somewhat savvier friend of his named Hicks grab all the glory by pretending to jump and squirm when the professor yelled, "Snake!"

By the fourth night Sammy was onto the game. He arose from the bench and became the most-mesmerized kid in the history of fake enchantment. He passed imaginary fire buckets. He went berserk over invisible steamboat races. He kissed phantom girls, caught gigantic make-believe catfish, debased himself in endless ways. Hicks never had a chance after that. He was a casualty of his own limited views on the possibilities of fiction. Not so Sammy: "Hicks was born honest, I without that incumbrance—so some people said."[17]

As Mark Twain embellished the differences between Hicks and himself on the mesmerizer's stage, he incidentally revealed his essence—as a representative child, and as a transformative literary artist. His essence lay in his respect for, and his uses of, enchantment:

> Hicks saw what he saw and reported accordingly, I saw more than was visible and added to it such details as could help. Hicks had no imagination; I had a double supply. He was born calm, I was born excited. No vision could start a rapture in him and he was constipated as to language, anyway; but if I saw a vision I emptied the dictionary onto it and lost the remnant of my mind into the bargain.[18]

The excitement and impact of these tin-and-sawdust diversions can be hard to imagine by a citizen of a culture that burns its images home unceasingly from everywhere to everywhere at the speed of light. And yet their impact, measured spectacle for spectacle against our late–twentieth-century onslaught, was incomparably greater. While long quiet intervals indeed existed, in the isolated villages, between these bursts of noise and flame and gaudy illusion, it was in those very intervals that the echoes of the pageants resounded and gained grandeur in the villagers' reveries; and no more so than in the children's; and no more so among the children than the attentive Sammy Clemens and his chosen chums. "The first of all the negro minstrel shows came to town, and made a sensation," the narrator of *Tom Sawyer* tells us. "Tom and Joe Harper got up a band of performers and were happy for two days. . . . A circus came. The boys played circus three days afterward in tents made of rag carpeting—admission, three pins for boys, two for girls . . . "

But enchantment still required an audience. For Sam Clemens's friends, the minstrels and the circuses and the mesmerizer were exhilarating, grand, formative—but fleetingly so, bright stories that faded to traces in adulthood ("—and then circusing was abandoned," we learn[19]). For Sammy, the stories never faded, the circus was never abandoned. Again, as he developed the tale of his eclipsing of Hicks in the mesmerizer's hall, he shed light on how he managed this—via his lifelong habit of noticing:

> Hicks . . . had shown several bad defects and I had made a
> note of them. For instance, when the magician asked, "What
> do you see?" and left him to invent a vision for himself,
> Hicks was dumb and blind, he couldn't see a thing nor say
> a word, whereas the magician soon found out that when it
> came to seeing visions of a stunning and marketable sort I
> could get along better without his help than with it.[20]

Sammy's acute noticing extended beyond Hicks, though, and into the subtlest nuances of the moment: into gesture and mood, into the critical information written on the faces of the crowd. As the mesmerizer stood behind his slow-witted rival and gazed at the back of his head, Sammy comprehended at once that, oblivious to Hicks, the man was trying to drive a mental suggestion into the boy. "If he had been noticing he could have seen by the rapt faces of the audience that something was going on behind his back that required a response."[21]

At first, "inasmuch as I was an impostor," Sammy dreaded the moment when the professor turned his gaze upon him. Surely now he would be exposed and denounced. And then, with the mesmerizer behind him and the audience's faces tense with expectation, inspiration struck: the artist's leaping impulse to connect an available artifact to the story-in-progress. His eye fell on an old revolver lying on a table onstage, a prop from an earlier routine. In a flash he recalled a drubbing he had taken from a school bully a few weeks earlier, during May Day celebration. The boy was now seated in the crowd, facing him, halfway down the aisle. Inspired, Sammy Clemens acted:

> I crept stealthily and impressively toward the table, with a dark and murderous scowl on my face, copied from a popular romance, seized the revolver suddenly, flourished it, shouted the bully's name, jumped off the platform and made a rush for him and chased him out of the house before the paralyzed people could interfere to save him. There was a storm of applause . . . [22]

The moment was such a success that the mesmerized mesmerizer could not resist prying himself into Sammy's story. "I assure you," he cried to the audience, "that without a single spoken word to guide him he has carried out what I mentally commanded him to do. . . . I could have stopped him at a moment in his vengeful career by a mere exertion of my will . . . "[23]

No greater comic moment occurs in any of Mark Twain's fiction. Nor a more revealing one. Tense and watchful because of his supposed "impostor's status" onstage—a lifelong source of anxiety for this famously divided soul—young Sammy uses his tortured, heightened awareness to seize upon a handy object, the revolver, and use it to effect a brilliant, improvised reversal: Now Sammy, and not the putative star of the show, is calling the shots, dictating the narrative, mesmerizing the mesmerizer himself into delivering the payoff line. Not even Tom Sawyer, conning his friends into whitewashing the fence, could have topped this moment.

Unless, of course, Mark Twain was dreaming it all up as he wrote.

But where, then, did the imaginative materials for the literary invention come from? What was the source of the dream? With either alternative, the final explanation seems the same: He was the average adolescent-minded American . . . plus genius.

Dream and reality were never far apart in Sammy's Hannibal. Throughout his childhood, men bearing learned credentials came to town to deliver lectures on witchcraft, on demonology, on human magnetism. In October 1844 he watched as a flock of worshippers from the Millerite sect wrapped themselves in ascension robes and flooded up the steep hill to Lover's Leap, there to watch as the world ended.

He watched as the fad of spiritualism took hold in Hannibal in the late 1840s. "Mediums" proliferated in household parlors. In *Life on the Mississippi,* he remembered a young woman named Roberta Jones, who thought to play a prank on a rapture-prone old woman who lived alone. Miss Jones appeared in the woman's house wrapped in a sheet, her face streaked white with dough. The resulting fright sent the old woman into the insane asylum.

Twain himself, with all his accumulated worldliness, would never be quite free from the phantasmagoric spell of his boyhood. In 1879, in Paris, he would try to talk to his brother Henry during a seance. "Talk with the departed," he would record in an aching notebook entry:

> To Henry, (through medium Mansfield)—Pray <move to> try the other place; <it is better to be less comfortable> you don't seem to have much intellect left, but even that is worth saving, & a change might help.[24]

He would rummage through mediums after Susy died, and, with his wife Olivia, kept up an active interest in what was then called "mind science."

Brimstone sermons invoking God the Avenger; mourning rituals that required the touching of a dead sibling; the lurid colors of the minstrel show; the thrall of the mesmerizer; the background voices of the nighttime-singing slaves on his uncle's farm, spellbinding, creating "something at once awful and sublime"; his own tendencies to dream of fire and to wander, dreaming, in the night: Both the inner and outer worlds of Hannibal must have seemed to Sammy, at times, engulfed in the supernatural, the paranormal, reality and fantasy always contending for the moment. "He did not believe in Hell," wrote Dixon Wecter, "but he was afraid of it."

Six

"I was always heedless.
I was born heedless . . . "

Will Bowen was his friend. Will Bowen of the yellow locks, pliable, genially conspiratorial.

In this solidly middle-class fire-insurance agent's son, Sammy the marginal young fantasist had struck a rare find: a boy who would reinforce and ratify Sam's fragile, romantic variations on his own identity. In this sense Will was much more than a sidekick. He was a splendid audience for the early dress rehearsals of a protean actor and master of psychic disguises. Sam, the lifelong devotee of twinning, of doubling, of mixed and fraudulent personas, seems to have perceived in spiffy Will his first idealized mirror image.

Only Bowen, of all the town boys, it seems, could approach Sammy's manic imaginings and keep up with his stage-managing of all the kidhood drama in town.

Years later Mark Twain would unify this chum and himself inside the persona of his most universally beloved literary creation, the blithe dream-meister Tom Sawyer. (Sometimes, when Twain's childhood self took up too much room, he would move Bowen over to occupy Joe Harper or Ben Rogers.)

He clearly needed a double—his Friar Tuck, his Black Avenger of the Spanish Main. Skinny and small-boned under his largish red head, Sammy lacked the mass to dominate his peers physically. The ritual pummeling of the "new boy" by the town kid in the opening chapter of *Tom Sawyer* may have drawn on painful memory. But he possessed, beneath his languid "long talk" drawl, a trait that was equally powerful: the sort of mesmerizing intellect that seemed almost to complete, or extend, the personalities of his playmates, and thereby seduce them into complicity. Bowen was a willing and amiable receptor.

Will was one of six children of Captain Samuel Bowen, who had moved his family to Hannibal from Tennessee several years before the Clemenses arrived. Captain Bowen had been a tobacco inspector and a warehouser, among his other accomplishments. He had put his family in a wing of the large brick warehouse that sprawled tantalizingly near the Clemens's poorer wooden digs, on the levee between Hill and Bird Streets.[1]

Sammy, the scion of fallen cavaliers, entered into the Bowens' plusher lives, in reality as in fantasy. Will's sister Mary was one of his many childhood sweethearts. Brother Sam served in Clemens's short-lived Confederate company at the outbreak of the Civil War, got involved in a tragicomic marriage while still a teen-ager, became a river pilot and died of yellow fever in 1878. It is likely that Bart and John Bowen may have sometimes joined their brothers and Sammy on "that distant boy-Paradise, Cardiff Hill."*

But it was Will whom Sammy chose as his alter ego, his collaborator in the most intense, encoded rituals of childhood: the signing of

---

*"Cardiff Hill" was the name Twain gave to Holliday's Hill in his fictions and in his autobiography. That is the name by which the hill later came to be known.

blood-oaths, the candlelit obeisances to superstition, the memorizing of medieval tales and their enactments deep in the green hillside woods. It was Will, paramount among others, with whom Sammy recreated the highlights of the circuses and raucous minstrel shows and stock-company performances that floated through town.

When imported stimulation was not available, Sammy created his own, with help from his trusty double. It was Will who tried to keep pace with truant, bookish Sammy in living out the classic storybook tales. "Guy of Guisborne wants no man's pass," calls Bowen/Harper in *Tom Sawyer*. "'Who art thou that—that—' 'Dares to hold such language,' said Tom, prompting—for they talked 'by the book,' from memory."

And it was Will Bowen who joined Sammy's early experiments at the border of life and death, in the years when many disturbing events were forming Twain's lifelong burden of guilt.

Will was at Sammy's side, straining, when they pushed the giant boulder ("about the size of an omnibus"[2]) down Holliday's Hill above the Mississippi. The two, with occasional help from other boys, had worked sporadically for weeks to dislodge the rock. One Saturday afternoon, after three hours' labor, they saw that it was ready to move. They waited for a picnic party on the road below them to pass beyond the likely path of descent, then they gave it their final shove.

"It was splendid," Twain wrote with arch detachment. The boulder tore up trees, flattened bushes, burst a woodpile to smithereens. Then in an instant bloomed horror. A Negro drayman—Simon by name—emerged into view on the low road behind his mule. As the boys watched helplessly, the boulder lurched and thundered toward him. A second before impact it launched itself from some impediment in the ground and sailed over the ducking Simon's head. It smashed into a frame cooper-shop, "and the coopers swarmed out like bees. Then we said it was perfectly magnificent, and left. Because the coopers were starting up the hill to inquire."[3]

This brush with manslaughter—however innocently begun—obviously left its imprint on Twain's memory.* But at around the same time in his boyhood, Sammy took another excursion to the edges of mortality. This incident was incomparably more calculated than the boulder misadventure; the other player, passive this time, was again Will Bowen.

Frontier towns and villages were vulnerable to lethal viral and bacterial waves, especially rivertowns with their constant influx of transients. In the summer heat of 1844, when Sammy was eight,† a measles epidemic swept through Hannibal. As was usual in such emergencies, children died daily. (The Hannibal *Gazette* reported in 1847 that "One quarter of the children born, die before they are 1 year old; one half die before they are 21, and not one quarter reach the age of 40."[4]) "The mothers of the town were nearly demented with fright," Twain recalled,[5] and none was more demonstrative in her fright than Jane Clemens, who grew obsessed with keeping her children protected from contagion.

In the midst of her frenzied barricadings, Sammy decided to expose himself to the disease. Will Bowen lay stricken inside his brick house.

---

*It played at his conscience as well. In his conversations with his biographer Albert Bigelow Paine around 1906, Twain softened the horror a bit: The boulder started moving on its own, he maintained; moreover, the incident occurred on a Sunday and the cooper-shop was empty.

†Mark Twain in his autobiography dated this incident at 1845, but other historians, including R. Kent Rasmussen (*Mark Twain A to Z* [New York: Facts on File, 1995]), locate it in 1844.

Sammy entered through the front door and crept along the hallways toward his friend's bedroom on the second floor, in the rear. He had made it inside the bedroom before Will's appalled mother noticed him and hustled him out of the house, scolding him all the way. "She was so scared that she could hardly get her words out and her face was white."[6]

The lesson Sammy drew from this was efficiently to the point: He needed to be more careful on his next attempt. "I hung about the lane at the rear of the house . . . until I was convinced that the conditions were favorable. Then I slipped through the back yard and up the back way and got into the room and into the bed with Will Bowen without being observed."[7]

He lay beside Will for a long time; he didn't know how long. His friend was too far gone in delirium to notice his presence. Finally Will's mother found him again—his head swaddled under a thin sheet against discovery—and dragged him all the way home by the collar.

Sammy achieved his goal, or part of his goal: "It was a good case of measles that resulted. It brought me within a shade of death's door."[8] He recalled the experience as placid, tranquil, sweet, delightful, enchanting. "I have never enjoyed anything in my life any more than I enjoyed dying that time."[9] The family assembled at his bedside; there was weeping. The effect on Sammy was vaguely pleasant: "I was the center of all this emotional attention and was gratified by it and vain of it."[10] Finally Doctor Cunningham managed to cure him by placing hot ashes on his chest; "and so, very much to his astonishment—and doubtless to my regret—he dragged me back into this world . . . "[11]

Twain's autobiography—far from a document of record in any case—leaves unclear the precise motivation for this morbid gesture. He says he grew tired of the anxiety he felt at the protracted threat of death the epidemic imposed: "I made up my mind to end this suspense and settle this matter one way or the other and be done with it."[12] Perhaps he felt that if his alter ego Will were dying he must logically die also—like the other half of the dog whose one-half Pudd'nhead Wilson yearned to kill.

Or perhaps he was trying in some inexpressible way to atone for his "treachery" to his recently departed brother Benjamin. His determination to climb into Will Bowen's sickbed and literally taunt the Grim Reaper bore some aspects of sacrificial atonement.

Will survived his measles affliction along with Sammy. The close affinity between the two continued after childhood. Something about Bowen connected Sam to the immutable flow of his boyish essence. He followed Will into the life of steamboat piloting in the mid–1850s; the two friends would copilot three boats on the Mississippi, kidhood fantasy consummated against impossible odds. ("Stop the stabboard! Ting-a-ling-ling! Stop the labbord! Come ahead on the stabboard! Stop her! Let your outside turn over slow," bellows "Ben Rogers," impersonating the steamer "Big Missouri" in *Tom Sawyer*.) After the Civil War and a money dispute briefly chilled their friendship, Clemens kept up a sporadic correspondence with Bowen throughout his life. Twain tended to write to his old chum (who had gone, Sawyerishly, into insurance sales in St. Louis) at moments of transition in his life, of artistic flowering or plunges into despondency. The urgency of these letters, alternately soul-baring and waspishly scolding, suggests the undercurrents of a conversation from the self to the self.

A few days after his wedding to Olivia in 1870, Mark Twain consulted Bowen in a famous letter addressed to "My First, Oldest and Dearest Friend." Bowen apparently had written him a nostalgic letter not long before, and the effect on Twain—coupled, perhaps, with his wedding—had been volcanic. "The fountains of my great deep are broken up," he proclaimed to Bowen, and then plunged into an inventory of old memories—the enabling blueprint of the great manuscript he would begin writing four years later, the enshrinement of the Bowen/Clemens boyhood in the rivertown:

> The old life has swept before me like a panorama; the old days have trooped by in their old glory again; the old faces have looked out of the mists of the past; old footsteps have sounded in my listening ears; old hands have clasped mine, and the songs I loved ages and ages ago have come wailing down the centuries.[13]

In the torrential stream-of-consciousness that followed, Twain seemed to see the episodes and characters of his childhood pass before him as in a vivid dream. It was nothing less, as the scholar James M. Cox remarked, than "the whole spectrum of experience which was later to constitute the adventures of Tom Sawyer and Huckleberry Finn."[14]

But six years later, in *Tom Sawyer* freshly published, Twain abruptly turned on Bowen—or on himself through his old friend. Declaring that "there is nothing . . . worth pickling for present or future use," he mocked his unsuspecting, nostalgic correspondent: "Man, do you know this is simply mental and moral masturbation?" It belonged, Twain raged, "eminently to the period usually devoted to *physical* masturbation, and should be left there and outgrown."[15]

It was nothing personal. This unprovoked assault was a *cri de coeur* from a former child in torment. Writing *Tom Sawyer*—a task that sagged in its middle, as many of his writing projects would—had not restored Twain to beloved memory as much as underscored his estrangement from it. In the summer of 1876, Twain was bunkered in at Quarry Farm in New York. He was fighting depression, revisiting the deaths of his father and siblings, and struggling hard with themes of conscience in essays and in the even more fatiguing manuscript that was to be *Adventures of Huckleberry Finn*. He believed in that summer that his creative forces were running out; he further brooded that the very youth now forever behind him had been wasted.

Another freighted event haunted him. In 1874 the famous "Siamese Twins," Chang and Eng Bunker, had died. These conjoined brothers, briefly voguish in P. T. Barnum's postwar entertainments, had reignited Twain's obsession with the nature of identity. He had probed the comic implications of their plight in an 1869 magazine sketch—which reappeared in a collection a year after their death—and they launched him into a widening series of twinning themes that would reach consummation in *Pudd'nhead Wilson*.

Little wonder that a communication from his distant mirror image would trigger such venom.

This would not be the last time Twain struck at Bowen. In one of his even more tortured, past-haunted moods in 1882, Twain lashed out again. He wrote that "The histories of Will Bowen, Sam, and Capt. McCune and Mrs. B. make human life appear a grisly and hideous sarcasm."[16] This was a curious outburst, given especially that Will was still alive; he would in fact visit Twain in Hartford in 1888.

Upon Bowen's death in 1893, Twain felt a pang of conciliation. He wrote to Will's widow, perhaps not entirely comfortingly: "I should like to call back Will Bowen and John Garth and the others, and live the life, and be as we were, and make holiday until 15, then all drown together."[17]

He formed other, less complicated friendships—vivid boys who would become less vivid men, like the eager faces in some school annual. Ed Stevens and John Briggs were close chums; Briggs, a future farmer, was one of the looseners of the boulder on Holliday's Hill. Sammy knew Arch Fuqua, who could double back his big toe and snap it so you could hear the noise thirty yards away. He knew Theodore Eddy, who could work his ears like a horse. He knew the sweet and gentle John Meredith, whose vividness would increase—he became a bloodthirsty Confederate guerrilla during the war. He knew the Levin brothers, the first Jews he had ever seen; his friends had a nickname for them, charmingly untainted by bigotry: "Twenty-two." Twice Levin—twenty-two. He knew George RoBards, whose streaming yellow locks surpassed even those of Bowen. He also knew Mary Moss, "that blooming and beautiful thing."[18] Unfortunately, RoBards knew her too, and laid siege to her and won.

The truly spectral figure among his childhood friends, of course, was Tom Blankenship. The model for Huckleberry Finn was everything that stolid, safe Will Bowen was not. Here was a dark, ravaged, primitive boy; unschooled, superstitious and wise in the uses of dead cats and midnight incantations; a creature of the wheel-rutted streets and free from every social restraint that bound Sammy and his other friends. He was one of many children of a drifting South Carolina drunkard named Woodson Blankenship, who had stashed his family in a spacious, tacked-together shack of dried wood amidst a jumble of hollyhocks, honeysuckle, cats, and rumors on a narrow street not far from the Clemens house. If Will Bowen represented middle-class respectability (and its face-washing discontents) to Sammy, Blankenship represented utter liberation, the disembodied catcall under the window that could release Sammy into the scary pleasures of the frontier night.

Tom Sawyer and Huck Finn were bosom pals only in fiction. Blankenship was royalty. Older than Sammy by a couple of years, he seems also to have commanded the natural aura of leadership that Sammy/Tom suggests in fiction. The family had a sinister aura: Among Tom's eight siblings, two or more of his sisters were suspected prostitutes. Tom's older brother Bence occasionally menaced the smaller boys, tying their clothes in knots when they went swimming.

And yet—fortunately for literature—the Blankenships weren't *merely* squalid. A kind of desperate nobility lay contained in their plight. At least that was true of Tom and his brother Bence. These boys revealed an essential kindheartedness beneath their rough appearances and manners. As for Tom, his liberation-within-poverty, his indifference to material wealth, captivated Sammy, who would bend his knee to wealth as an adult as he bent it to hard times as a boy. "He was the only really independent person—boy or man—in the community, and by consequence he was tranquilly and continuously happy and envied by all the rest of us," Twain wrote.[19] In the character Huck Finn, he maintained, "I have drawn Tom Blankenship exactly as he was."[20]

A hazier presence in 1840s Hannibal—obscured, now, in the confusing claims of history—is the figure of Injun Joe.

The fictional Joe, who saturates the latter passages of *Tom Sawyer* with fiendish menace, is among the most horrific characters Twain ever created: a depraved half-breed who stabs Dr. Robinson in the graveyard, coolly arranges the evidence to indict his companion Muff Potter, testifies against Potter at the murder trial, then lurks about the town, invisible but threatening, after Tom bravely accuses him in court. The scene in which Tom and Becky Thatcher, lost inside the cave, realize that Joe lurks there also in the darkness, is among the most chilling passages of nineteenth-century children's literature.*

Whether a real-life model for Injun Joe existed has been a mystery. Twain referred in his autobiography to a harmless town drunk by that name, whom his father once tried, without success, to reform. The consensus among Hannibal people for many years was that "Joe" was drawn from a man named Joe Douglas, a part-Osage who had been scalped as a boy and was about two years older than Sam Clemens. Douglas lived until 1923, when he died, probably at the age of 102. Douglas was known to resent the connection with Twain's villain and always denied that he had been the character's real-life referent.

Sam's world did not consist solely of boys, but also of far more mysterious strangers: girls. In addition to Will's sister, Sam's other love-interests included Mary Miller, twice his age at eighteen, and Artimisia Briggs, who was even older; and he fancied the wild and ungovernable Mary Lacy, also older, who married and became quite governable indeed. (The older, married Mary Fairbanks, whom he met aboard the Quaker City, would summon the Victorian gentleman from his repertoire of identities across a thirty-year span of unctuous friendship.) At nine, he was smitten by the fourteen-year-old Margaret Sexton, the daughter of a woman who boarded in the Clemens house.

---

*Tom Sawyer's stature as a "children's" book is in fact ambiguous. Upon its completion in the summer of 1875, Twain wrote to William Dean Howells, "It is *not* a boy's book, at all. It will only be read by adults." Howells, upon reading it, urged him "to treat it explicitly as a boy's book. Grownups will enjoy it just as much if you do . . ." In the event, its initial publication in 1876 was delayed by scheduling errors; the book appeared with no distinct marketing identity, and only with the passage of years did it emerge as the most popular of all his books. It has never gone out of print.

And of course, there was Annie Laurie Hawkins, blue-eyed and yellow-haired—the Becky Thatcher of his writings, who lived across the street from him (in the house that is now a bookshop bearing her fictional name), who inspired Sammy's handstanding showoff antics. She outlived Mark Twain by eighteen years and recalled on learning of his death exactly how he'd looked the first time they'd met: a barefoot and mulberry-stained seven-year-old, sorting berries in the palm of his hand; and she remembered exactly what people found funny about him—his "drawling, appealing voice."[21]

His drawling, appealing voice. How he shaped and flavored words in his mouth. Words intoxicated and thrilled and terrified him—his own words, other children's, his mother's, the mincing words of Sunday School superintendents and the specialized jargon of riverboat captains, the knee-slapping snappers of the end-men in minstrel shows, the highblown words of visiting orators such as Senator Thomas Hart Benton, the sham Shakespeare of the sly circus blackface Dan Rice. And all the inventories of language unscrolled by strangers off the riverboats, the clipped Connecticut Yankees and the filigreed Virginia planters; his uncle's slaves telling their coded tales out on the farm; the lofty bad poetry of household homilies and serenades.

The words of all those American relatives and comrades and slaves and strangers, the thick broth of the culture then brewing.

That broth was brewing not only in spoken language, but also in books, and the love of books.

Somewhere, Sammy Clemens learned to read. Learned not only to read, but to hunger for reading. When, exactly, this avidity ignited, or from whose spark, remains unclear. His detestation of schooling and his love of hooky-playing were part of his personal and fictive myth. During his summer visits, he looked in on a country schoolhouse near the Quarles farm where he claimed his greatest educational experience was the eating of corn dodger and buttermilk at noon. (He also learned to smoke there.) In Hannibal, he went as a small boy to a "dame school" presided over by a Mrs. Horr, at the southern end of Main Street near Bear Creek. Later he enrolled in a school near the town square, at Center Street, which was kept by one William O. Cross. After his father's death in 1847, he labored under J. D. Dawson—the unfortunate model for his uproarious schoolmaster caricatures in *Tom Sawyer*.

Perhaps his most influential reading teacher was a spinster associate of Mrs. Horr's named Mary Ann Newcomb. Twain rendered her mercilessly as "an old maid and thin" in "Villagers," but more importantly, she drilled him and his fellow pupils in McGuffey's Reader, Webster's Speller, and selections from the Bible.

Mark Twain would develop a deep and complex relationship with the Bible. He read it continually from boyhood through old age: Some twenty-five copies of the Good Book would pass through his extended family. He would make more than four hundred Biblical allusions in his work. In sequence, they would describe the arc of his deepening alienation from its authority, even as his respect for its language and fascination with its characters increased.[22] His attitude toward its doctrine came almost to suggest the attitude of a spurned lover for a fickle beloved. An unquestioned oracle of authority in his boyhood, the Bible shifted over the decades into a vessel of "blood-drenched history; and some good morals; and a wealth of obscenity; and upwards of a thousand lies."[23] His conscious distancing from it may have begun toward the end of his years as a Mississippi River pilot, when he read Thomas Paine's *The Age of Reason*, and saw for the first time an intellectual skepticism over the claims to miracles or to the justness of the Christian God.

Yet the Bible fascinated him, Genesis and the Life of Christ sections especially. He was passingly familiar with at least thirty-seven of the sixty-six books in the Bible; whether out of curiosity, love or contempt, he read it. Miss Newcomb was chief among his early prompters. "She compelled me to learn to read," he confessed on his last visit to Hannibal in 1902.[24]

One might conjecture that his icily intellectual father, who organized a small library in Hannibal, encouraged his reading at home. As a young man Sam twitted his mother as a romantic disciple of James Fenimore Cooper.[25] As Mark Twain he found Cooper's prose hysterical, but the remark suggests that Jane may have read aloud to him as a small boy. And certainly a craving for books would have been a natural result of the many stories, tall tales, and narrative songs and spirituals in which he luxuriated throughout his childhood.

Whatever the exact impetus, by middle childhood Sam Clemens was a book-saturated boy without being "bookish." He had virtually memorized *Robin Hood,* as *Tom Sawyer* suggests, and worked it into his fantasizings with Bowen and the others. The same went for *Ivanhoe, Robinson Crusoe, Gulliver's Travels, The Arabian Nights,* and *Don Quixote.* Language and performance, in a quest for an irreducible self. His life's work, and his nation's representative voice, in chrysalis.

His enchantments with language and with reenacting the bright pageants that came to Hannibal brought him more immediate benefits as well. They fortified him against the terrors that had already begun to enflame his dreams: the instances of undertow, of conflagration, of abyss that the Edenic river and hills and cave suggested in their *ur*-images.

Sammy had already experienced the deaths of two siblings, and had made an impulsive gesture toward suicide. (He would revisit that impulse at least once more, pressing a pistol to his head in an alcoholic depression in San Francisco in 1866. "Many times I have been sorry I did not succeed," he remarked several decades after that, "but I was never ashamed of having tried."[26]) But by 1844, the year in which *Tom Sawyer* was by implication set, Sammy had also witnessed the first in a series of extraordinarily gruesome spectacles and events—bloody corpses, acts of murder and manslaughter, drownings, vivisection, immolation—*ur*-images, themselves, of the new-forming culture in its fondness for violence and danger.

These spectacles and events found their way into his literature and into the hollows of his soul. Mark Twain, for all his deserved acclaim as a champion of justice and a critic of aggression, could be astonishingly sardonic about the loss of human life. "We pine for murder— these fistfights are of no consequence to anybody," he joked darkly in his coverage of a brawl for the Virginia City *Enterprise* in 1863.[27]

The string of horrors commenced as Sammy's family took up life in what would become one of the most famous frame houses in America. Sometime around 1844, John Marshall Clemens developed the last little plot of land he'd bought when he moved to Hannibal: a cramped space just up the street from the Virginia House. There he commissioned the building of a spare two-story wooden house, painted white. This house, at 206 Hill Street, is the one that was restored and enshrined in 1912 as the Boyhood Home of Mark Twain. Sammy and his younger brother Henry shared a small upstairs bedroom; his older brother Orion and his sister Pamela each had their quarters; in the coming desperate time Pamela would give music lessons in the downstairs parlor, and Orion would try to run a newspaper for awhile out of one of its tiny anterooms. More importantly for American myth, it was from this house that Sammy would steal, through his bedroom window, meowing to his friends' meows, and then down all the ledges of grown-up habitation for his escapades in the Hannibal graveyard night.

Seven

"Three times he stretched his hand a little way out into the dark, gingerly; and snatched it suddenly back, with a gasp—not because it had encountered any thing, but because he felt so sure it was just going to."

Night—the Dark—would form one of Mark Twain's most enduring metaphors. He and his young comrades knew its absoluteness; knew the primitive profundity of it, the purity of its majesties and terrors, its capacity to engulf and transform, to render themselves and their village as small as microbes under its great indifferent bell. Night would become, in his life and in his art, a source of unappeasable dread, but also a sort of sanctuary to which he would return again and again. It would become a dreamscape of memory and invention where grief and fright and risk and oblivion took on, finally, an almost ennobling patina that at once magnified and redeemed his losses and his horror.

Catcalled, he would crawl from his window along the roof of the ell, then drop down to the top of the woodshed, and then to the ground. Joined perhaps by Will Bowen and John Briggs and the wraithlike meowing Blankenship, this small-framed boy would slip into a night-time demimonde nearly impossible to evoke from the perspective of a later, illuminated and amplified century.

By day the village offered its diversions; by night, it offered the pleasures of risk. "A phantom town inhabited largely by ghostly presences," as the critic Cynthia Griffin Wolff characterized it.[1] A place where restless children would shine their inner beacons on a vast dark slate.

The boys would make their way through a stark black village innocent of vaporlights, of auto headlights, of neon; a village in which only the occasional dim candle or banked hearth fire broke the gloom. An ominous labyrinth of incipient violence. The houses, where adult Hannibal slept, would be stupefied shapes under the moon or the glow of the Milky Way; if the sky were covered by clouds, the Mississippi itself might be invisible—heavy-scented, alive with the low lappings of its current, but without form, river as dream. Barking dogs, roused by the boys' passage, would often be the only other sources of sound, of commentary, save for the clock booming on the hour or an owl far beyond the town borders. A who-whooing owl was mourning the dead; a barking dog meant that someone was about to die.

They felt their way over earthen streets toward the levee, toward the tanyard where the town drunk Jimmy Finn slept with the hogs; toward the slaughter pens, toward the woods, toward the old-fashioned western graveyard on the northern hill; toward a night filled with intimations of hoodoo and magic spells, of witches and devils and walking bones, all the layers of American guilt and terror and sorrow gathered and palpable in the dark air. Perhaps they were on their way to add to the ambient superstition—toward a certain dead hillside tree or down to the cave by skiff to enact rituals of gang initiation, imitating what they knew of the real gangs that menaced the region: candles and sulfur matches in their pockets, and knives for pricking the fingertips. With school-hating bookworm Sammy supplying all the literary citations.

"Must we always kill the people?" [Ben Rogers asks Tom during the gang's blood-oath ceremony in the cave, and Tom replies:] "Oh, certainly. It's best. Some authorities think different, but mostly it's considered best to kill them. Except some that you bring to the cave here and keep them till they're ransomed."

"Ransomed? What's that?"

"I don't know. But that's what they do. I've seen it in books; and so of course that's what we've got to do."

"But how can we do it if we don't know what it is?"

"Why blame it all, we've got to do it. Don't I tell you it's in the books?"[2]

Perhaps they were only going to swim naked in Bear Creek in the moonlight or set cats loose inside the guest-rooms of the Western Star tavern, or steal peaches, or knock over some farmer's stable. It hardly mattered; or rather, it all mattered. The common referent to all this was the night, the supernatural night. The town boys took ownership of the night—invested it with their mimetic, improvising maleness—to a degree that they could never invest the grown-up matriarchal day.

They did so knowing the possible consequences. The frontier night's terrors were by no means all fanciful. The invisible Mississippi could devour, and placid Bear Creek had its submerged hazards. The sulfur matches could ignite other things besides candles. Not all the adults were asleep.

There lurked the constant prospect of an encounter with maleness unconstrained. Drunks littered the darkened streets outside the taverns. Older herds of boys, less romantically disposed than Sammy and his friends in the mid–1840s, might gather at Main and Bird—within earshot of the Clemens household—and scream obscenities and bawdy songs. Perhaps a genuine sociopath or two, like the wild Hyde brothers, Dick and Ed, would be on a boozy prowl with their revolvers, intimidating whomever they met for the hell of it. Nor could the boys venture into the darkened woods with the absolute assurance that they would not encounter a fugitive band of cutthroats, one of the many that worked the Mississippi river valley in those days. "'Twas always said that Murrel's gang used around here [sic] one summer," mutters Injun Joe's cohort in the haunted house, unearthing the treasure box as Tom and Huck listen from the upstairs floor. The reference is to the actual leader of a murderous thousand-member gang that prowled the region in the 1820s.

Some of the most terrifying things Samuel Clemens ever witnessed across his seventy-five years of world travel occurred in his Hannibal boyhood, often at night. Even the daylight horrors returned to him at night, in the form of dreams.

One winter night in the late '40s Sammy and Tom Nash, the postmaster's son, went on a midnight ice-skating spree on the Mississippi. They likely sneaked out of their respective houses to do it. "I cannot see why we should go skating in the night unless without permission," Mark Twain mused in his autobiography, "for there could be no considerable amusement to be gotten out of skating at midnight if nobody was going to object to it." The boys had swirled and glided more than half a mile outward from the Missouri shore when they began to hear the grinding and rumbling sounds that could mean only one thing: that the ice between them and dry land was breaking up.

The Mississippi was preparing to devour them. Twain recalled that they struggled for an hour toward shore, flying along when they were sure of the ice-surface, then, when darkness overtook them, waiting for the moon to break through the clouds and reveal a new route. Near the Missouri banks, they began to leap in desperation from fragmenting cake to cake. Tom Nash made the wrong leap, Twain recalled. "He got a bitter bath . . . then his feet struck hard bottom and he crawled out. . . . He took to his bed, sick, and had a procession of diseases. The closing one was scarlet fever and he came out of it stone deaf."[3]

But Tom Nash's frigid struggle in the nighttime river was by no means the only brush with mortal crisis that Sam Clemens experienced during his boyhood. Given that Nash lived, it in fact ranked among the least jarring in a litany of gruesome incidents. The decade from 1843 until 1853—essentially, the Hannibal boyhood era—contained the richest experiences of Mark Twain's life and literature. No other period drew him back so insistently; no other period so saturated the wellsprings of his literature. And although these years supplied him with many satisfactions and ecstasies and lyric yearnings—"I can call back the solemn twilight and mystery of the deep woods, the earthy smells, the faint odors of the wild flowers. . . . I can call it all back and make it as real as it ever was, and as blessed"[4]—these pleasures existed in a dialectic with the terror and the intimation of violence that always lurked, on the American frontier, at the edges of one's vision. Just as he had heard the slaves on the Quarles farm work their terrors into songs and stories of deeply textured beauty, Mark Twain listened ever afterward to the pitch of anguish that sounded through his youth and made it a theme in his great tragicomic symphony.

The shadow world lay perfectly conjoined within the sunlit one, its dark twin. It was steeped in human savagery; in beatings, knife-wielding, gunplay, and less lethal cruelties. The natural elements themselves were demonic. Fire could spread from a spark and roast the flesh. Water could imprison a careless boy in its deep sucking currents. The wind and lightning could sound like God's hard judgment come to claim a sinful child who lay quivering in his bed.

The aftershocks of such episodes never abated in Twain's memory, but erupted at the most unexpected moments and went throbbing into his work. Wandering through the white marble cathedral of Milan in 1867, while disembarked from the *Quaker City* cruise that would produce *The Innocents Abroad,* he was shown a "coffee-colored piece of sculpture" reputedly from the hand of Phidias—a figure of a man without skin, at once flawlessly beautiful and evocative of hideous pain. The image plunged him into dark night. "I shall dream of it," Twain wrote, "I shall dream that it is resting its corded arms on the bed's head and looking down at me with its dead eyes . . . touching me with its exposed muscles and its stringy cold legs."[5] In the next instant, his mind went free-associating back to Hannibal and a moonlit horror in 1843.

"It is hard to forget repulsive things," he observed by way of preamble, and then disgorged the now-famous story of the white human hand on the floor of his father's law office. He had played hooky from school that day, capered well into the September night—he was not yet eight—and climbed into the window of John Marshall's small first-floor office to sleep and forestall the inevitable thrashing. A dark shape on the floor caught his attention. A pale square of moonlight, inching slowly along, illuminated the form by excruciating degrees: first a hand, then most of a naked arm, then the pallid face of a corpse, "the eyes fixed and glassy in death."[6]

This was the body of one James McFarland, a farmer who had been stabbed with an eight-inch shoe knife earlier that evening by his drinking companion Vincent Hudson. The two had been arguing over a plow. The corpse had been brought to Judge Clemens's office to await the embalmer's attentions the next morning. This was the first recorded murder in Hannibal's history. Like some other equally morbid firsts of that region, it bore Sammy's witness.

Mark Twain's description of his exodus from that office would become a comic staple in the routines of his drawling twentieth-century impersonators:

> I went away from there. I do not say that I went away in any sort of a hurry, but I simply went—that is sufficient. I went out at the window, and I carried the sash along with me. I did not need the sash, but it was handier to take it than it was to leave it, and so I took it. I was not scared, but I was considerably agitated.[7]

In the literary conversion of that almost proto-Freudean discovery—the corpse of a murdered man in the habitat of his father—into a comedic scene of detached ironic elegance lies a recurring paradigm: Mark Twain's childhood darkness, infused and sanctified with his imaginative light.

Two years after his first viewing of a murdered man, the boy witnessed his first murder—which happened to be the first premeditated murder in Hannibal's history. He was nine then. The spectacle gestated a fresh round of bad dreams and a chillingly unforgettable literary character.

The victim was a neighbor of the Clemenses, one "Uncle Sam" Smarr, an innocuous soul when sober, a belligerent fool when in the bag. Smarr, when drunk, liked to abuse the reputation of a local businessman named William Owsley. Smarr had grown obsessed with the notion that Owsley had weasled a friend of his out of two thousand dollars, and would publicly announce, after taking on a load, that he, Smarr, considered Owsley a son of a bitch who ought to be whipped, if not killed. One January day in 1845, after Smarr had ridden his horse up to Owsley's establishment and renewed his tirade, a customer noticed that Owsley began to twitch and turn white around the mouth. This proved not a good symptom for Smarr. Several days later, when "Uncle Sam" returned to town sober to sell a side of beef, Owsley stepped up to him from behind at the intersection of Hill and Main, just down the sloping street from the Clemens house. As several witnesses, including Sammy, looked on, Owsley drew a pistol from his pocket and called out: "You, Sam Smarr." Then, as Smarr turned and began to protest, the merchant—from a distance of about four paces—calmly extended his arm and fired off two bullets into the man's chest, measuring his second shot after he had discharged the first.

A friend of Smarr's named Brown testified to Judge Clemens that Smarr fell backwards and cried—in the flawless syntax that all mortally wounded people of the nineteenth century seemed obliged to employ—"Brown, come take me up, I am shot and will soon be a dead man." The victim was dragged into the drugstore of one Dr. Orville Grant at Hill and Main. (The strapped Clemens family would move into the second story of that building within a few months; death and dwelling-places seemed to converge for young Sammy.) There he was laid on his back on a table, where a crowd gathered to watch him for about half an hour, until he died.

Sammy squeezed in, and his dreams were enflamed with a particularly macabre detail. "In them I always saw again the grotesque closing picture," he would write,

—the great family Bible spread open on the profane old
man's breast by some thoughtful idiot and rising and sinking to the labored breathings and adding the torture of its
leaden weight to the dying struggles. . . . In my nightmares
I gasped and struggled for breath under the crush of that
vast book for many a night.[8]

The Bible was an interesting detail—interesting partly because no one
else remembered it being there. (Dr. Grant didn't mention it in his
later testimony.) The vessel of "blood-drenched history" had itself
become drenched in blood, whether in actuality or in the writer's
imagination.

"O Lord, don't shoot!" Mark Twain makes Smarr (renamed
"Boggs") cry in *Adventures of Huckleberry Finn,* as Owsley (now the
gothic cold-blooded Colonel Sherburn) stands at ease in the street,
holding the pistol with the barrel tilted up towards the sky. In Twain's
famous fictionalizing, the scene has shifted to the little one-horse town
of Bricksville, deep in Arkansas, where Huck, Jim, the duke, and the
king have put ashore to bilk the locals with an evening of fractured
Shakespeare. Huck, loafing through the town, witnesses the noisy arrival of Boggs on horseback and his drunken challenge to Sherburn;
he hears Sherburn's warning ("I'll endure it till one o'clock . . . ") and
later watches as the ascetic Colonel shouts, "Boggs!" and slowly low-
ers the pistol, both barrels cocked. After the shooting, Boggs is carried
to "a little drug store," where not one but two Bibles are supplied for
him—one under his head, the other spread on his breast. His shirt is
torn open, and "I seen where one of the bullets went in." Twain supplies the dying man with a sixteen-year-old daughter, who arrives on
the run just at the moment of gunfire and weeps, screaming, over her

father, whose gasps lift the Bible about a dozen times before he expires. Afterwards, a lynch mob forms in front of Sherburne's house; the Colonel steps through a window onto the roof of his front porch holding a double-barrel shotgun and calmly shames the crowd into dispersal by mocking their cowardice. "I could a staid, if I'd a wanted to," Huck assures his readers, "but I didn't want to." In the next sentence he wanders off to the circus. The murder of Boggs, its aftermath, its significance—all these vanish forever from the narrative.

Huck Finn, unlike Twain, does not seem likely to suffer nightmares from the bloody violence he has witnessed. His "but I didn't want to" is a piece of comic mock-bravado, a wink at his own inclination to slink on out of there with the crowd, get on with the day, and leave the villagers and Boggs's daughter and Sherburne to the almost unimaginable next phase of their lives.* Similarly, the adult Twain, unlike the child Sammy, seems unvexed by anything stronger than amusement at his own long-ago reaction to the stabbed corpse in his father's office.

In artistic terms, this clipped detachment exemplifies the sweeping revolution of diction that Mark Twain brought to American literature: the vast paring away of ornamental language by fast, edgy, suggestive talk. (If Smarr really did offer up that flowery supplication to Brown, he could have used a fast rewrite by Huck.) It suggests another Twainian bequest to the twentieth century: the existential hero, the unmoved

---

*In *Mark Twain on the Loose: A Comic Writer and the American Self* (Amherst: University of Massachusetts Press, 1995) the scholar Bruce Michelson analyzes Twain's oeuvre as a protean series of "escapes and evasions" from the culture's calcified adherence to numbing consistency and logic. He sees in Huck's "curt excuse for leaving the scene" a bracing example of Huck's capacity to conserve his own psychological liberty—to forestall the "disaster of becoming." "This is the Huck that matters," Michelson writes, "as a breakthrough in American realistic narrative, and as an American cultural icon."

mover on the lam; the psyche as camera with its shutter open, quite passive, recording, not thinking.

Mark Twain indeed played at notions of determinism in his late, grief-stricken years; he came to imagine Man as mere machine. But from boyhood through most of his writing years his camera-eye was anything but passive and unthinking. Mimetic, rapt, almost helplessly susceptible to the thrall of story and environment and experience, he relieved the pressure of memory by unloading it into narrative. Spoken language—the language of slaves, silver-miners, steamboatmen, roughnecks, boys; all the rich terse patter and coded lingo of his formative years—proved for this compulsive scribbler the most efficient way of getting it all down, including the hollows, that which was left unsaid.

Sammy seemed almost magnetically drawn to bloodshed. At age ten he was shocked to see a white slavemaster take offense at something that one of his charges had done awkwardly; the overseer smashed the man's head with a lump of iron-ore. It took the victim an hour to die. He happened along a town street one day just as a "young California emigrant" found himself on the receiving end of a knife attack from his drunken comrade. "I saw the red life gush from his breast," he later wrote,[9] a line that in its distinctly youthful-American bravado echoes Whitman ("The suicide sprawls on the bloody floor of the bedroom/It is so . . . I witnessed the corpse,"[10]) and anticipates Ben Hecht, the tough Chicago journalist of the early 1900s ("A man lay on his back in Barney Grogan's saloon with a knife sticking out of his belly, and I made notes"[11]).

Violence did not always find him. Sometimes he went looking for it. Once he had the bad judgment to rush up Holliday's Hill one dark and threatening night, with his friend John Briggs, to investigate the uproar triggered by an "invading ruffian." This was another California emigrant who had decided, after a bout of drinking, to go and raise hell in front of "The Welshman's house," which was occupied by the Welshman's elderly widow and her daughter. The Californian's obscene tirade had awakened most of the village by the time the boys arrived. On the porch stood the two women, the mother cradling a musket in her arms.

As Sherburne would do in literature to Boggs, the widow gave her tormentor a warning. If he were still in front of her when she finished counting to ten, she would kill him. Like Boggs, the drunk abuser was slow to appreciate his peril. By the count of five, he was still laughing. He was silent but still standing defiantly through "seven . . . eight . . . nine"—and likewise through a long pause, "we holding our breaths," before "ten!" and a burst of fire from the musket that tore the man's chest apart.

The crowd surged forward toward the house then under a sudden thunderous downpour, but by this time Sammy's appetite for such amusements had dulled: "I went home to dream and was not disappointed."[12]

Not even his beloved Mississippi gave him sanctuary from the horrors. In *Huckleberry Finn,* Huck and Jim remain generally free from the world's grotesqueries as long as they are out in the Mississippi's current. It is onshore that their brushes with depraved civilization occur. This was not altogether true in Clemens's life. The river, in time, would extract from him the most excruciating loss of his young manhood. But in its very denial of sanctuary, the river invested Twain with the greatest imaginative and moral inventions of his greatest book.

Sammy had nearly experienced the river's lethal grasp in the Tom Nash incident. When he was eleven, he received an even more ghastly preview of its doleful powers on a hot August day in 1847, when a corpse raised itself out of the water to grin at him.

Catfishing one day off Sny Island, across from Hannibal near the Illinois shore, Tom Blankenship's older brother Bence stumbled onto the hiding-place of a runaway slave, one Neriam Todd. The fugitive had a bounty on his head, but Bence ignored that. For several weeks the white boy ventured across the river in his skiff with stolen food for the man.

The arrangement could not last indefinitely, given that there are few secrets in a small town. Toward the end of the summer, Todd was rousted out by a group of men, woodchoppers by trade, who had heard rumors and gone to the island to investigate. They chased Todd through the underbrush and into a shallow, sandy stretch of water between the island and Illinois, a dank spot known as Bird Slough. Apparently they caught him there. He was never again seen alive.

But he was seen again. A few days later Sammy was foraging around on the island, along with John Briggs and the Bowens. They were wading in the water of the slough when "suddenly the negro rose before them, straight and terrible, about half his length out of the water. He had gone down feet foremost, and the loosened drift had released them."[13] Later accounts reported that he had been "much mutilated."[14] The boys, who had been rummaging for pecans and berries, splashed away in terror—in their hysteria they believed that the corpse was after them.

Twenty-nine years later, as he began work on *Adventures of Huckleberry Finn* in Hartford, Mark Twain revisited the steamy, frightful episode of Bird Slough, and found in it many of the foundation elements of his immortal story.

In chapter 8 of *Huckleberry Finn,* Huck surprises Jim on "Jackson's Island," much as Bence Blankenship had come upon the runaway slave on the Sny. (Huck had just escaped from father's cabin and counterfeited his own death; he had drifted downriver in his canoe toward the island, which was "standing up out of the middle of the river, big and dark and solid, like a steamboat without any lights.") Jim has run off from Miss Watson, who has decided to sell him down the river to New Orleans. Huck is shocked that Jim has escaped, but promises not to tell, much as Bence must have promised his desperate discovery. This is the first transforming moral decision of Huck's great odyssey:

> "Jim!"
>
> "But mind, you said you wouldn't tell—you know you said you wouldn't tell, Huck."
>
> "Well, I did. I said I wouldn't, and I'll stick to it. Honest *injun* I will. People would call me a low down Ablitionist and despise me for keeping mum—but that don't make no difference. I ain't agoing to tell, and I ain't agoing back there anyways. So now, le's know all about it."[15]

Later in the narrative, in Chapter 16, the "raftsman" chapter, Twain imagines the conflict of conscience that Bence must have endured—it was thought to be a shocking failure of decency in that society, not to mention a felony, to abet a runaway—and transfers it to Huck. Here, as the two imagine themselves near the mouth of the Ohio River and their route to the free states, Huck starts to consider that he is to "blame" for Jim's imminent freedom: "Conscience says to me, 'What had poor Miss Watson done to you, that you could see her nigger go off right under your eyes and never say one single word?'"[16] In a celebrated passage of unintentional irony, Huck then describes his private decision to turn Jim in, his opportunity to do so when he meets a couple of canoeing slave-hunters on the river; and his last-minute inability to betray his friend—which he sees as a puzzling kind of weakness:

> "I knowed very well I had done wrong, and I see it warn't no use for me to try to learn to do right. . . . Well, then, says I, what's the use you learning to do right, when it's trouble-some to do right and ain't no trouble to do wrong, and the wages is just the same? I was stuck. I couldn't answer that. So I reckoned I wouldn't bother no more about it, but after this always do whichever come handiest at the time.[17]

This rumination in turn foreshadows the utterance that, more than any other single passage, propels the novel outside its century and anneals its claim to moral and literary greatness. Far down the phantasmal river now, below the town of Pikesville, with Jim having been caught and held in custody at the Phelps farm, Huck's guilt over abetting a runaway overtakes him again. Thinking himself "wicked," "low-down," "ornery" (and watched by "Providence" for it, but unable to pray), he composes a letter to Miss Watson up in Hannibal, disclosing Jim's whereabouts. Now he is no longer lost, no longer on his way to hell. But then a com-peting guilt grips him: He reviews the whole trip down the river, Jim and himself in the moonlight, sometimes in storms, floating along, talking, singing, and laughing. He studies his letter again, "because I'd got to de-cide, forever, betwixt two things, and I knowed it." And then Huckle-berry Finn utters, to himself and to history:

"All right, then, I'll *go* to hell." And tears the letter up.

In this way did Samuel Langhorne Clemens elevate the most sordid horrors of his youthful consciousness to the highest levels of his literary art: by handing them over to Mark Twain, whom Robert Penn Warren called the "double that he had summoned into existence in order, himself, to exist at all."[18]

Yet the sublime transference did not necessarily put the long-standing trauma of the childhood memories to rest. The image of a sudden-vitalized corpse never stopped haunting the edges of Mark Twain's reverie. He made digressive use of it in two of his most substantial works. In *Life on the Mississippi,* he related a double-framed tale in which a dying man recounts his memory of an enemy of his rearing up in his shroud in the "corpse-room" of a Bavarian mortuary-house.* And in *Huckleberry Finn,* in a long-lost section discovered in 1990 and officially restored to the text in 1992, Jim tells Huck of an encounter he'd had with an eerily moving body at a "doctor college" many years before. Sent at night by a medical student to the second-floor dissecting room of the college to "warm up a dead man dat was dah on de table, en get him soft so he can cut him up," Jim first notices the corpse's eyes pop open; then the toes move; then, as the village clock strikes midnight, *"down he comes,* right a-straddle er my neck wid his cold laigs, en kicked de candle out!"[19] Jim's tale is presented simply as a kind of "ghost story," with no intrinsic relation to the plot. It is interesting, however, that Jim—whose creation seems to have been inspired at least in part by the up-bolting body in Bird Slough—here himself experiences the terror of a suddenly animated corpse.

---

*This is chapter 31, "A Thumb-Print and What Came of It."

What, then, drove Sammy into the night? Perhaps it was a welcome, if eerie, distraction from the horrors at home—not within the family, but within his own mind.

What guilts he suffered. What responsibilities he accepted in life for the sufferings of others, even as he pushed those guilts away, under irony and humor, in his art. Little wonder that he liked to escape his bedroom on Hill Street and glide into the actual night with his friends. Too often the alternative was to lie in bed, listening to nature itself remonstrate with him for his sins, or bombard his village with peals of predictive thunder after snatching away one of his comrades.

He recalled the drownings of two friends, each drowning associated with a thunderstorm. In *Life on the Mississippi* he revisited Hannibal and brooded on the memory of "Lem Hackett"* who had fallen out of a flat-boat one Sunday afternoon, probably on Bear Creek. "Being loaded with sin," Twain wrote wryly, "he went to the bottom like an anvil. He was the only boy in the village who slept that night. We others lay awake, repenting." A storm came up in the night, rattling windows, turning the wet houses white with horrid lightning. Sammy sat up in bed quaking and shuddering, "waiting for the destruction of the world, and expecting it. . . . Not a doubt entered my mind that all the angels were grouped together, disucssing this boy's case and observing the awful bombardment of our beggarly little village with satisfaction and approval."

He recalled cravenly trying to draw the angels' attention away from himself, to the sins of his friends—"Tom Holmes's" swearing, "John Smith's" fishing on Sunday. Then it struck him that in calling atten-

---

*An alias for Clint Levering, whose relatives were still living when the book was published. In "Villagers," the entry for Levering reads: ". . . drowned. His less fortunate brother lived to have a family and be rich and respected."

tion to his comrades, he had assured his own damnation. "Doubtless the lightning had stretched them all dead in their beds by this time!" Beside himself with guilt and panic, Sammy made wild promises into the noisy darkness: He would go to church and Sunday school; he would be attentive to the poor; he would become a missionary. The awful night passed, the storm subsided, daybreak arrived, the world looked safe again, and Sammy decided that perhaps it had been a false alarm. His sense of security lasted three weeks, until the next drowning, and the next storm.

This time the victim was a star of the Sunday school classes, a German immigrants' son nicknamed Dutchy. In Twain's recall, Dutchy's memory was so prodigious that one Sunday he recited three thousand verses of Scripture without missing a word. The next day he drowned. This time, Twain remembered his boyhood self as being directly implicated. The venue, again, was probably Bear Creek.

Sammy and Dutchy were with a group of boys swimming around a calm, deep stretch of the creek, near a spot where the village's caskmakers, or "coopers"—perhaps the same coopers who scattered under the onrushing boulder down Holliday's Hill—liked to submerge hickory hoop poles to soak into a state of pliancy. As Twain tells it in *Life on the Mississippi*, their game was to dive under the surface, hold onto the poles, and "see who could stay under longest."

Here Twain's reminiscence takes on the contours of a fable—suspicious contours, in the view of some critics: clumsy Dutchy is having trouble staying under very long; the boys tease him and distort their counting; he seems hurt and pleads for an honest count "just this once"; he dives again and the laughing boys scamper behind a cluster of blackberry bushes to imagine "Dutchy's humiliation, when he should rise after a superhuman effort" and find no one there to applaud.

But Dutchy doesn't rise. The boys grow apprehensive, then panic-stricken. Someone must dive down and find out what has happened. The reluctant boys draw straws for the onerous duty. "The lot fell to me and I went down." Feeling among the hoop poles, Sammy grasps a limp wrist. Dutchy has become ensnared among the poles and is drowned. "I fled to the surface and told the awful news." The formerly mocking boys are paralyzed with horror. "We did not think of anything; we did not know what to do, so we did nothing—" They scurry away and give the alarm. Dutchy's corpse is hauled out of the creek. That night the damning thunderstorm returns.

The lesson for Sammy this time is mordant: "if Dutchy, with all his perfections, was not a delight [to heaven], it would be vain for me to turn over a new leaf."

Twain was nothing if not a self-mythifier, and many of his chroniclers have approached his boyhood "disaster" narratives with skepticism. In his introduction to the 1986 Penguin edition of *Life on the Mississippi,* the distinguished scholar James M. Cox points in particular to "the episodes that Mark Twain recounts of his boyhood as he reaches Hannibal," which would include the drownings and the vagrant's fire. These stories, Cox warns, "often betray aspects of indulgent as well as invented guilt fantasies."*

Certainly Twain's memory betrayed him at times in his old age, and certainly this master of the tall tale was never a slave to objective truth—least of all, perhaps, during his journalism years in Nevada and California. But while the contours of the disaster recollections are

---

*Yet Cox himself has commented at length on the famous letter of February 6, 1870, that Twain wrote to Will Bowen—a letter in which Twain refers explicitly to the time "we accidentally burned up that poor fellow in the calaboose . . . "

suspiciously formalized, these stories do not seem entirely invented. Twain's memory could also be uncannily accurate, as Walter Blair has shown by his independent verification of most of the names mentioned in "Villagers." The greatest scholar of Twain's boyhood, Dixon Wecter, verified the dates of nearly all the 1843–53 episodes from old records and newspaper files.

In his autobiography, Twain wrote that with each witnessing of a childhood tragedy (each one of them "on my account"), he felt a new impulse toward repentance: "the patience of God will not always endure." And yet he privately believed that it would—at least he believed it in the daytime. "But not in the night. With the going down of the sun my faith failed and the clammy fears gathered about my heart. . . . Those were awful nights, nights of despair, nights charged with the bitterness of death." Wherever he writes of them, Samuel Clemens's boyhood nights emerge as unrelieved orgies of guilt and mortal terror.

"In my age as in my youth," he wrote in his autobiography, "night brings me many a deep remorse. I realize that from the cradle up I have been like the rest of the race—never quite sane in the night."

In Mark Twain's dark night lay America's literary dawning. In his deep remorse, as in Huck Finn's remorse, lay the seeds of liberation. Like his greatest boyhood fictional creation, Samuel Clemens (mistakenly) thought himself wicked, low-down, ornery, watched by Providence for it, unable to pray. As Huck composed a letter to Miss Watson disclosing Jim's whereabouts, Twain would grope toward redemption many times in his adulthood by making himself the status-seeking pretender to "polite" literature, of the type approved by refined women. But at necessary times—the fragmented composition of *Huckleberry Finn* most prominent among them—he would review the phantasmal downriver trip of his most representative consciousness: his *doppelgänger* "Jim" and himself in the moonlight. ("Jim" in these reveries being perhaps the sum of all the nights, all the storms, and all the talking, singing, and laughing of all the black slaves who invested Clemens with the freedom of the spoken word.) And Mark Twain would say, in effect: "All right, then, I'll *go* to hell." And thus, without quite ever knowing it, he would bring the celestial light of his genius into the darkness.

Eight

"A week drifted by, and all the while the patient sunk lower and lower. The night drew on that was to end all suspense. It was a wintry one. The darkness gathered, the snow was falling, the wind wailed plaintively around the house or shook it with fitful gusts."

If Sammy's nighttime escapades contained an element of escapism—and the furtive, daredevil aura of them strongly suggests that they did—there could be little question as to what, or from whom, the boy was seeking, however fleetingly, to escape. The tall, spare, spectral presence that dominated the Clemens household was claiming more and more of his fourth son's rueful attention. And the son, for whom the mysteries of shifting and divided identity would be a lifelong preoccupation, could hardly have failed to fasten upon one eerie, deepening quality of his father's existence: John Marshall Clemens seemed to be two entirely separate persons inhabiting the same body: Siamese twins of circumstance.

On the one hand was the imposing prince of Hannibal's civic and cultural life. On the other was the borderline pauper constantly foraging for a livelihood and haunted by the prospect of ruin.

The princely side of John Marshall was dazzling enough, from a boy's perspective. Here was the "prodigious personage," the august creation who might at any moment roar. As he'd done in Florida, John quickly advanced to the rank of Leading Citizen in his newly adopted town: a promotor, a chairman of committees. He became Hannibal's Justice of the Peace—elected, probably, in 1842. Beginning in 1844 he superintended the surveying of roads around the village. By 1846, he was at the center of a civic group that was organizing a railroad from Hannibal westward across Missouri to St. Joseph, at the Kansas border. (The railroad was in fact chartered and completed in 1859, but by that time John Marshall was long dead.)

His civic strivings reflected a mighty man of public affairs, "sternly and irreproachably moral." But while the "public" man struck these lofty poses, the private man scrounged to keep his wife and four children housed and fed.

Nothing was working. His landlord-and-merchant dreams had evaporated: None of his tenants felt much like paying their rent, and Clemens had his usual luck in collecting it. As for the general store and its expensive stock of goods, they diminished under Orion's hopeless management—the boy had a way of extending credit to customers, then forgetting about it. There seemed to be no way out of the constant, deepening poverty.

Through it all, John kept up his personal aura of what his son would lampoon as "F.F.V."—First-Family Virginian—by every means available to him. He read poetry aloud (albeit tonelessly) to the family; he attended lectures on grammar; he wrote letters and opinions with a fine-honed intellectual precision. As for playfulness, he had none—at least for his sons. He could be indulgent with Pamela, who adored him. But Sammy soon learned that to appear lively or spontaneous in John Marshall's presence seemed to give his old man goose-flesh.

One thing had to be granted John: His imperious, planter-macho posture was no mere affectation. He backed it up. Once, in his court-house, when an enraged witness fired off a clumsy pepper-pot revolver in the general direction of the plaintiff, filling the room with smoke, the Judge stepped forward and sent the shooter sprawling with a hammer blow to the head.[1] He found a hammer useful another time, when the owner of a stonecutter's shop by the name of Dave Atkinson started trading haymakers with a local troublemaker known as "Fighting" MacDonald. The shop was next door to John's law office, and the noise of the scuffle distracted him. He hurried outside, commanded the peace, was ignored, took hold of one of Atkinson's stonecutting mallets and administered a pair of shots with it to the side of MacDonald's head. Then he summoned both men into his court and fined them.[2]

Nor did John Marshall find it necessary to explain or apologize for any gulf between his stern, irreproachable morality and his embrace of Southern racial assumptions. In every recorded dealing with a slave, Clemens displayed a heartlessness so chilling that it formed a revul-sion in Sammy. Twain's own written reflections suggest that this re-vulsion in turn may have formed his empathy, radical in its time, for black people, and may further have annealed his dependence on black vernacular speech as the foundation of his literary voice.

In 1840 John kept his household solvent for a few more months by selling Jennie. ("She was tall, well formed, nearly black, and brought a good price," noted the ever-approving biographer Paine, blandly.) The young but maternal slave woman had even more to recommend her: She had become part of the fabric of the family. Having accompanied the Clemenses from Tennessee, she had cared for Sammy through his sickly infancy and had likely saved him from drowning once in Bear Creek.* And she endured some stinging strokes from John for her lapses into high spirits.

None of it mattered. John not only cashed Jennie in; he sold her to a speculator whose cruelty toward slaves made him a scourge in Hannibal. Vilified covertly around town as "the nigger trader," this man, contrary to his promise, promptly resold Jennie down the river.

To be sold "down the river"—into the unforgiving hands of the brutal overlords of the great plantations of the Delta—was, for a black slave accustomed to the relatively humane precincts of Missouri, quite literally a fate worse than death, as Mark Twain took pains to establish in more than one of his novels. ("Dey sha'n't, oh, dey *sha'n't!* yo' po' mammy will kill you fust!" he has Roxana wail over the endangered child she believes to be her own in *Pudd'nhead Wilson.* And when it becomes clear that the raft has missed the mouth of the Ohio in *Huckleberry Finn,* Jim understands his predicament at once: "Doan' less' talk about it, Huck. Po' niggers can't have no luck. I awluz 'spected dat rattle-snake skin warn't done wid it's work.")

Apparently Jennie escaped the worst that could happen to a downriver slave—a short, brutal life in the cottonfields, under the unforgiving sun. "Was seen, years later, a [chambermaid] on a steamboat," Twain wrote of her.[3]

Chambermaiding on a Mississippi riverboat is one of the fates that befalls Roxana in *Pudd'nhead Wilson.* (She is later sold downriver,

---

*Albert Bigelow Paine writes that time and again, as a swimmer, Sammy "had . . . been dragged ashore more dead than alive, once by a slave-girl, another time by a slave-man . . . "

and becomes a common field hand.) Roxana is generally held to be Twain's most richly realized female character, an uneducated but noble woman of fierce, unrequited decency and moral brilliance. Although only one-sixteenth African, she suffers, in the novel, the full range of indignities visited on American slaves of the mid-nineteenth century. But she rises above her victimhood to offer enduring insights into the issue not only of slavery, but of motherhood. In her defiant love of her own child and her willingness to condemn her master's child to slavery, and also in her many decisive actions that drive the novel's conclusion, she breaks the stereotype of fictional black women "as mammies, not mothers," as David Lionel Smith has shown.[4] Critics who have chastised Twain for not creating a symbol or a story of the antebellum South at the visionary level of *Uncle Tom's Cabin* might do well to revisit Roxana. And Roxana, in turn, might owe her complex character and affronted humanity to the lost figure of Jennie.

"My father was not a reformer," Mark Twain wrote dryly, with barbed understatement.[5] The Judge's anti-Abolition sentiments were icily unshakable. In 1841, he served on a jury that famously handed down twelve-year, hard-labor sentences to each of three men who had tried to help a group of slaves escape across the Mississippi River to Illinois along the Underground Railroad.

John Marshall Clemens had one further notable dealing with a slave. This one revealed a curious mixture of his callousness and his selective, self-defeating compassion.

In the winter of 1841–42, two years after the family's arrival at Hannibal, John had set off on a long, excruciating journey into the South: to Mississippi and then to New Orleans, by steamboat, and then back upriver and overland into Tennessee and Kentucky. Parts of the purpose of this trip were honorable by any standards: John Marshall intended to visit his aging mother, who lived on the family homestead in Kentucky; to investigate the sales prospects of the maddeningly unmarketable Tennessee land; and to collect the payment for a $470 loan he had made twenty years earlier to a Mississippi man named William Lester. When he finally tracked Lester down, after days of hard cold riding, he let the debtor sweet-talk him into reducing his demand, in "these hard times," to $250—payable the following March. As it turned out, John Marshall never collected a penny.

But he had taken care to have with him a hedge: a bit of property in the person of a slave named Charley, whom he had purchased in Missouri and whom he hoped to sell at a profit in the Deep South. Here, John Marshall was not merely making a "downriver" sale, he was escorting his terrified captive personally into the abyss.

Yet John Marshall, cruising the Mississippi with Charley in tow, seems not to have suffered a single tremor of conscience. He had tried to unload the man for $50 at New Orleans, then for $40 at Vicksburg. "I expect to sell him for whatever he will bring where I take water again, viz. at Louisville or Nashville," he blandly informed the family in a letter. A surviving promissory note suggests that he finally traded Charley for ten barrels of tar somewhere on the river.[6] After more than two months he returned home about $200 the poorer for his overall fundraising efforts.

Poring over his father's records half a century later, Mark Twain could not contain his contempt—for either half of John Marshall's nature. "If even the gentlest of us had been plowing through ice and snow, horseback and per steamboat for six weeks to collect that little antiquity, wouldn't we have collected it, and the man's scalp along with it? I trust so," he hissed in a private jotting.[7]

As for his father's treatment of Charley, Twain was even more explicit in his distancing. "Thank God I have no recollection of him as house servant of ours; that is to say, a playmate of mine," he wrote, in a passage almost palpably aimed, retroactively, at his father's values; "for I was playmate to all the niggers, preferring their society to that of the elect, I being a person of low-down tastes from the start, notwithstanding my high birth, and ever ready to forsake the communion of high souls if I could strike anything nearer my grade."[8]

All right then, Samuel Clemens seemed to be saying, even at that early age. "I'll *go* to hell."

Justice of the Peace, chairman of commissions, man of letters, slave-holding squire: such were the princely aspects of John Marshall Clemens. But always the pauper lurked, biding his time; inevitably, the pauper became ascendant.

John Clemens's financial humiliations in Hannibal began early. In October 1841, just two years after the family's arrival in town, the small windfall from Jennie's sale ran out. Fallen some $2000 in debt, he was obliged to hand over the title of his Hannibal property—the $7000 quarter-block he had bought from Ira Stout in 1839—to satisfy his dry-goods creditor in St. Louis.

Clemens's creditors showed a good deal less compassion with him than he showed with his man in Mississippi. In October 1842 the St. Louis merchant, James Kerr, actually put the lot up for sale at auction, including the Clemenses' living space. Only their neighbors' reluctance to exploit this chance at a windfall saved the family from indigence. Frantic for income, John and Jane Clemens sent dreamy Orion, now seventeen, down to St. Louis to learn the printing trade. Orion would prove a spotty success in publishing, but in his new calling he would launch his younger brother into literary fame.

A year after that—in the autumn of 1843—after the Clemenses had managed to move out of their corner of the Virginia House and into quarters across the street, Kerr finally liquidated his holding: He subdivided the property and unloaded it for just under $4000. This sum exceeded John Marshall's indebtedness and left him with a little cash after settling the expenses of the sale.

One purchaser was the wealthy lawyer James Clemens Jr. of St. Louis, the distant cousin from whom John Marshall had already borrowed $250. This Clemens paid $330 for the twenty-foot-wide lot halfway up Hill Street, an act of compassionate salvaging. There, he allowed John to build the little woodframe house—the Mark Twain Boyhood Home that still stands.[9]

John Marshall Clemens could be cold, irascible, and even cruel toward his male children. But Sam, who perhaps suffered the most under this callousness, and who learned to dread the prospect of poverty, took a penetrating assessment of his father's rigid gallantry in the face of ruin. True to his code of honor as a Virginian, John insisted on satisfying every claim against him, even though it meant parting with nearly everything of value that he owned: household furnishings, silverware, tables and chairs. At some point this required the family to leave, temporarily, the little house that John had built and accept the charity of rent-free quarters offered by the family of the druggist Dr. Orville Grant across the street. The arrangement was that Jane would "board" the Grants—cook them their meals and see to their laundry. The prospect was a godsend.

John Marshall never stopped believing that his tribulations were about to end. Someone would soon buy the Tennessee land. Was it not abundant in iron ore; in yellow-pine timber; in tar, pitch and turpentine; in wild grapes for wine; in grazing lands, land for corn, wheat, potatoes? Was it not Eden? How could anyone not want to purchase Eden? Someone would arrive soon, "the long-delayed but always expected something that we live for," as a playwright nicknamed "Tennessee" would phrase it a century later.

Meanwhile, John Marshall would have to hock his soupspoons and candlesticks.

The mimetic boy preserved the memory of this stoic divestiture. He preserved another quality as well: a resentment against the circumstances that made it necessary, a resentment so radiant that it burned him into a kind of predator after wealth throughout his own adulthood: He would literally scrape the earth for it as a young man in the silver and gold mines of Nevada and California. It is impossible to know whether this resentment was directed in part at his father—the "prodigious personage," the "most august creation," now revealed not only as an unloved husband but as a failure at provider as well—or even at himself, yet another instance of young Sammy laying claim to ambient guilt.

This much is certain: Fifty-one years later, Mark Twain got his chance to reenact his father's noble ordeal, and when that chance came, it beggared John's small-time penury. The Paige-driven stakes were $100,000, the scale was global, equatorial, and his triumph of paying back 100 cents on those dollars established for all time who was the bankruptcy-recovery champion in the Clemens line.

A shadowy figure in John Clemens's downfall was the original seller of the quarter-block. "Big Ira Stout," John calls him in a fragment of handwritten notation[10]—probably from a creditors' case against Stout that the Judge presided over. The gangsterish moniker may have fit: A lot of Hannibal people sued this speculator for bad debts, and he apparently took creative refuge in the bankruptcy laws, emerging flush and property-rich in 1845, and even flusher in 1847, the year of John's death. (In that year he put up for sale some seven hundred lots in Hannibal, among other blue-chip holdings.)

Mark Twain was capable of deep, virulent, and irreversible hatreds against anyone whom he thought had wronged him or those close to him, especially in matters of money. He left no doubt of his conviction that Ira Stout had violated his father's good faith and pauperized him. "He did the friendly office of 'going security' for Ira Stout," Twain wrote in his autobiography, "and Ira walked off and deliberately took benefit of the new bankrupt law . . . a deed which ruined my father [and] sent him poor to his grave . . ." In a later section Twain explicitly states that John Marshall had lent Stout "several thousand dollars—a fortune in those days and in that region."

But that, of course, is just the problem with that particular memory: John Marshall did not have a fortune to lend, or at least he left no evidence of having had one. The scholar Dixon Wecter, whose research is definitive, could find no trace of a legal claim against Ira Stout by John Marshall Clemens among the many on record against him. Still, the juxtaposition of the Judge's final fall into penury and Stout's sudden emergence as a property broker cannot be denied. Nor can Twain's conviction that the trusted businessman stole his father's security, as well as his family's.

The illusory comforts of money, and the all-too-substantial chaos engendered by its sudden loss, especially through treachery—this took root as a source of anxiety for Twain and grew throughout his life. It must have fueled his dreams; it certainly fueled "Which Was the Dream?", one of the several tortured "dream-stories" he wrote, or began, as a broken man in the months following his daughter Suzy's death.

He launched into it less than a year after the tragedy, in the half-crazed summer of 1897, having remained in England after receiving the thunderclap of news. The story, deeply narcissistic, is on its surface devoid of reference to Hannibal or boyhood; it is filled with coded references to Twain's illustrious years in Hartford, his wealth, his literary fame, his friendships with such giants of the day as Ulysses S. Grant. But at its edges one can detect the irrational, compulsive fantasizing of an anxious boy lacerating himself with the macabre question: *What would it be like if I had a nightmare, and the nightmare turned out to be real?*

The nightmare for "Thomas X," the story's protagonist, is the disappearance of a fortune, a happy home life, a tremendous reputation, and, for a time, his sanity. The culprit is a grossly deceitful boyhood playmate and lifelong confidante. Destructive fire—a staple, along with engulfing water, of Twain's brooding motifs—also figures in the plot.

Thomas X is an almost impossible success at the story's beginning: a Senator, a former military hero, and a prospective future President at age thirty-four. Like Twain, he is married to a woman of society and has sired three daughters. But one evening, as the happy household prepares for a pageant to entertain their illustrious friends, Thomas falls asleep while writing in his study. He awakes to find that his house is on fire. Thanks to the coolheaded leadership of an on-the-skids army lieutenant named Grant (and nicknamed "Useless"), the house is evacuated. But from that moment, Thomas's future is destroyed. He is humiliated to learn that his bank accounts are overdrawn, his insurance policies are no good, and that a gold mine in California in which he had invested his wife's fortune is nonexistent. (Its name, X had been led to believe, was the Golden Fleece—even in his despair, Twain could not resist a mordant pun; he doubtless had James W. Paige's fortune-draining invention in mind.) Gradually it becomes clear that he has been betrayed by his wife's cousin Jeff, whom Thomas has known from boyhood. Thomas had entrusted everything to Jeff: investments, bookkeeping, even the composition and signing of Thomas's business letters. But Jeff has developed and nursed a longstanding irrational hatred of Thomas, which his wife Alice had suspected but which Thomas refused to believe.

Not only is Thomas's life ruined: He must also undergo a humiliating inquisition by a delegation of bankers and creditors—leading citizens—whose outrage at his apparent private perfidy is the more galling because they remain somewhat in awe of his public distinctions. In the throes of his helpless fury and mortification at his encircling accusers, Thomas blacks out. When he comes to his senses, eighteen months have passed; his splendid trappings are all vanished and he finds himself in a clean but meager mining cabin in California, where his brave, uncomplaining wife and daughters have removed to begin a new life of stoic subsistence. Here, Twain abandoned the story.

The contrived bathos of this tale, its pervading note of self-pity (a highly uncharacteristic trait of Twain's writing at its long zenith), and its ultimate formlessness hint at a kind of regression, if not a brush with insanity. In fact Twain began and abandoned many similar "dream" manuscripts in the two years following Suzy's death. Pre-Freudean theories about the "unconscious," and its mysterious power over the conscious mind, were part of fashionable intellectual thought during these years, and Twain, ever alert to the cultural currents, had fastened on them. (He had read and been swayed by Robert Louis

Stevenson's *Dr. Jekyll and Mr. Hyde,* published in 1886; he also read Poe and Hawthorne for their probings of the otherworldly.) The biographer Justin Kaplan has suggested, persuasively, that Twain's own dream-life in those years bordered on madness, and that by exposing himself to madness—"by turning his dream life into a literary problem"[11]—he was able, at last, to escape madness's permanent grip.

If "madness" it was, its traumatic roots were deep. While the surface connections in "Which Was the Dream?" to Twain's Hannibal years are nonexistent, much else binds it to deep boyhood memory: the public/private divisions of the father, his bankruptcy and accompanying humiliation, the shadowy presence of a malign deceiver. What is missing in this construction is the observing boy. But the boy has not gone far. Ever-guilty, he has entered the persona of the suffering father.

In 1846, the gulf between the public and the private fortunes of John Marshall Clemens was at its widest. This was the year of his leadership in the Hannibal–St. Joseph railroad venture and the macadamized road project. In this year he also thumped—unsuccessfully—for a Masonic college to be built at Hannibal. He did manage to establish the "Hannibal Library Institute"—which amounted to a gaggle of books stored in Dr. Meredith's office. In November he filed his candidacy for Clerk of the Circuit Court. The election was to be held the following August, and his chances for victory appeared to be good.

But 1846 was also the year the Judge hit rock-bottom financially. In September he made what was to be his last attempt at cashing in on the Tennessee land: He hired a land-agency firm in New York to market the seventy thousand acres at twenty cents an acre. A complete sale would have brought the family $14,000. But the agency was not able to unload even one acre. In that same summer and autumn, the Judge got ensnared in yet another claim of indebtedness. This one was complicated. Clemens had for several years held two notes against William Beebe, the businessman known as the "nigger-trader" who had sold Jennie down the river. Pressured to pay up, Beebe instead lashed out: He got hold of a note of indebtedness against Clemens, for $290.55. He brought suit and won a favorable ruling, plus $126.50 in damages. The local sheriff was ordered to sell John Marshall's "goods and chattels and real estate" to satisfy the claim, but the sheriff could find no goods to sell. The Clemenses had already been picked clean. They were living now above the Grants' drugstore on the corner of Hill and Main, where Smarr, mortally wounded, had been dragged the year before.

It was in this debased state of affairs that John Marshall Clemens set off on horseback, on a frigid day in March 1847, for the village of Palmyra, about twelve miles northwest of Hannibal. His purpose was to attend a judicial hearing there and receive what proved to be the last good news of his life: a circuit court judge's decision that the Judge's pitiful notes of indebtedness against Beebe offset Beebe's niggling claims on him.

Slogging homeward back to Hannibal, Judge Clemens was overtaken by a sleet storm. It was nothing compared to the forty miles of rain and sleet he had endured on horseback five years earlier, in his futile quest to collect his $470 debt in Mississippi, but this time John Marshall had no reserves left. He stumbled into the living quarters above the drugstore benumbed with cold. Pneumonia set in. Thin, ravaged, he took to bed and clung feverishly to life for about two weeks. Orion hurried home from St. Louis to be at his bedside; Jane and daughter Pamela hovered; Sammy and little Henry watched, helplessly.

On March 24, 1847, Sam sourly recalled, John Marshall displayed his "First instance of affection."[12] (He apparently had forgotten John Marshall's kissing of Jane when Benjamin died in 1842.) It was also his dying gesture. He beckoned to the weeping Pamela, then twenty, to come to his bedside—an action that may have inspired the image of Boggs's distraught sixteen-year-old daughter rushing to her father's bloodied, heaving breast in *Huckleberry Finn*. Then he extended his arms, pulled the girl down to him, kissed her "(for the first time, no doubt)"[13] and moaned, "Let me die." About ten minutes later the Virginia gentleman was gone—having neglected to bid farewell to his loveless wife or to any of his unloved sons. He was forty-nine.

"I am leaving you in cruel poverty. . . . But courage! A better day is—is coming. Never lose sight of the Tennessee Land! . . . There is wealth stored up for you there—" cries Squire Hawkins, one of Judge Clemens's fictional surrogates, on his deathbed in *The Gilded Age*. In his autobiography and in Paine's work, Twain has his father saying, as his "dying charge," "Cling to the land and wait; let nothing beguile it away from you." Twain told Paine that at some point during his throes, his father had said, "I believe if I had stayed in Tennessee I might have been worth twenty thousand dollars to-day." The advisability of whatever "clinging" he recommended might have been summed up in an aside in "Which Was the Dream?": "But unfortunately none of us can see far ahead; prophecy is not for us. Hence the paucity of suicides."

What lay immediately ahead for Sammy, who was eleven, was more distress, followed shortly by a trauma of unknowable effect. His boyhood had on the day of his father's death come to an abrupt end.

The distress came first. Jane Clemens, as Twain recalled it, augmented his distress with her usual deathbed histrionics. Noticing that Sammy was wandering about the Grant house "fairly broken down"[14] with grief, the new widow worked her special power of persuasion: As she had when Benjamin died, she took his hand and led him back into the room beside John Marshall's body.

"Here by the side of him now,"[15] she told him, she needed a promise. The scene, as recounted by Paine on the writer's testimony around 1906, is a florid classic in the Twainian mythos:

> He turned, his eyes streaming with tears, and flung himself into her arms. "I will promise anything," he sobbed, "if you won't make me go to school. Anything!"
>
> His mother held him for a moment, thinking, then she said:
>
> "No, Sammy; you need not go to school any more. Only promise me to be a better boy. Promise not to break my heart."
>
> So he promised her to be a faithful and industrious man, and upright, like her father. His mother was satisfied with that. The sense of honor and justice was already strong within him. To him a promise was a serious matter at any time; made under conditions like these it would be held sacred.[16]

That night, and for several nights afterward, Sammy sleepwalked. On the first night, he wandered, entangled in a white sheet, into the room where his mother and sister were sleeping in the same bed, waking them with his footsteps. The "form in white" terrorized the already distraught women until they grasped its identity.

Well he might have sleepwalked. He had just watched his defeated father die in a room not his own, addled with visions of wealth just out of grasp. Then his mother (at least as he recalled it) had led him beside the warm corpse, where she'd begged him to "be a better boy" and promise not to break her heart. Such a double bombardment of grief and censure might have saturated any reasonably sensitive boy with guilt; and Sammy Clemens was nothing if not a sponge of self-recrimination.

This moment in fact is what some scholars have identified as the origin of Mark Twain's "wound"—the culminating sorrow of a ravaged boyhood and, as some hostile critics claimed, the premature death of his genius. Jane Clemens's "awful ceremony,"[17] in this view, stamped a cloture on the great wild conversation that was then welling up inside Sammy, deforming what might have matured into a truly subversive American literary voice and reducing it to mere cleverness and a constant quest for genteel respectability and the approval of women.

The leading proponent of this darkly eccentric view was Van Wyck Brooks. Brimming with Freudean theory and burdened by his sober-sided brahmin's tin ear, Brooks swooped down on this episode and used it to form a pathological view of Twain that would set the terms of debate for forty years.

". . . We feel with irresistible certitude," Brooks wrote, "that Mark Twain's fate was once and for all decided there." He continued:

> He is broken down indeed; all those crystalline fragments
> of individuality, still so tiny and fragile, are suddenly shat-

tered; his nature, wrought upon by the tense heat of that hour, had become again like soft wax.... He is to go forth the Good Boy by *force majeure,* he is to become such a man as his father would have approved of, he is to retrieve his father's failure, to recover the lost gentility of a family that had once been proud.... Hide your faces, Huck and Tom! Put away childish things, Sam Clemens; go forth into the world, but remain always a child, your mother's child![18]

So much for going willingly to hell. Brooks met with his own withering disdain, in time, from critics who homed in on his reductionism. (Bernard DeVoto, among several others, doubted that Jane's bedside exhortations ever occurred.) The enduring value of his book lay, in the end, not in the accuracy of its summation of Twain as in its indictment of stultifying American culture generally, and in its loosening up forever of "polite" literary criticism. Yet even in his stance of preemptive malice, Brooks asked some penetrating questions about the foundations of Twain's wound.

"... We are told he was 'broken down' by his father's death," Brooks wrote; "remorse had 'laid a heavy hand on him.' But what was this remorse; what had he ever done for grief or shame?"[19]

Brooks had pinpointed one of the abiding mysteries of Sammy Clemens's boyhood. What *had* he ever done?

We know some of the things he had seen—things that might have invested a small boy's thoughts with dread and pain. He had seen his father's constant struggle against poverty. He had seen the corpse of the stabbed man in his father's moonlit office. He had seen Smarr shot down, and watched him die. He had seen his friend Will Bowen bedridden with measles, dying for all he knew, and had tried stubbornly to join him. He had seen the white slavemaster murder a charge of his with a lump of iron-ore. He had seen the "young California emigrant" receive a fatal knife wound from his drunken comrade. He had experienced the drownings of two of his friends, and recalled diving under the surface of Bear Creek to feel the limp hand of one of them.

In the years just after his father's death, he would see the fugitive slave's corpse rise up staring out of the Bird Slough morass. He would see the widow lay open the California marauder's chest with a musket-shot. And at seventeen he would see (if we are to believe his own testimony) the vagrant burning alive in the calaboose, having struck a match that Sam offered him.

He later wrote explicitly of his "remorse" over all these fatalities, though of course witnessing is not the same as perpetrating.

There exists one further possible source of Mark Twain's wound. Paine is mum about it, although he doubtless knew of it, having read the manuscript of luckless Orion's unpublished autobiography, which contained an account of it. (The manuscript was unpublished partly because Paine lost it.) Brooks, fastened as he is on the toxic maternalism of Jane Clemens, never seems to notice it—perhaps because Twain himself never mentioned it directly. Fastidious William Dean Howells certainly knew about it: He read Orion's manuscript, was shocked to his foundation, and pleaded with Twain to suppress the offending passage, among some others:

> But the writer's soul is laid *too* bare; it is shocking . . . and
> if you print it anywhere, I hope you won't let your love of
> the naked truth prevent you from striking out some of the
> most intimate pages. *Don't* let any one else even *see* those

passages about the autopsy. The light on your father's
character is most pathetic.[20]

The autopsy. Twain alluded to it twice, each time with a chilling
flatness, an imposed distance. In "Villagers," the allusion is just
that—those two words—at the bottom of his long entry regarding
"Judge Carpenter." And in his Notebook entry of October 10,
1903—three years before Paine began compiling the official biography—Twain wrote: *"1847.* Witnessed post mortem of my uncle
through keyhole."

Mark Twain did not have an uncle who died in 1847. Clearly, even
as a worldly sixty-seven-year-old man, he could not bring himself to
confront, or record, exactly whose autopsy or postmortem he had
clandestinely witnessed.

Postmortem; autopsy. Each term refers to the medical examination
of a human body after death: a dissection. The inference is over-
whelming that Sammy Clemens, keyhole-peeping, saw his father's
body cut open by the attending physician, Dr. Hugh Meredith.

Why such a procedure was necessary can only be guessed at. Dixon
Wecter has surmised that Dr. Meredith, a longstanding family friend,
was intent on surveying the effects on John Marshall's body of his
"lifelong mysterious maladies": the attacks of "sunpain," nervous ex-
haustion and shortness of breath that bedeviled the Judge.

But echoes of what he must have seen ripple through his memory,
and his literature. Dead or dying men with their chests laid open, both
real and fictional (or some complex admixture of the two) recur: the
stabbed corpse in his father's office; Smarr shot in the breast and laid
out to die weighted down by a Bible; his fictional counterpart Boggs
likewise bleeding slowly to death and encumbered by two Bibles; the

widow-shot marauder on Holliday's Hill; the stabbed California emigrant ("I saw the red life gush from his breast").

The themes of dissection, sundered chests, and concealed observation are combined, and recombined, in the famous murder scene in *Tom Sawyer*: Tom and Huck are prowling the town's hilltop graveyard at midnight seeking to cure warts via a ritual involving a dead cat and a newly buried wicked person. They hear men's voices and duck behind a stand of elm trees. A lantern freckles the ground, and the young Dr. Robinson enters the hilltop cemetery with Muff Potter and Injun Joe; he has paid them to rob a grave and supply him with a corpse, inferentially for dissection purposes. After they dig up the body of the reprobate "Hoss" Williams, Injun Joe flares into a rage at Robinson over an old insult. With the hidden boys gaping in horror, he drives a knife "to the hilt" into the doctor's breast—a killing that will be blamed on the drunken Muff. The would-be dissector is thus himself opened up.

Judge Clemens was buried in the cemetery that served as the model for the one in *Tom Sawyer,* the hilltop Baptist cemetery north of town, on the same ridgeline that formed Holliday's Hill. Orion was named executor of John Marshall's estate, such as it was, and maintained his printer's job in St. Louis, sending what money he could upriver to the family. Pamela gave her piano lessons, and Jane looked over her four children as best she could. The bereaved family continued to struggle. Soon Sammy would have to fulfill his promise to his mother: He would have to become a good and responsible boy. He would have to go to work. His first sustained, serious work would be as a printer's apprentice—the physical making of words. Perhaps his mother was not such a hindrance to his destiny after all.

Nine

"Everything human is pathetic.
The secret source of humor itself is not joy but sorrow.
There is no humor in heaven."

What possibly connected him to a destiny of humor—to his permanent legacy as a man of laughter?

Given the terrors, the griefs, the guilts, the angers and the hallucinating obsessions that strung their path through his boyhood like ice floes on a turbulent river, it is plausible to wonder how Samuel Clemens could ever have emerged as a "humorist," much less as the transforming embodiment of American humor.

But given an understanding of the wellsprings and the functions of American humor as these were taking shape during his early life—and given the accuracy of Sam's status as "the average American . . . plus genius"—it is hardly plausible to imagine him emerging into any other fate. The arresting, the bittersweet aspect of his long ascent into his comic genius was not so much that he achieved it, but that he never consciously grasped what it was he'd achieved, or why the achievement was so important.

Humor was not merely a component of the distinctly American culture that was coalescing in the 1840s: Humor *was* that culture. More acutely than music or painting, more intimately than architecture or poetry or literature, and more universally even than religion, humor was the irreducible medium through which the new nation understood itself. Our humor's origins lay in the confluence of a thousand nascent myths and archetypes that channeled themselves, over time, into a great flow of comic voices: the conversation of a new country slaying its dragons, facing down its demons, with outrageous words.

Outrageous—and often hard, loud, and rough. The invention and function of frontier humor had less to do with genial amusement than with building a psychological structure against chaos. The rattlesnake wilderness that stretched outward from Boston and Philadelphia and New York was not yet ready for drawing-room aphorisms or comedies of manners. Here lay vastness, loneliness, alienation, depravity, and many interesting varieties of sudden death. Thus the hard edge of those nascent myths and archetypes matched and amplified (and was intended largely to oppose) the edginess of the frontier itself. In rough laughter, the new settlers sought coherence and psychic survival.

The gush of immigrant settlers who followed Daniel Boone west along the Wilderness Trail had swelled the American population from fewer than 4 million in 1790 to more than 10 million just thirty years later. Still, the terrain was enormous, and even those millions tended to sink into its wilderness, to thin out and get lost inside the dark fields of the republic. When they did make human contact, it was often with a gothic lot indeed: earlier settlers who by the closing years of the eighteenth century had grown profoundly estranged from the comforting predictabilities of Eastern Seaboard manners, which were themselves imported from the ancient, densely settled cities of Europe.

Pioneer America was in fact an environment designed for violence: tiny isolated villages in which eye-to-eye grievances festered; brutal cycles of subsistence clearing and farming and hunting; cold and end-less winters; the constant shock and despair of infant death; the per-vading fear of a hostile and semi-visible native population that might at any moment attack from the deep woods with arrows and toma-hawks. Even strangers of one's own colonizing race were suspect. Large outlaw bands and the occasional sociopathic loner roamed the Mississippi and Ohio river corridors and the hills and hollows of Ken-tucky, Tennessee, and the remoter northern regions of Alabama, Geor-gia, Mississippi, Carolina. "American lawlessness towered everywhere on the border and reached its zenith on the Mississippi," wrote Bernard DeVoto. "Islands and bayous held confederacies of outlaws. . . . Before 1840 there were few places on the border where solitary travel was safe; barges couldn't tie up at night."[1]

The big rivers were especially attractive to organized cutthroats and to men of violence generally. The psychotic John A. Murrell, the God-father of his time, ruled a gang of thieves, robbers, murderers, and barge-pirates, perhaps a thousand in number at its peak, that infested the Mississippi shores from Hannibal southward—"the most wide-spread criminal organization in America," DeVoto called it. Murrell's signature crime was a morbid practice known as "nigger-stealing." Posing as an abolitionist, and sometimes as a Methodist minister, Mur-rell or one of his henchmen would coax a slave off the plantation with the promise of safeguarding him to free soil. Instead, the outlaw would sell, steal, and resell the helpless slave for a while, then kill and disem-bowel him. This atrocity recurred hundreds of times.

This is the same "Murrel" that Injun Joe's cohort mentions in *Tom Sawyer* as the likely source of the treasure. It is reasonable to imagine that John Murrell haunted Sammy's troubled dreams every bit as much as Injun Joe haunted Tom's.

In the days before steamboats had replaced the timber-rafts and keelboats, Sammy stood on the Mississippi levee and watched and listened as the lesser hard cases floated past:

> . . . hoards of rough and hardy men; rude, uneducated, brave, suffering terrific hardships with sailor-like stoicism; heavy drinkers, coarse frolickers in moral sties like the Natchez-under-the-hill of that day, heavy fighters, reckless fellows, every one, elephantinely jolly, foul-witted, profane . . . [2]

The morals, the manners, and the restraints of Eastern and European civilization could not answer to these realities. Whether among hardened criminals or everyday people, every aspect of the Interior seemed to reinforce "the peculiar melancholy and death longing of the Western frontiersman."[3] If nothing else, the interlacing rhythms of struggle, boredom, and terror fed an ever-present recourse to hard liquor, which in turn fueled bursts of crazed aggression. Inevitably, violence came to form an aesthetic of its own. Inevitably, violence came to be enjoyed for its own sake.

Blood sports had existed in the American colonies long before the westward push. Bareknuckled boxing, an English importation, was a routine skill of young Virginians a hundred years before Sam Clemens was born. Death was not infrequently the result. Swordplay, ritualized as dueling, eventually became a darkly elegant replacement to fisticuffs among the planter aristocracy. But as white settlers trickled out beyond the Appalachian wilderness in the mid– and late–eighteenth century and got a taste of the abyss, their recreational fighting took on a quality of ritualized sadism that became the stuff of European legend. It seemed to offer satisfying proof, especially following the shock of the Revolution, that the American experiment was nothing more than a regression into barbarity. The predominant symbols of this barbarity were the ripped testicles, the bitten-off nose, and the gouged eye.

"We found the combatants . . . fast clinched by the hair, their thumbs endeavoring to force a passage into each other's eyes," ran an entirely typical piece of correspondence from a British visitor in Georgia near the nineteenth century's turn, "while several of the bystanders were betting upon the first eye to be turned out of its socket."[4]

This sordid brawl was no aberration. Gouging matches, supported by cheering encircling crowds, were a routine culmination of backwoods gambling wagers, insults, grudges, drinking sprees, and plain meanness. "Rough-and-tumble" was the name for it, or "no holts barred," and the strategy was brutally simple: try to get your thumb inside your opponent's socket, feel for his eyestrings and make him "tell the news" before he did the same to you. In certain hamlets, scarcely a grown man had the use of both eyes. Davy Crockett, a real-life figure who briefly became a cuddly Disneyfied TV icon in the 1950s, was once heard to casually remark that "I kept my thumb in his eye, and was just going to give it a twist and bring the peeper out, like taking up a gooseberry in a spoon," when a bystander interrupted the fight and his pleasure.[5]

As paradoxical as it may seem, this primitive aggression enjoyed—depended upon—an intimate relationship with language. This relationship largely formed the American vernacular and inspired several of our characteristic national myths and folkloric figures. And it created the outlandish terms for a sense of humor which was unmistakably American, and which the young Mark Twain would refine, on the strength of one brilliantly told comic tale, as uniquely American.

Frontier violence formed the vernacular through its elicitation of boasting. Men who were about to plunge into bloody hand-to-hand combat needed to bolster their own courage and to intimidate their opponents. The resulting "wit-combats" preceded physical fighting and would produce champions of verbal as well as physical dominance. Among the greatest of these was the self-made legend Mike Fink:

> I'm a salt River roarer! I'm a regular screamer from the old Massassip! Whoop! I'm the very infant that refused his milk before its eyes were open and called out for a bottle of old Rye! I love the women and I'm chockful o' fight! I'm half wild horse and half cock-eyed alligator and the rest o' me is crooked snags an' red-hot snappin' turtle. . . . I can out-run, out-jump, out-shoot, out-brag, out-drink an' out-fight, rough an' tumble, no-holts barred, any man on both sides of the river from Pittsburgh to New Orleans an' back ag'in to St. Louiee. Come on, you flatters, you bargers, you milk white mechanics, an' see how tough I am to chaw! I ain't had a fight for two days an' I'm spilein' fer exercise. Cock-a-doodle-doo![6]

These word-combats would linger in the American culture and echo in the bench-jockeying that flavored American baseball from its nineteenth-century origins and amplified into the pervasive trash-talking of late-twentieth-century sports. They would echo in the boasts of Muhammad Ali (formerly Cassius Clay of Louisville, Kentucky, and the descendant of slaves), who proclaimed before a championship fight in Zaire in 1974 that "Last night I murdered a rock! injured a stone! hospitalized a brick! I'm so mean, I make medicine sick!"[7] They would echo in "standup" comedy, and in the rapping and "dozens"-style duels that preceded (and sometimes supplanted) urban streetfights.

Mark Twain, with his limitless ability to imitate and send up spoken language, enshrined the wit-combat in his literature. It appears most famously in the so-called "raft chapter," featuring an exchange between two heel-cracking, head-shaking Mississippi keelboatmen, "Bob" and "The Child of Calamity," and includes this tirade by a suspiciously erudite Child:

> Whoo-oop! Bow your neck and spread, for the kingdom of sorrow's coming! Hold me down to the earth, for I feel my powers a-working! Whoo-oop! I'm a child of sin, *don't* let me get a start! Smoked glass, here, for all! Don't attempt to look at me with the naked eye, gentlemen! When I'm playful I use the meridians of longitude and the parallels of lattitude for a seine, and drag the Atlantic Ocean for whales! I scratch my head with the lightning and purr myself to sleep with the thunder! . . . I'm the man with a petrified heart and biler-iron bowels! The massacre of isolated communities is the pastime of my idle moments, the destruction of nationalities the serious business of my life! The boundless vastness of the great American desert is my enclosed property, and I bury my dead on my own premises![8]

Twain had the typic dialogue down, but in the fracas that follows this exchange of insults, he submerges the orgy of eye-gouging and nose-biting and replaces it with broad comedy. Listening, on the fringes, to the blood prophecies of Bob and the Child, is a "little black-whiskered chap." As the two would-be gladiators end their bragging and tactfully edge away in different directions, this interloper, Little Davy, halts them with this conspicuously terse challenge: "Come back here, you couple of chicken-livered cowards, and I'll thrash the two of ye!" And he does, too, in a hilarious but mostly bloodless knockabout that ends with the two warriors washing their faces in the river and all hands resuming the idyllic life of the keelboat, fiddling and singing and drinking from the convivial jug.

Mark Twain was always protective, almost primly so, about life on his Mississippi. His seminal reminiscing account of it treads very lightly, for example, upon the explosive dangers of steamboat travel, although Twain had more than ample reason to brood upon those dangers. But in altering the course of the keelboatmen's fight from grotesquerie to farce, he was also tracing a shift in the function of American humor itself—from an incitement to violence and toward its substitute. (And he was, to complete the symmetry, announcing a shift in representative American vernacular: the overwrought verbosity of the Child of Calamity giving way to the conquering electric terseness of Little Davy. It was a shift that Twain's own writing made legitimate and universal.)

For this violence was so extreme, and so pervasive, and so apparently ingrained in man's brutish nature, that even its avid witnesses were capable of feeling defiled by it. Some sort of distancing attitude from one's own savagery was needed if one were to keep from falling into a pervasive self-loathing or, worse, a condition of true depravity.

Here, language proved useful again—just as it had in creating the elaborate, folk-poetic boasts that had helped motivate men to fight and risk disfigurement in the first place. The boasting took on a comic life of its own, at the expense of its subject-matter. The exaggerations became exaggerated. Instead of being aimed solely at one's opponents, the big brag took on violence itself as its target, sought to diminish it by making the invented story larger and more extreme than the physical act.

Here lay the origins of the fundamentally American art form that would be known the world over as the tall tale.

The folkloric historian Kenneth S. Lynn has summed it up most acutely: "By burlesquing savage emotion, [the tale-teller] remained true to himself as a human being—however obscene his language became—because burlesque turned brutality into a theatrical performance, released the frontiersman into a detachment about himself, and allowed him to laugh in the very teeth of his fears."[9] The scholar Henry B. Wonham concurs: "By exaggerating the conditions that made life virtually unbearable, inhabitants of the frontier were at the same time expressing their defiance and taking refuge in laughter."[10]

The tale-teller began to realize another benefit of his comic art. Not only was he preserving his humanity, he was gaining prestige. "The humorist established himself at the very center of frontier society," writes Lynn. "When he spoke, all eyes turned toward him. Many of the most gifted humorists were either politicians or revivalist preachers."[11]

Not to mention the combatants themselves. The Tennessean Davy Crockett, in most respects a cold-blooded, prideful, dangerous man, possessed gifts of phrase-turning and wicked mimicry that delighted his squatter countrymen. His wit propelled him from the slaughtering of Indians to the U.S. Congress in 1827. Mike Fink's droll allusions to cock-eyed alligators knocked them dead when Fink himself was not knocking them dead. Jim Bowie, the cold-eyed knifemaker, could elicit grins with his overheated challenges to duels. And Abraham Lincoln, who had been in a brawl or two in Illinois, once answered and disarmed a call to honor by suggesting cow-dung at five paces.[12]

Those who would seek this prestige, and the social and political advantages it conferred, found that they needed to draw on skills not available to everyone. A knack for mimicry helped, an ear for spoken language and the wit to invent variations on it. (Mark Twain's mimetic gifts were striking; he could "do" conversation and song in dialect as well as write it.) The storyteller also needed a discerning sense of the *changes* in the spoken language he heard and mimicked. The vernacular changed rapidly on the frontier after the Wilderness Trail was opened. New settlers, new situations, new political alliances, new exposures to cross-cultural currents—all these produced new hybrids of metaphor, swearing, slang.

But not only was the content of American English changing, the sound of it was changing as well: Various twangs, drawls, and other inflections were moving it swiftly from its Scotch and British origins. Twain, nothing if not a slave to verbal nuance, apotheosized these early-century varieties in the 1880s. In his "Explanatory" at the front of *Huckleberry Finn,* he advised the reader that a number of dialects would be used: "the Missouri negro dialect; the extremest form of the backwoods South-Western dialect; the ordinary 'Pike County' dialect; and four modified versions of this last." These shadings, he paused to point out, had not been done by guesswork, but painstakingly, and out of personal familiarity with these forms. The resulting book handed American literature its representative voice.

The silver-tongued raconteurs who could keep up with these proliferating tales and styles, and who could add a few refinements of their own in the retelling, discovered themselves at the centers of a populace starved for laughter, enchantment, and the theatrics of storytelling. And they discovered something even more wonderful: Their racy, bawdy, grotesque tall tales were being taken at face value by the Europeans and the Yankees who were flooding into the American Interior in the early nineteenth century.

These outsiders arrived because the Interior, along with the North and South poles, was among the last areas on earth unexplored by representatives of northern European civilization. Many of the visitors—an astonishing percentage of them—were travel writers, and their resulting books—"uncounted hundreds of them," in the historian M.H. Dunlop's estimation—established the Interior as "the most important locale for the most detailed examination of landscape ever conducted in North America and the vantage point from which to inform [their readers] of the greatest and most rapid experiments in social equality and landscape alteration that had ever occurred anywhere on the globe."[13]

The quality of observation varied widely. Alexis de Tocqueville arrived from France and consecrated everything he saw. Charles Dickens arrived and desecrated everything he saw. Frances Trollope arrived from Britain and believed everything she heard. The visitors agreed, disagreed, were charmed, repelled, but nearly always they were staggered at the boiling intensity of what they encountered. On certain themes there was general agreement: on how much landscape there was ("probably too much," in the opinion of one writer[14]); how fast the new country was transforming itself; how much and how fast the Americans ate; how grubby they tended to be, especially in the fingernails; and, most preponderatingly, how incredibly violent everyone was.

It did not take the Europeans long to notice the gouged eyeballs and the bitten-off noses that, in some of their accounts, practically littered the countryside. "I saw more than one man who wanted an eye, and ascertained that I was now in the region of 'gouging,'" came the nervous titter of a young Presbyterian minister headed downriver for

Louisiana in 1816.[15] This same worthy was shocked to encounter a hairy denizen of a riverside settlement and hear him described as the "best" man there, only to learn "that best in this context meant not the most moral . . . but the local champion who had whipped all the rest, the man most dextrous at extracting eyes."[16]

It did not take long for the locals, especially the storytellers, to notice that the refined visitors had insatiable appetites for being horrified. From their point of view, the exotic travelers "came to the West as to a zoo, with notebooks and pens poised to record the mating calls and other bizarre noises of the inhabitants."[17] The frontiersmen were only too happy to oblige. They had sensed the Easterners' condescension; they had caught the visitors' disdain for their table manners and their dirty fingernails. The more talented storytellers began to embroider the very real violence in their society, to see how far they could go with their ludicrous exaggerations. Pretty far, as it turned out. The Europeans scribbled down their outrageous lies as gospel and reported back that the lost colonies were a land of unspeakable depravity. The frontier storytellers were much gratified.

And thus another root-characteristic of American humor took seed: the convention of the rustic turning the tables on the sophisticate; the mock-innocent's "splendid revenge" on those who thought themselves his betters. The laughers, as Lynn put it, made laughable. Lynn added: "For the Clown, after all, was not impressed by the Gentleman—nor had he ever been . . . by deliberately playing up their own loutishness they may very well have mocked the dandy to his face."[18]

Through the late eighteenth century and into the early nineteenth, the formation and spread of American humor had been overwhelmingly oral: songs, myths, and tall tales, refined and embellished by traveling tellers; archetypal characters (the Yankee Peddler, the Keelboatman, the Negro Minstrel) endlessly reinvoked and refined along the inland trails and waterways. (Traveling plays, semi-scripted minstrel shows, and the occasional memoir of a planter-in-exile from London society were transitional exceptions.)

It was only in the early 1830s—just a few years before Sam Clemens's birth—that the oral form began to find its resonant echo in print.

A number of converging trends brought this about. Among the most important were the spread of the "penny press" in the 1820s from urban centers to small towns, and the onrushing formation of a distinctly Southern, or "Southwestern," political and cultural identity.*

As for political/cultural identity, it cohered around a generation of literate, educated Southwestern men, disaffected supporters of Andrew Jackson whose writings would eventually form the concept of Southern patriotism. Their ideas and passions would infuse the Whig Party when it was organized to oppose Jackson in 1834. (Orion Clemens, like his father, was a Whig.)

These men—widely scattered over the region and not necessarily in contact with one another—tended to be professional by class, conservative by philosophy, political by habit and romantic in their literary tastes. Kenneth Lynn discerned two additional unifying traits: "a sense of humor . . . and in a surprising number of cases a notoriously

---

*The "Southwest," as it was called until the Civil War, must be distinguished from the region that now bears the title: Arizona, New Mexico, and Texas. In the early nineteenth century, "the Southwest" referred to the states and territories stretching southward and westward from the great cities of the Eastern Seaboard. It comprised Virginia, the Carolinas, Appalachia, and other elements of what is now known as the Deep South.

bad temper."[19] The backwoods dichotomy began repeating itself in the parlors and the courthouses of the Southwest.

The bad temper might have owed itself to a collective sense of betrayal. These new mandarins of Southern society had championed Andrew Jackson during his heroic military years and his subsequent political rise. They accepted his populism, his campaign to remove power from the plantation "gentry" and the urban mercantile interests, and bestow it upon the farmers and the mechanics of the new republic. They helped elect him President in 1828, assuming that this son of Carolina would move to relieve them of the "abominable" tariffs that Congress had enacted earlier that year: 50 percent taxation on imported raw wool, similarly high levies on hemp and pig iron. Instead, Jackson shocked them by standing firm. (He was, after all, a populist.) When South Carolina, spurred by John C. Calhoun, moved to declare the tariff law null and void, President Jackson countered aggressively: In 1833 he demanded and gained the power to use military troops to enforce the tariffs. He won this fight, but at a cost that changed American history.

Jackson's ironfisted federal posture unhinged his former boosters. The so-called Nullification Crisis activated something primal in the good mandarins of the Southwest. It jolted them into an angry consciousness of themselves and their region as an entity apart, a culture-within-a-culture, taken for granted and now aggrieved. Suddenly, in 1833, the Southwest's traditions, its myths and its ideals (including, not incidentally, the "ideal" of slavery) seemed to constitute a kind of nationhood. Now this mythic nation was under assault from a distant government.

Here, perhaps, could be found the key to John Marshall Clemens's grinding contradictions: his rigid code of honor and dedication to humanitarian justice, coexisting with his chilly acceptance of slavehold-ing. He was a Virginian, after all, and Virginians understood these ideals in ways that the world outside the South could not.

The penny presses enabled this new culture of the Southwest to ex-press itself. First came the literature—a spontaneous combustion that flared into two distinct genres. The lofty style was claimed by the so-called "plantation novelists," men who represented an aristocracy al-ready deep-rooted in America and who wanted to keep it that way. These sonorous writers turned for their literary model to Sir Walter Scott, whose florid fantasies of bygone chivalric romance, sacred homelands and terrific costumes colored their own idealizations of the South. (It didn't hurt any that Sir Walter's native Scotland had pro-duced the Stuart line, tragically deposed from the British Crown in 1688 and poignantly unsuccessful in an attempt to regain it in 1745. Here was a writer who understood the exquisite tragedy of the privi-leged dispossessed.) These imitators of Scott tried to impose the tem-plate of his courtly feudal myths on their time and place. Hoop skirts, derringers, mustachioed cavaliers, and lots of misty-eyed *yearning* filled their pages.

(Mark Twain, who in certain ways owed his lineage to Sir Walter Scott, perceived the romanticizer's influence more clearly than most, and detested it. Twain saw through Scott's rambling novels as mere-tricious sentimentality, puffing up a "sham civilization." Scott, he said, "sets the world in love with dreams and phantoms . . . with the silli-ness and emptiness, sham grandeurs, sham gauds, and sham chivalries of a brainless and worthless long-vanished society."[20] Having deliv-ered that pleasantry, Twain turned a little peevish and blamed Scott for the American Civil War. "Sir Walter had so large a hand in making

Southern character, as it existed before the war," he wrote in the 1880s, "that he is in great measure responsible for the war." It was Sir Walter, he jeeringly maintained, "that made every gentleman in the South a major or a colonel, or a general or a judge . . . for it was he that created rank and caste down there, and also reverence for rank and caste, and pride and pleasure in them."[21])

Meanwhile, and with far greater impact than that of the "plantation novelists," a grittier attack was being launched by the new humorists. Their style was livelier, but their agenda no less serious. The comic writers who burst into print in 1833, mostly in periodicals and weekly papers throughout the Southwest, had their eye on Scott as well. They noted how he had reinforced the grandeur of his leading characters, the knights and kings and their ladies, by his contrasting use of "low" bit players: gardeners, maids, assorted peasants. In their unabashed efforts to imitate Sir Walter's lowdown caricatures, and thus toss a little mud on those annoying, tariff-bloating Jacksonian democrats, the new Southwestern wits dipped into their region's flourishing oral repertory. They gave new, lasting life in print to the bumptious brawling bad boys of the tall tale.

These fictional bad boys seized hold of the region's consciousness in the years between 1833 and the onset of the Civil War. Their names were as whimsical as their language was coarse and their deeds dark: Ransy Sniffle and Flan Sucker and Sammy Stonestreet and Simon Suggs and the truly sulfurous Sut Lovingood. Different in their make-believe particulars, these loutish creatures had many general traits in common. They were physically ugly. They feasted on bloodshed and cruelty. They were spoilers of the civilized order, the sworn destroyers of Whig manners and moderation. They all spoke in brilliantly rendered backwoods dialect. And they were, for the most part, literally *boys*: the new egalitarian order depicted as demon-child. Their collective behavior was wittily reprehensible. And yet they established a rough prototype that made the world safe, if not vice versa, for Huckleberry Finn.

There was plenty of method in this badness. The Whig wits enlisted these comic traits and mannerisms in a cause no less solemn than the salvation of Southwestern society. Unlike the backwoods fans of Davy Crockett and Mike Fink generally, these educated gentlemen were not amused by violence—either the physical violence of their white-trash fellow citizens, or the political violence that they saw in the Jacksonian leveling of wealth. Thus the shiftiness of Suggs, the sadism of Sniffle, and the saturnine sass of the inevitable addition to the gallery in the 1850s: the Happy Darky, who generally came to grief at the hands of snickering Sut.

But as vividly as they were drawn, these villains were never the *point-of-view* characters of the stories in which they appeared. The intent was always to show them through the eyes of a detached, condescending or disapproving onlooker who represented, on the page, the shared enlightenment of the author and the reader. The need to make this separation utterly clear led to the insertion of a second "main character" in the stories—a narrator, always unnamed, but understood to be the author's alter ego. This character, besides his air of calm good manners, was as distinctive for his impeccable use of English as the bad boy was distinctive for his misuse of it. In fact this narrator spoke for the bad boy, reproducing his dialect in the manner of an oral yarnspinner telling a tall tale, but always conveying his distaste for the tale being told.

This was the important literary device known as the "frame": the two-tiered structure of the comic story, in which author introduces civilized speaker who then "recalls" the central action for the reader. A crusty Georgia newspaper editor named Augustus Baldwin Longstreet, thumping for state's rights and Nullification, brought the "frame" into vogue in 1833, with his newspaper sketches centering on Ransy Sniffle. But the device had a distinguished lineage. A century earlier, the British essayist and wit Joseph Addison had used "framing" to contrast his own Man-of-Reason stance with the irrational biases of the peasantry.

So much of the American psyche was encoded and packed into those brilliant, unruly old tales and sketches. So much of the nation's political ferment and cultural disputation were caught in their sly deft metaphors. So much has been lost to all but the most meticulous scholars. Kenneth Lynn offers one example among many for analysis: A. B. Longstreet's cultivated narrator recalls a journey through the lovely Georgia woods; his serenity is broken by the sound of a terrible fight issuing from behind a clump of bushes. He replicates the comic dialogue of threat and challenge. But to the narrator's surprise, there emerge from the bushes not two combatants but just one, an eighteen-year-old boy "jist seein' how I could 'a' *fout*." The ground around the boy, the narrator notices, bears "the prints of his two thumbs, plunged up to the balls in the mellow earth, about the distance of a man's eyes apart; and the ground around was broken up as if two stags had been engaged upon it."[22]

Twentieth-century readers might sift through this antiquated piece and be amused at the feast of rustic dialogue, but beyond that, the tale's point would almost surely elude them. This loss of connection to the device is unfortunate if only because the "frame" story and its encoded secrets also hold the key to Mark Twain's abrupt burst from obscurity into national celebrityhood in 1865, on the reputation of one similarly arcane twenty-six hundred-word comic tale.

The scholar Lynn has decoded the Longstreet story's probable meaning. "The conservative political allegory" in the sketch, he assures us, "was recognized at once." The boy's mindless gouging of the soft Georgia earth, Lynn suggests, parallels the equally ridiculous (and to Whig sensibilities, violent) assault being waged by President Andrew Jackson against the Biddle Bank, a consortium of commercial interests who wanted to establish a Second Bank of the United States. "The violent boy," he concludes, "represents what to the Whig mind was the central quality of Jacksonianism."[23]

The "frame" story was part of the cultural air that Sam Clemens breathed as a boy and a young man. He certainly read A. B. Longstreet among some of the others; Lynn notes that in *Tom Sawyer,* Twain rewrote and defanged the Georgia boy's phantom fight in the scene that depicts Tom's imaginary "pummeling . . . kicking and gouging" of the dandy Alfred Temple: "Oh, you do, do you? You holler 'nough, do you?" He read and favorably reviewed George Washington Harris, and drew heavily on a Harris/Sut Lovingood tale as he lampooned the weaving, raving preacher in the camp-meeting scene in *Huckleberry Finn.*

It was to be partly through the radical redefinition and, finally, the exploding of the frame that Twain secured his place in storytelling history.

The tall tale that transformed him was first published late in 1865 as a magazine and newspaper sketch called "Jim Smiley and His Jumping Frog." Two years later it resurfaced as the title essay in his first book, a collection called *The Celebrated Jumping Frog of Calaveras County, and Other Sketches.* Like its ancestors, the nearly forgotten Whig allegories of Longstreet, Harris, and the rest, the full range of this story's comic complexity is unavailable to the late–twentieth-century general reader. "The hilarity is gone from it now," Bernard DeVoto acknowledged as early as 1933. "No one will ever laugh at it again as all America, in the actual presence of the life it wrought with, laughed at it in the closing weeks of 1865."[24] Since then, untold numbers of American schoolchildren, while amused perhaps at the cartoonish aspects of the story, have strained to understand why this strange little riff is regarded, in the words of Richard Bucci, as "one of the most effective pieces of humorous writing in American literature."[25]

The outlines of the tale were nothing new. Versions of it had been floating around the West for years. The boy Sammy may have heard a version of it from his Uncle John Quarles back in Florida. A stranger comes to town and meets a local braggart and compulsive bettor who tells him that the frog he is holding in a box can outjump any other frog in the county. The stranger says he'd like to bet on that, but he doesn't happen to have a frog with him at the moment. The local man offers to go out and find one. While he's out searching, the stranger takes the opportunity to fill the champion frog's gullet full of lead shot; at the critical moment the champion cannot budge; the stranger pockets the wager and disappears.

After hearing this tale at a mining cabin in a rustic spot known as Jackass Hill one winter night in 1864, Twain worked it up into a classic Southwestern "frame" story—a sedate narrator reproducing a yarn told in rough, comic dialect—but there the conventional aspects of the "Jumping Frog" forever vanished.

It vanished partly into the persona of "Simon Wheeler." Here was no ordinary stock-company rustic spouting amusing malaprops, but a fully-fleshed literary figure of masterful compression and novelty. "Wheeler" is American story personified, a fountain of fantastical character (both human and animal), incident, drama, and surprise, who erupts into talk when the narrator makes a simple inquiry about the whereabouts of a friend, and is still spieling away when the narrator takes his leave. Any fellow who tells a tale of a bull pup named Andrew Jackson whose fighting specialty is "freezing" his teeth to the hind leg of the other dog, and who is finally defeated by a dog with no hind legs—and who makes it clear that *that* tale is just a throwaway digression from his *main* tale—there is a fellow worth paying a little attention to. It is the voice of Wheeler, then, that gives the Frog story its initial boost out of the ordinary. Unlike most Southwestern narrators, Twain's gentleman never interrupts Wheeler once he has begun, which enhances the illusion (as Lynn has pointed out) that this tale is being told instead of written.

But wild fluency is only part of Wheeler's special fascination. He is also a highly enigmatic character. Here, Twain leaves the Southwestern tradition even further behind. Wheeler is not on the page just to drive home some transient social or political point. He's a sorcerer, of sorts. He has already thrown Twain/the narrator off balance by shifting the talk from *Leonidas* Smiley (whom the narrator had asked about) to *Jim* Smiley (the frog's owner and a person utterly beside the point). And now, Wheeler's compulsive comic banter kicks in to overdrive: eerily gifted racing nags, a wager on the recovery prospects of a dying parson's wife; straddle-bugs and rat-tarriers and chicken-cocks and frogs that could whirl in the air "like a doughnut" and hoist up their shoulders "like a Frenchman." Is this rustic innocence—or is it something else? Soon there arises a surreal air of confusion as to exactly where (if anywhere) reality lies.

Once "Wheeler" gets to the central action of the tale, he scores a fairly obvious comic point by the deadpan telling of the critical action:

It is in the middle of a blandly phrased paragraph that the stranger sits thinking to himself, then "got the frog out and prized his mouth open and took a teaspoon and filled him full of quail shot—filled him pretty near up to his chin . . . "

At the end of the tale the narrator gets up, in a state of stupefaction, and leaves Simon Wheeler rattling away about "a yaller one-eyed cow." He has learned—what? That a stranger to him has been outwitted by another stranger? And this on the testimony of yet a third stranger, "Simon Wheeler"? What about the party the narrator has come to find, the Rev. Leonidas Smiley? His whereabouts are still as much a mystery as, say, the existence of the jumping frog.

For the first time in the history of Southwestern humor, the gentlemanly narrator himself has become the butt of the joke. Political agendas be hanged, along with Smiley and his afflicted cow. Here at the close of the traumatic Civil War, a war that the nation would spend the ensuing decades trying diligently to forget, an absolutely new and cleansing comic viewpoint had been opened up.

The future, not the past, was what mattered now: reinvention, possibility, a liberation from constricting and bankrupt old aristocratic myths. In this sense Mark Twain was reigniting (or jump-frog-starting) the entire American experiment. That experiment, after all, was at its origins a "lighting out for the Territory"—a bursting free from old Europe's enslavement to history, encoded and petrified in the Greek and Latin texts. In the early years of the nineteenth century the Old South had mimicked and replaced Old Europe as a repository for hardened assumptions about class, caste, privilege, and fixed destiny.

The War ended those assumptions militarily. But it took the Jumping Frog to end them culturally, to redirect America's gaze back to the future. An ironic achievement, perhaps, for a writer who came to distrust that future, mythify his personal past and embrace his century as the culmination of history. But of all Mark Twain's contributions to the twentieth-century American temperament—plainspeaking, egalitarian, wisecracking, centered in its fanfare for the common man—this tale, perhaps, beat all. It foreordained the proletarian comic stances of Will Rogers, Ring Lardner, Finley Peter Dunne as "Mr. Dooley" in the *Chicago Tribune*. Even such early cinematic icons as Charlie Chaplin in his "Tramp" persona and Groucho Marx, riotously deflating the pompous Margaret DuMont, owed a debt to the frog.

The postwar nation recognized it at once, and rejoiced. "The finest piece of humorous literature yet produced in America," James Russell Lowell called it.[26]

As for the creator himself, he was (typically) the last to get it. Mark Twain considered the tale, as he wrote to his mother, "a villainous backwoods sketch." In another letter, he pleaded with his bride-to-be, Olivia Langdon, to not read a word in it. And to his brother Orion, even as he was drafting the tale, he grumbled that "I *have* had a 'call' to literature, of a low order—*i.e.* humorous. It is nothing to be proud of . . . "

Mark Twain never surrendered his childhood stories. And yet in the ambitious middle years of his life, Twain seemed to recoil a little from the Panlike beckonings of his Hannibal-boy muse: the go-to-hell subversive note he struck with Huck and the jumping frog. Thankfully for American literature, the Hannibal boy never recoiled from the man.

Ten

"Honest poverty is a gem that even a King
might feel proud to call his own, but I wish to sell out."

After John Marshall's burial, Orion plodded back to St. Louis and his printing job, sending money home and visiting as often as he could. At twenty-two, he had been at printing for five years now and had begun to half-believe he was young Benjamin Franklin, imitating what he'd read of Franklin's life as an apprentice. As executor of the family estate, Orion also took over responsibility for his father's little Hannibal Library Institute and ran it with his customary prowess: He forgot to collect dues from members and misplaced several of the books. He did succeed in leasing the house on Hill Street from the compassionate James Clemens, and in April the family moved back in to remain until Sam's departure in 1853.

Pamela, twenty now, came home from Florida and Paris—that is, from the nearby villages of Florida and Paris, where she had been giving piano and guitar lessons—and began receiving pupils in Jane's household. Like her niece Clara, Pamela's life would be devoted to music and duty, mostly duty. Pale, sickly, and humorless, she took up watch over her mother, whose great vitality had suffered a setback with John's death.

Jane's red hair was showing streaks of gray now, and her trademark laughter sometimes revealed a sharp, impatient edge. She herded Sam and Henry toward school, played cards when she could, tried smoking a pipe for awhile, watched out for omens and the prophecies revealed in people's dreams, wept, embroidered, worried about money, and found pleasure in the color red.

Henry, not quite nine, remained the household pet, the Good Boy. He liked school, read a lot, obeyed his mother and older sister, developed into a bit of a snitch, occasionally traded clods and cobblestones with his brother, but generally depended on Sam for protection.

The red-haired boy emerged from the bereavement as he always seemed to emerge from bereavements until they piled up in his whitened old age: unaffected and sunny again, after a brief period of sleepwalking and inflamed dreams. His father's death; the effects of whatever he had witnessed through the keyhole; his mother's admonitions, whatever they might have been—these left no apparent imprints on his behavior.

Perhaps he had perfected his mask of stoicism by then. Mark Twain's writings would always show an emotional detachment from violence and death. Keen interest, to be sure, and diamondlike precision of detail, and often a mordancy of wit that could be, and was, taken for callousness. Describing his introduction to newspapering in Virginia City in *Roughing It,* he recalled exaggerating the arrival of a hay truck from the country ("I multiplied it by sixteen . . . ") and then casting about for more filler material: "Presently, when things began to look dismal again, a desperado killed a man in a saloon and joy returned once more." A bit later on, he and a colleague hear pistol shots on the street at night and get the particulars "with little loss of time, for it was only an inferior sort of bar-room murder, and of little interest to the public . . . "

This sort of thing became a grisly routine. Late on another night he was sitting peacefully in his hotel room writing a letter to Jane and Pamela when his attention was again disturbed by gunshots. He got up from his writing desk, went outside to investigate and returned to add a laconic postscript: A gunman—a fellow from Jackson County, Missouri, as it happened—"shot two of my friends (police officers) through the heart—both died within three minutes. Murderer's name is John Campbell."

Interest, detail, and mordant wit. But never a show of hand-wringing, or mourning, or eulogy. Not, at least, until Suzy was taken from him, and later Livy.

In his autobiography, Mark Twain recalled going virtually from John Marshall's funeral into a printer's apprenticeship, but in fact that did not happen for another year. Instead, at age eleven, he enrolled at Dawson's School about three weeks after his father died and took on a succession of odd jobs remarkably similar to those available to a small-town Midwestern boy a century later. With Sam, each job contained the seeds of its own comic termination.

Through the spring and summer of 1847 he clerked in a grocery store until he was fired for eating too much sugar; he was a book-seller's clerk for awhile until "the customers bothered me so much I could not read with any comfort"; he clerked in a drugstore "but my prescriptions were unlucky, and we appeared to sell more stomach pumps than soda water." He tried his hand in blacksmithing, was a newspaper delivery boy; at some point in his boyhood he studied law, or played at it, for a week, then gave it up "because it was so prosy and tiresome."*

---

*He detailed these memories in chapter 42 of *Roughing It*.

In his spare time he ran with his nighttime gang, agitated his mother, tried once in awhile to joke around with Pamela but always had to explain he was joking, and dipped into the romance and adventure books whose contents he seemed to transfer intact to his memory.

Gangly Orion, as he always would, provided some doleful comic relief. On one of his returns home that summer, he apparently forgot that his family had moved back into the Hill Street house. Arriving in town at night, his dreamy mind elsewhere, he ambled like a drayhorse to the old address, trudged up the stairs, undressed and dropped into the bed on the second floor, and found himself in close company with Dr. Meredith's spinster sister.

The year 1848 was to be a time of transition for Sam Clemens and for the western half of the continent he lived on, and for the combined destinies of the two.

Sam finally went to work full-time as a printer's devil in the summer of that year. Six months earlier and two thousand miles away, the eccentric partner of a sawmill proprietor in the California territory, one James Marshall, had approached the proprietor with a few slivers of ore in his hand; he thought they looked like grains of gold. The proprietor, whose name was John Sutter, thought Marshall was acting like a fool again. But just to be sure, he got out his encyclopedia and read up on the description of gold. A year later the California Gold Rush would stampede its way through Hannibal, trailing prosperity in its wake of the kind John Marshall had only dreamed of.

In the meantime, strapped and fatherless in the white town, the Clemens family needed relief from the price of food and clothing. "Pretty hard sledding" was the way Twain recalled this period. In fact the family was desperate, so desperate that Sam, at age twelve, was sent into a kind of servitude. Happily, his place of toil was only half a block from the family house, and the kind of work he did began to prepare him for his life in words.

Among the artifacts of the new American culture spreading westward at about that time—in addition to the carnival, the minstrel show, the traveling theater troupe, and the outlaw—was the newspaper. Back East, in 1833, the publisher Benjamin Day had dropped the price of his *New York Sun* from six cents to a penny, gestated the modern mass-circulation newspaper, and created the conditions for a self-aware working-class "public" that would in time identify Mark Twain as its literary champion. Day's radical experiment meant that ordinary people, and not just an economic and intellectual elite, could have access to his paper, and thus to information about matters that bore on their lives. (It also meant that newspapers began to be *about* information, as opposed to vested political opinion.) Its immediate success ignited a conflagration of penny presses—first in other urban centers such as Philadelphia, Boston, and Baltimore, and then west across the hinterlands. Their spread was hastened by the development of railroads and the technological shift from creaky, hand-powered wooden presses to two-cylinder, steam-driven iron ones. A nation that counted only 650 weekly papers and 65 dailies in 1830 saw those numbers double within a decade, and more than double again by 1850.*

---

*Their readers grasped the Jacksonian benefits of the new form right away. A nonplussed Frances Trollope reported that when she chided her Cincinnati milkman about his time spent reading the paper, he snapped back at her: "And I'd like you to tell me how we can spend it better. How should free men spend their time, but looking after their government, and watching that them fellers as we gives offices to, does their duty, and gives themselves no airs?" (The exchange is cited by M. H. Dunlop in *Sixty Miles from Contentment.*)

In most smaller towns, like Hannibal, the cachet of newspapering took hold well ahead of steam. At midcentury, editors made do with equipment that had not changed much from Ben Franklin's time, or Gutenberg's. They worked with "Ramage"-type presses, whose right-angled iron platens and type-beds were small enough to set up in one room of an ordinary house. Their assistants, printer's-devils, made up news pages letter by letter, handpicking the symbols from a case of assorted metal typefaces, stored alphabetically and numerically in rows of cases. They arranged the letters into words and words into lines, or "sticks." Each stick was then placed inside the "tray," the emerging skeleton of the newspaper's page. When an entire tray had been assembled, the printers covered the surface of inked type with paper made from rag-stock, and then pressed the plate down by use of a triple-threaded screw. The work was draining and precise, but two skilled workers could produce about 250 sheets an hour this way.

Newspapers began cropping up in Hannibal as soon as the village gathered a critical mass of merchants willing to run ads. The first paper was launched in 1837, the year of the town's incorporation. Called the *Commercial Advertiser*, it required four days to set up and discharge a printed page. In 1840 a new owner renamed it the *Pacific Monitor*. It took on a number of fanciful names after that—*Price Current* and *Hannibal Journal and Native American* among them—before finally settling down to become merely the *Journal*.

The *Gazette* came along in November 1846. One of its first advertisements was for "The Writing Academy of Messrs. Jennings and Guernsey," promising "A chance for Hannibal people who have never had an opportunity to learn to write, to do so now."[2] Two years later the *Gazette* moved from the Pilaster House to the second floor of the L. T. Brittingham drugstore at the town hub, Hill and Main. There in that same year it was bought by Joseph Ament, a stingy Tennessee-born editor then working in Palmyra. Ament renamed the paper for his Palmyra sheet—the *Courier*. It was the ancestor of the present-day Hannibal newspaper, the *Courier-Post*, and the venue for Sam Clemens's first physical contact with print.

Jane Clemens sent Sam to work for Ament around June of 1848. His original duties were to fetch water, build the fire in winter, sweep the floor, and learn what he could about setting type. Ament paid him nothing. But the boy was allowed to eat his meals at the Ament house, which eased the pressure of scarcity half a block up Hill Street, and he was entitled to two suits of clothes a year. Before long, like the rest, he began to learn to set type, and set it fast. He worked long hours and sometimes slept on the printing-room floor, amid smells of turpentine, lye, soot, and thick black printer's ink.

Sam found the clothes bad and the food worse. He and two other apprentices had to eat in the kitchen, where an elderly slave cook and her daughter starved them to the point that they stole onions and potatoes from the cellar. As for wardrobing, the boy received one suit of clothes, not two, and that one suit had belonged to Ament, who was twice Sam's size. "I had to turn up his pants to my ears to make them short enough," he later wrote.[3]

Bleak House it may not quite have been, nor a blacking factory, but Sam was thrust up against some Dickensian characters, or ordinary folks whom he appraised with a Dickensian eye: the first few in a vast repertory of American innocents whom he would encounter in his overland travels and on the big river.

There was Ament himself, pennypinching, peevish, and sour-tempered, whom Sam would later characterize in Orion's rival paper as "a diminutive chunk of human meat."[4]

There was the hawkish Judith D. Ament,* the editor's aunt or elder sister, whose microscopic apportioning of coffee-sugar marked her as the stingiest figure in this gothically stingy household. "You could not tell her breast from her back if she had her head up a stove-pipe hole," Twain pleasantly remarks of a fictional character quite similar to Miss Judith in an unpublished story.[5]

There was the apprentice Pet McCormick, a human caricature in his red goatee, plug hat pulled down low over grease-cultivated curls, pungent Cuban cigars, and strangely mannered prance.

There was Wales McCormick, the other apprentice, a gigantic seventeen-year-old who satirically "made love" to the demure mulatto slave-daughter† and who pulled off the most audacious prank of Sam's tenure at the *Gazette*.

It was set in motion by the arrival from Kentucky of Alexander Campbell, the charismatic founder of the Campbellite religious sect and among the organizers of the Disciples of Christ. Campbell swept into town on a cloud of celebrityhood and preached a tremendous sermon that jammed the public square in Hannibal. His dazzled followers took up a collection of $16 and brought it to Ament's printing establishment—it was the largest mass of money that had ever entered the office at one time—to have the sermon printed in book form. When the three young apprentices had it all set in type—hour upon hour of excruciating labor—they were aghast to find that they had left out a couple of key words.

---

*Dixon Wecter established her name through a search of census records.

†"Make love" in that time generally meant what "flirt" means today, but Twain casually alluded to a more physical interpretation. "The old mother's distress about it was merely a pretence," he wrote in his autobiography. "She quite well understood that by the customs of slaveholding communities it was Wales's right to make love to that girl if he wanted to."

Wales McCormick had a brilliant idea: He would reduce the name of Jesus Christ, which showed up in the same line as the missing words, to its initials: "J. C." He made the fix, and the line fit. The three sent a proof-sheet of the correction to the great man of God. Then they waited, a little doubtfully, for his reaction. They did not have to wait long. Campbell was soon looming in the doorway of the print-shop. He threw some brimstone at young McCormick and finished by roaring, "So long as you live, don't you ever diminish the Savior's name again. Put it *all* in."

McCormick decided to obey Campbell, to the letter, as it were. At the expense of resetting the entire last three pages of the eight-page booklet, he restored the Savior's name to its fullest majesty. He gave it an extra syllable that had gained popularity among swearers of that time and place, so that it stood out proudly in the text of the sermon: Jesus H. Christ.

"I don't remember what his punishment was," Mark Twain wrote, still delighted more than half a century later, "but he was not the person to care for that. He had already collected his dividend."[6]

To complete this gallery, there was Sam Clemens himself—shaggily red-haired, still tiny at twelve, propped up on a cigar box to reach the type-case, his baggy clothes sagging on his frame, puffing away on a cigar as he worked.

As he worked and smoked, he was building his literary conscious-ness—letter by letter, word by word, line by line. More than the adventure books of his young boyhood, more even than the Bible, these years of typesetting would anneal him to language by making it a tactile presence in his hands, with weight and shape and scent, the scent of the ink.

The paradigm of typesetting remained a lifelong guiding principle of Mark Twain's writing and even speaking style. As fast and torrentially as his work could flow, twenty manuscript pages a day in the throes of inspiration, his sentences were always *constructed,* never dashed. The right word obsessed him, like an "elusive and shifty grain of gold."[7] Even more: "The difference between the *almost right* word and the *right* word is really a large matter—'tis the difference between the lightning-bug and the lightning."[8] He knew that the average English word was exactly four letters and a half, and "shaved" his own rhetoric, he claimed, until the average was three and a half. The unspoken word (like the unused sliver of type) was, to him, "capital. We can invest it or we can squander it."[9] He became a connoisseur of the last words of great men; those of Franklin, that other printer's devil cum-aphorist, delighted him: "He pondered over his last words for as much as two weeks, and then when the time came, he said, 'None but the brave deserve the fair,' and died happy. He could not have said a sweeter thing if had lived till he was an idiot."[10]

As for the influences on his speaking style, he learned to use the pause almost as a thing of weighted substance, as a length of solid lead to place between his well-constructed words. "The right word may be effective, but no word was ever as effective as a rightly timed pause," he wrote.[11] In Utica in 1870, on tour as a lecturer, he proved the point and daringly took the pause to its limit. Walking onstage in his trademark shuffle, he peered at the audience but did not at once begin to speak. He continued to hold the silence until well beyond the limits of comfort. The crowd looked back at him in tense confusion. Then, as he held his pose, someone tittered, and the tension erupted into convulsive laughter. Describing the moment in a letter to Livy, he relived his delight in this power of the pause. "No man will dare more than I to get to it," he exulted. "An audience captured in that way *belongs* to the speaker, body and soul . . . "

Besides the tactile presence of words, his career in Joseph Ament's shop (and later in Orion's) sharpened his literary interests in more direct ways. Newspapers of that era had limited resources for the actual gathering of news; among their most fertile sources were other newspapers. The editors' access to one another's newspapers was greatly facilitated by the Postal Act of 1792, which allowed every publisher to send one free copy of his paper to every other publisher free of charge. Even allowing generously for loss, inertia, and jealous withholding, this Act ensured a lively exchange of local papers around the country and reprintings of topical essays, sketches, and poetry.

This flow became an important carrier of the emerging American culture. In particular, it carried the loud, rude, no-holts-barred verbal violence and wild invective with which that new culture was announcing itself. It amplified well beyond their own regions, for instance, the boozy mayhem and the thuggish practical jokes of George Washington Harris's Sut Lovingood and the shrewd con-artistry of J. J. Hooper's Simon Suggs. The weekly flow of distant "Southwestern" newspapers into the *Gazette*'s tiny office is almost certainly how Sam Clemens became acquainted with Sut, Simon, Ransy Sniffle, and the literary structure behind them.

Sam's days as a printer's devil did not lead exclusively to happy consequences. The recollected feel of weighted words in his hands would resonate with his darkest reversals as well. Mark Twain never lost his memory of the excruciating repetitive tasks of the printer. His passion for investing in the ill-fated Paige typesetting sprang partly from those memories.

His sense of humor, flavored with hot Southwestern spices, was maturing. Contrary to his denatured twentieth-century image, his wit had an aggressive edge; in fact it existed on that edge, and always would. His passion for hoaxes and practical jokes was nourishing itself here, as was his detached glee at the comic sufferings of others. The very prospect of fun at others' expense could leave him "in a radiant heaven of anticipation."[12] Among his earliest and most favored victims, as he began his printer's apprenticeship, was one Jim Wolf, a naïve and bashful seventeen-year-old from a Missouri settlement who had come to the Clemens household as a boarder.

Mark Twain mined Jim Wolf's bashfulness for one funny and relatively innocuous story that he eventually published in California. One winter night Pamela gave a candy pull. Late in the moonlit evening the guests spilled out into the small courtyard with their saucers of hot candy; their laughter apparently activated the yowling of a couple of tomcats on the annex roof below Jim's bedroom. The cats disturbed Jim; Sam dared him to climb out on the roof and shoo them away; the boy took him up on it, climbed out onto the snow-covered roof in his nightshirt, lost his balance "and, like a rocket he darted down the roof feet first, crashed through the dead vines and landed in a sitting position in fourteen saucers of red-hot candy. . . . There was a wild scramble and a storm of shrieks and Jim fled up the stairs, dripping broken crockery all the way."[13]

A comically authentic "tall tale," as far as it went, and given permanence in print by Twain's teasing buildup to the moment of Jim's slip, and by the incomparable rush of visual nuance: the boy darting like a rocket feet-first, the sitting position, the fourteen saucers of red-hot candy.

But Sam's appetite for Jim Wolf's misadventures went far beyond mere pratfall. The following summer he enjoyed laughter at the young rustic's expense that by any standard except, perhaps, the American frontier's, tended uncomfortably toward sadism.

Sam was on hand one warm evening as Wolf entered Jane's small parlor and was confronted by "two majestic old maids,"[14] who had seated themselves directly in his path. Paralyzed, Wolf took a seat in the nearest chair and went rigid. Sam entered not long after, "was charmed with the situation and sat down in a corner to watch Jim suffer and to enjoy it."[15] Presently Jane entered and began a conversation. Jim Wolf sat unmoving; but Sam noticed the promise of real distress in his face: "There would be a sudden twitch of the muscles . . . an instant distortion which in the next instant had passed and left no trace."[16] The twitches grew in frequency; after a while, tears formed in Jim's eyes. As Sam watched, Jim finally moved: His right hand inched along his thigh and clutched at the cloth of his trousers.

The boy's legs were being invaded by wasps. He had sat above a colony of them, and now they were moving up, under his clothing, stinging as they went. Sam took in the most subtle details of Jim's torment, and the aged Twain savored them in his autobiography:

> . . . for a quarter of an hour one group of excursionists after another climbed up Jim's legs and resented even the slightest wince or squirm that he indulged himself with in his misery. When the entertainment had become nearly unbearable he conceived the idea of gripping them between his fingers and putting them out of commission. He succeeded with many of them but at great cost, for as he couldn't see the wasp he was as likely to take hold of the wrong end of him as the right; then the dying wasp gave him a punch to remember the incident by.

The stings, the suffering, the obliviousness of the others, the bashful young hick's choice between pain and the embarrassment of drawing attention. None of it was lost on Sam. "Jim never could enjoy wasps," was his later conclusion. But he'd already known that. A few nights earlier, he had not only enjoyed Jim Wolf's torture by stinging insects, but had initiated it.

On that night he'd entered the bedroom he sometimes shared with the young boarder and found the window encrusted with wasps. "I turned the bedclothes and, at cost of one or two stings, brushed the wasps down and collected a few hundred of them on the sheet on that side of the bed, then turned the covers over and made prisoners of them."[17] That night he had watched as Jim climbed into bed, suffered several stings, and climbed out again, "his shirt . . . black with half-crushed wasps dangling by one hind leg"[18] and several dozen more in his hands. Sam's reaction—or so he wrote—was to laugh himself to sleep. He awoke not long afterward with Wolf astride him, pounding his face with both fists. This only made Sam laugh some more, an amused spectator now at his own brutalizing. "It hurt—but he was knocking all the restraints of my laughter loose; I could not contain it any longer and I laughed until all my body was exhausted and my face, as I believed, battered to a pulp."[19] For a few moments there, under the covers in the upper bedroom of the house on Hill Street, Sut Lovingood lived.

Sam may have begun to publish scraps of his own work on Ament's press. The record is ambiguous. It seems clear that in spare moments he liked to copy out other writers' poems that caught his fancy, print them on scraps of cotton or silk, and send them to girls. A tantalizing possibility of his authorship surfaced twice in the early summer of 1849: two bursts of florid but highly literate love poetry addressed to someone named Juliet and signed "Mark." Sam did not adopt his famous pen name until 1863, and Mark Twain does not cite a "Juliet" among his recollected childhood sweethearts. Nonetheless, scholars believe the quality of the diction was within Sam's range at age fourteen, given the saturation of romantic poetry at the time.

Another pivotal and highly dramatic literary event—dramatic enough to suggest Twain's self-dramatizing touch—was his memory of his nearly supernatural first encounter with the figure of Joan of Arc. As Twain told the story to his biographer Paine, this "Turning-Point" was triggered when, walking home from Ament's shop one day, he spotted a page from a book fluttering along the street. He picked it up, scanned it, and grew absorbed in the plight of some "Maid of Orleans" held prisoner in the fortress at Rouen, her clothes confiscated by two "ruffian English soldiers."[20] According to his self-announced legend, Sam was inspired by this accident to plunge into medieval history; he also felt an awakening of passion on behalf of the downtrodden and oppressed. (As he read into the Maid's eventual fate, he also grew obsessed with her death by fire.) He also took on a curiosity for foreign languages; he would teach himself the rudiments of French within five years, and he also embarked on his lifetime of comic battles with "the awful German language," in which he grew rather proficient.

Hannibal received several shocks in 1849. A cholera epidemic swept the town in the early summer. In November of that year a young black slave known as "Glasscock's Ben" was accused of a hideous double crime: killing a boy of ten with a rock from a quarry, then raping his twelve-year-old sister and slitting her throat. (He was hanged early the following year.) Yellow fever struck the town in the early winter; then cholera again.

The biggest ongoing news, however, was the Gold Rush. Hannibal had started feeling its effects as early as April, when the streets became glutted with emigrants from the East on their way to Sutter's promised land. Eighty of the town's citizens joined the rush that year; six of them were dead by May, casualties of cholera and Indians. In all, more than three hundred Hannibalians would head west. Years later Mark Twain would run into some of them in Virginia City and San Francisco.

The red-haired boy stood and watched the throngs pass through his town. He watched as one of them knifed another and saw the red life gush from his breast. Twelve years later, when it was thankfully too late, he would finally join the migration and find his riches in another vein. But before that, he had a couple of other lives to finish living and a mythos to consummate.

Eleven

"My good opinion of the editors had steadily declined;
for it seemed to me that they might have found
something better to fill up with than my literature."

O n September 16, 1852, a certain refined young gentleman
named J. T. Hinton, the "local" correspondent for the Hannibal *Tri-Weekly Messenger,* plucked forth a copy of the rival Hannibal
Journal and was thunderstruck to find himself wickedly caricatured in a
woodcut cartoon: His head the head of a dog, the Hinton-figure is leaning on a cane, carrying a torch, and advancing toward the moonlit waters
of Bear Creek with a liquor bottle suspended in space in front of him.

The headline above the drawing announced: "'Local' Resolves to
Commit Suicide," and the caption beneath it extended the caricature to
words, explaining, in mortifying clarity, the significance of every object
in the drawing. Below the caption, a brief paragraph summed it all up:

> The artist has, you will perceive, Mr. Editor, caught the
> gentleman's countenance as correctly as the thing could
> have been done with the real *dog*-erytype apparatus. Ain't
> he pretty? and don't he step along through the mud with
> an air? 'Peace to his *re*-manes.'[1]

The paragraph was signed, "A DOG-BE-DEVILED CITIZEN."[2]

About three weeks earlier, J. T. Hinton had made the grave, if unsuspecting mistake of ridiculing Orion Clemens in print. Orion, writing in his own newly established *Journal,* had composed a mild complaint about barking dogs in the town at night. Hinton, a newcomer to the town, had responded in the *Messenger* with a ponderous bloc of elephantine scorn: "A fierce hater of the canine race pours out his vials of wrath, as if to add a fresh stimulus to our worthy dog-exterminator, whose active exertions have already silenced the plaintive wail and mournful howl of many a pugnacious cur and ferocious mastiff," etc.[3] Now came the response to the response, not by phlegmatic Orion (who was out of town in any case) but from his younger brother. J. T. Hinton had just become the first public victim of the compressed satiric vengeance of the young man who would become Mark Twain.

The stage for Sam's debut as a rough-and-tumble Southwestern slag-artist had been set two years earlier. In January 1850, Jane Clemens wrote a letter to Orion in St. Louis, alerting her son to an opportunity for putting his printing skills to work close to home. Jane had learned that the Gold Rush was about to entice another Hannibal citizen, one "Big Joe" Buchanan, who had published the Hannibal *Journal,* a Whig paper, since 1842. Buchanan had already turned the paper over to his brother Robert, or "Little Bob," who had found a couple of partners, but Jane sensed that inevitably, Little Bob would follow his brother out of town. She advised her son to round up some financial backing in St. Louis and make his pitch for ownership. "I could board the hands [at the house on Hill Street] and you could have Henry. Sam says he can't leave Ament, he intends to make him pay wages and you would want him to wait."[4]

Jane's instincts were correct. Little Bob could not stand to be left behind by Big Joe, and in mid-April the two brothers headed off toward the Oregon Trail. They left the paper in the hands of an associate, but Little Bob donated the Buchanan family piano to Pamela for use in her music classes. Pamela, meantime, wrote to Orion urging him to come home for a family gathering that would include Jane's brother James Lampton, a doctor with a bit of financial resources. Apparently Dr. Lampton was forthcoming, because that summer Orion quit his printing job in St. Louis, bought about $50 worth of type and press equipment and, while waiting for the *Journal* to become available, set up the Hannibal *Western Union*, on Bird Street down near the Mississippi, between First and Main. He brought out the first issue in early September 1850. A year later he was finally able to acquire the Buchanans' paper. He published the consolidated *Journal and Western Union* for a while, then called his product the *Journal*.

Quiet Henry, twelve then, came aboard as Jane had promised, but Sam did not join him right away. His two-year apprenticeship with Ament ended in the spring of 1850, but the boy stayed on, hoping, as his mother had written, to earn some actual wages.

Although he probably helped his brother informally in the last months of that year, he was fully available by January 1851 to join Orion and young Henry as a printer and an all-around assistant. Sam was fifteen now; his schooldays had been over for almost two years, and his critical education was finally in full swing.

Orion needed all the help he could get. Within a few months of his debut as a publisher, he had lost his initial excitement and had grown depressed. Already, in certain ways, he was turning into his father: serious, studious, oppressively honest; a young man who like John Marshall had never really been a boy. Like his father, he was born to failure. Unlike stern John, however, Orion was gentle and distracted. Sam noticed, and would later write about Orion's large, earnest eyes that always seemed to be searching for something. In the few available photographs of him, all taken when he was in middle age, those eyes have a glinting, fixed quality. Along with his beard, his thin face, and his big shock of brushed-back hair, Orion bore a surprising resemblance to the fanatical abolitionist John Brown. But fanaticism was far from his makeup; he lurched and drifted, through his long life, from one impulse to another, never quite surrendering himself to any one thing.

He would later write that he'd never really wanted to be an editor or a printer in the first place. The role he always saw for himself in those early days was as orator—a singularly absurd daydream given that, confronted by every Fourth of July crowd or church gathering he spoke at, Orion's nerve failed him and he lapsed into a whisper.

Sam studied Orion's abiding futility at close quarters in this period. Newly released from the despondent gravitational field of his father, Sam would now become a kind of lifelong connoisseur of his older brother's hopelessness. In later years he would recall how eager Orion could be at the start of the day—"three hundred and sixty-five red-hot new eagernesses every year of his life"[5]—and he would recall how those eagernesses gave way always to his "deep glooms." "Every day he was the most joyous and hopeful man that ever was, I think, and also every day he was the most miserable man that ever was."[6]

This close exposure to familial failure seems to have hardened him. If American humor had its roots in aggression, Samuel Langhorne Clemens with his verbal violence was as American as a blackened eye.

Orion proved a handy whetstone for Sam's satiric blade. As Mark Twain's literary fame consolidated he would berate and lampoon Orion ruthlessly, while helping himself to the sibling's neuroses as fodder for characters. (Orion is the undisguised "Secretary" in *Roughing It,* and traces of him show up in Colonel Sellers and in Angelo Capello in *Pudd'nhead Wilson.* He was also the star of a malignant, unfinished Twain story, "Autobiography of a Damned Fool," which did not see publication until 1967.*)

Yet he was not merely sadistic. A great yearning for Orion's transcendence shone beneath these attacks. In the midst of his Cain-like aggression, Sam was literally giving his older brother the clothes off his back. He pitied, bankrolled, and safeguarded his sibling, and in a way grieved for him. He once confessed to Howells that he imagined Orion on the stage, a melancholy harlequin, forever shifting his political and religious passions, "and trying to reform the world, always inventing something, and losing a limb by a new kind of explosion at the end of each of the four acts."[7]

Viewed in the context of this yearning, Sam's thunderbolts aimed at J. T. Hinton were more than haphazard adolescent spleen. They have the quality of veiled exhortation; of a passionate boy offering a model of defiance for the remaining father-figure in his life. Here were the early glowings of the pen warmed up in Hell.

Whatever the motive, Sam's pen (and knife) treated the unfortunate Hinton to a roasting the likes of which had not been witnessed in the brief annals of Hannibal journalism.

He had waited for his chance to pounce on his mark. It opened up "on a lucky summer's day" several weeks after Hinton's initial broadside. Orion was preparing to leave town for a week, headed for Tennessee in another futile attempt to cash in on the Land. "He . . . asked

---

*In Franklin R. Rogers, ed., *Mark Twain's Satires and Burlesques* (Berkeley: University of California Press, 1967).

me if I thought I could edit one issue of the paper judiciously. Ah! Didn't I want to try!"[8]

"Judiciously," of course, was scarcely the point. Presented with this unobstructed chance for revenge, the sixteen-year-old boy pounced with a ferocity that Sut Lovingood himself might have applauded. The "'Local' Man Resolves to Commit Suicide" headline and cartoon, for example, made ruthless fun of a recent matter of some delicacy for Hinton: his half-hearted attempt to drown himself in Bear Creek one night after being jilted. Hinton had slogged about halfway in, thought better of the impulse and waded back to shore. In the meantime a friend of his had found his suicide note and made for the creek in time to see Hinton sloshing back to safety. "The village was full of it for several days, but [Hinton] did not suspect it."[9]

Directly under the woodcut cartoon—which he had carved out, suggestively enough, with his jackknife—Sam offered the arch caption suggesting that Hinton's aborted suicide (and his imputed drinking) had to do with a lack of response to his attack on Orion:

> "Local," disconsolate from receiving no further notice from "A Dog-be-Deviled Citizen," contemplates Suicide. His "pocket-pistol" (i.e. the *bottle*) failing in the patriotic work of ridding the country of a nuisance, he resolves to "extinguish his chunk" by feeding his carcass to the fishes of Bear Creek, while friend and foe are wrapt in sleep. Fearing, however, that he may get out of his depth, he *sounds the stream with his walking-stick.*[10]

Sam and his helpers inked the plates, churned the edition out, and then sat back to wait for the inevitable howl of outrage from down the

street. It came with satisfying shrillness and speed. "This newly arisen
'Ned Buntline'* shall be paid in his own coin," the *Messenger* warned
a couple of days later. Then, in the next edition, Hinton attempted a
shift to dignified condescension: "Such controversies are adapted
only to those whose ideas are of so obscene and despicable an order
as to forever bar them against a gentlemanly or even decent discus-
sion," etc.[11]

This flotilla of heavily armored prose, so conventional in its midcentury context, was no match for the sleek torpedoes that came foam-
ing back. In the September 23 *Journal* two more jackknife-wrought
woodcuts appeared. (Sam would be a sketcher and napkin-doodler all
his life, and a few of his line drawings, awkward but comically intelli-
gible, would accompany his published work.) The first showed the
dog-headed "Local" mincing in excitement over "something interesting in the *Journal*." The second cut, metaphorically shrewd, showed
the same "Local" being blown away by a discharge from his own cannon, which he had "chartered" to wage war on the *Journal*. "Lead
being scarce," the caption continued with insolent glee, "he loads his
cannon with *Tri-Weekly Messengers*."

After a little more verbal nose-thumbing, Sam adroitly declared the
feud to be at an end:

MR. EDITOR:
I have now dropped this farce, and all attempts to again
call me forth will be useless.
A Dog-be-Deviled Citizen[12]

---

*A lurid "dime-novelist" of the period.

Arriving back in Hannibal (empty-handed, for all purposes), gentle Orion was horrified by Sam's swashbuckling breach of decorum. Virtually clucking mollification, he rushed an editorial into print (crammed into the same edition as the last pair of woodcuts) that genuflected to the *Messenger:* "The jokes of our correspondent have been rather rough; but, originating and perpetrated in a spirit of fun, and without a serious thought, no attention was expected to be paid to them, beyond a smile at the local editor's expense."

This brought forth one final, tremendous harumph from the *Messenger*, and there the vendetta ended. But Sam Clemens had tapped the lode of invective that would irradiate his satiric voice forever afterward.

Years later Mark Twain would protest that he had no idea Hinton would take the whole thing so hard: "I thought it was desperately funny, and was densely unconscious that there was any moral obliquity about such a publication."[13] This is a plausible mindset for an adolescent boy accustomed to the white-hot blisterings of the Southwestern papers, which in certain respects were the Comix of the frontier. But Twain's penchant for getting under people's skin lasted well beyond his adolescence. Nobody was going to cross him without paying a price. Sometimes Twain himself drew first blood. He spoiled for a good fight, and on occasion he went to bizarre, even self-destructive lengths to provoke one.

The poison-pen salvos he fired and the hoaxes he dreamed up as a young journalist in Nevada in the 1860s, for example, were often recklessly aggressive. The most notorious was the one that nearly led him into a duel in Nevada in 1864. Like the Hinton incident, it was ignited while he was temporarily left in charge of a paper—the Virginia City *Territorial Enterprise.* Out of boredom or cussedness, he dashed off an item ridiculing a charitable auction, set to raise money for Union Army medical supplies; he said the money was really earmarked "to aid a Miscegenation Society somewhere in the East."[14] This slur infuriated Virginia City society and several other newspaper editors who had already grown disgusted with Twain's insolence. One of these editors, James L. Laird, attacked him in print; Twain responded, and soon found himself obliged to challenge Laird to a duel. Horrified at the prospect, Twain scurried out of town for California on the thinnest pretext of dignity. He would make several efforts in later years to dismiss the whole incident as a prank, but he lived out his years feeling mortified by the episode.

The filleting of J. T. Hinton was not Sam's first identifiable appearance in print. That event had occurred eighteen months earlier, on January 16, 1851, within days after Sam had left Joseph Ament to come over and help Orion on his *Western Union*. (Orion had promised him the extravagant wage of $3.50 a week. "[B]ut Orion was always generous. . . . It cost him nothing in my case, for he never was able to pay me a single penny as long as I was with him."[15]) As with most of Mark Twain's humor, this brief piece took aim at a comic foil, if good-naturedly. The foil, unnamed in the item, was the long-suffering Jim Wolf, who was working the shop alongside his good pal Sam.

The previous week an early-morning fire had broken out in the grocery store next door to the *Western Union* shop. The two boys, laboring late, had spotted it. Wolf became a little unhinged. Snatching at the first items in the shop that caught his eye—which happened to be a broom, a mallet, a wash-pan, and a dirty towel—he cradled them in his arms and bolted out the door. He kept on rushing, for about "ten squares," or half a mile, as Sam calculated it, before deciding that the materials were out of danger. By the time he made it back to the office to grab some more valuables, the fire had long been extinguished. Sam got all of this into a one-paragraph item headlined, "A Gallant Fireman,"* which he finished off with a little sampling of Wolf's rustic dialect and a mannered condescension a bit beyond the reach of the average fourteen-year-old school dropout:

> . . . He returned in the course of an hour, nearly out of breath, and thinking he had immortalized himself, threw his giant frame in a tragic attitude, and exclaimed, with an eloquent expression: "If that thar fire hadn't bin put out, thar'd a' bin the greatest *confirmation* of the age![16]

If Sam's own voice was absent from Orion's papers from early 1851 until late 1852, it was not because he had fallen away from writing. In his sixteenth and seventeenth years, he'd spent at least part of that time getting himself published in the widely circulated newspapers of the East.

It is generally agreed that Samuel Clemens came upon the writing life haphazardly, without ever having planned it as a boy or a young man. He all but stumbled over the wild newspaper demimonde in Nevada, and joined up only when digging for gold had worn him out. Later, in the East, his need for money, social status, and business success would take precedence over his identity as a writer—until it was obvious that writing was his only chance at money, social status, and business success.

---

*Some scholars, including Edgar Marques Branch, an editor of *The Works of Mark Twain: Early Tales & Sketches,* believe that Sam composed this piece as he stood before the "case," setting it by hand into type.

All of which, of course, are good working descriptions of journalists and writers. Here, as in other ways, Clemens was far ahead of the evolving American style.

But in Orion's print shop he must have had some glimmerings of his future profession; the work he did clearly shows it. Every day he climbed the stairs to the second floor of the little shop and hunkered down for several hours putting words together with his hands; usually someone else's words, but once in awhile his own. Those little eruptions were generally better than anything else in Orion's damp pages; and Orion, typically after it was already too late, would recognize that and offer his kid brother a column. Sam stuck to the sheet music mostly, the texts of what he was supposed to set in type; but now and then he would break free and run off his own dizzy riffs, imitating styles, improvising his own rhythms of language and making it all spill into some mad dangerous flow, its force fed by playfulness, anger, and maybe a little terror mixed in.

What motivated him? Perhaps in this dry period of poverty and loss and struggle he daydreamed back to his uncle's farm and those stormy "abysses of the slaves' estate," the songs and stories by which those lost black people managed to save their sanity. Just as likely he was acting out a more practical dream, equally dear to his heart: his lifelong dream of making a dollar. The printed word led to money in the pocket—if not in Orion's office, then somewhere; the evidence was pretty clear on that. And Sam Clemens, the boyhood barterer of marbles and fishhooks and good-luck charms, was ready to fill his pockets with something even more negotiable.

Whatever the motive, he taught himself to write. With no one to encourage him except for Miss Horr and Miss Newcomb (and they had encouraged him as a reader, as distinct from a writer); with no models of any sort from his own people except models of unrealistic ambition—his dead failed wealth-obsessed father, his flailing brother, and the assorted merchants and Gold-Rush dreamers in the town—with no realistic prospects of any sort for "rising" in America, or even of escaping his subsistence life, the teenaged Sam Clemens was plumbing the well of voices within himself.

He learned to write by reading, and internalizing what he read. Most of what filtered into the office, Orion shuffled Sam's way, including the other newspapers, the poetry, and the "polite literature" that he was constantly culling for filler. (Among the problems that dulled the *Western Union's* journalistic cutting-edge was Orion's inability to get a telegraph wire strung across the Mississippi to connect him with civilization.) Sam read the papers with interest and the rest of it with wicked imitative glee; he would seize many occasions to send up the bad poetry and the polite literature in his own work.

Any kind of mannered writing at all, in fact, would forever run the risk of attracting his deadly eye and ear (unless of course he was appropriating it for his own commercial uses). His "Fenimore Cooper's Literary Offenses" remains as definitive and hilarious a hatchet-job today as when he wrote it in 1895. As for newspaper "society" writing, it was never quite the same after "The Lick House Ball," which he composed in September 1863 in San Francisco: "Miss B. wore an elegant goffered flounce, trimmed with a grenadine of *bouillonnee,* with a crinoline waistcoat to match; pardessus open behind, embroidered with paramattas of passementerie . . . with a frontispiece formed of a single magnificent cauliflower imbedded in mashed potatoes. Thus attired Miss B. looked good enough to eat."[17] (This sort of antic patter, with its free-associating orgies of verbal excess, was almost unknown in the nineteenth century—which took its verbal excesses quite seriously. But Twain's showoff riffs would point the way for the next century's leading overdoers. "Her white evening gown, accented at the bodice with pompons, appeared at first glance to have been improvised from a candlewick bedspread, though it admittedly complemented her olive skin and pneumatic *balacon*,"[18] froths S. J. Perelman in the 1950s—himself the screenwriting voice of Groucho Marx. Woody Allen doubtless has taken some notes as well.)

Back in the *Western Union* office, Orion even pressed on Sam a copy of *Bleak House*, which he was excerpting. Sam declined, perhaps feeling that the theme was a bit close to home—although on New Year's Eve 1867, his first evening out with his future wife, Sam would escort Olivia to a reading in New York by Charles Dickens.

He did read the papers, though, and imitated what he found in them. He would always immerse himself in the popular culture, like his own description of the German language-speaker diving headfirst into a sentence. He would always emerge from it with the best of his material, like the German emerging with the verb in his mouth. These *Journal* days were the beginning of Sam's long dive. He caught some action almost immediately. By the spring of 1852, at only sixteen—six months before the attack on Hinton—he had broken into the circles of Eastern newspaper publishing.

His debut was a facetious sketch called "The Dandy Frightening the Squatter," printed in the May 1 edition of the Boston *Carpet-Bag*, a comic weekly magazine, over the initials "S.L.C"—his first direct attribution.

A crude fragment of frontier slapstick by many standards, its special cachet all but incomprehensible to a late-twentieth-century reader, "The Dandy" nonetheless shows Sam paying close attention to the literary conventions of his time. It has some aspects of the "frame story," with young Sam himself in the role of the gentlemanly observer, who is recounting an incident that transpired thirteen years previously, when "the now-flourishing young city of Hannibal . . . was but a 'wood-yard.'" A brawny woodsman is observed leaning against a tree, gazing riverward toward an approaching steamboat. Among the boat's passengers is a "spruce young dandy, with a killing mustache," who is keen on impressing the ladies on board. Spotting "our squatter friend" on the bank, he alerts the ladies that a good laugh is at hand. Then he sticks a bowie-knife into his belt, takes a large horse-pistol in each hand, and strides up to the woodsman, whom he engages in badinage:

> "Found you at last, have I? You are the very man I've been looking for these three weeks! Say your prayers!" he continued, presenting his pistols, "you'll make a capital barn door, and I shall drill the key-hole myself!"[19]

The *denouement* to all this is basically that the squatter takes a squint at the dandy, draws back his fist and drills him into the Mississippi. He then offers a bit of rustic advice: "I say, yeou, next time yeou come around drillin' key-holes, don't forget yer old acquaintances!" The ladies are amused. End of story.

The gentleman/ruffian archetypes, of course, would have been instantly recognizable to political readers of the period. But there are subtle reversals in Sam's point of view. He had dipped into an older and more democratic storytelling tradition, one that regarded any outsider "putting on airs" as decadent and alien. Sam's squatter is by no means a stock-company backwoods thug, enlisted to illustrate some departure from Whig good manners. On the contrary, he is the aggrieved party, an innocent bystander (or bysquatter) who is affronted by the fatuous traveler—who himself is, by implication, a sojourner from the perfumed east. Already Sam's social-class anxieties were showing. But this was a defiant way of expressing them, this punch in the snoot for the Dandy's Boston peers from a sixteen-year-old Missouri truant.

Like Tom Sawyer's dream of becoming a Detective, Sam had spotted a fantasy for himself and lived it out: he'd become a Boy Writer. Something had impelled him to do it. Perhaps it was those exotic by-lines on those far-away papers trickling into his brother's shabby upstairs office. (Perhaps it was his brother's shabby upstairs office.) At any rate, one week after his "Dandy/Squatter" debut, the Boy Writer had struck again. This time in the Philadelphia *American Courier,* and this time Sam's Huck Finnish attitude had given way to an experiment in the stoutly Tom Sawyerish: His errand was a gilt-edged homage to his native town. This was the first published product of what was to be a lifetime of Hannibal-conjurings.

Encrusted with high-toned flourishes that fit him as badly as Joseph Ament's clothes—"Then the war-whoop of the Indian resounded where now rise our stately buildings"—the brief descriptive piece is flat and unremarkable, except for another hint of Sam's Southwestern edginess regarding the snob culture of the Seaboard: "Your Eastern people seem to think this country is a barren, uncultivated region, with a population consisting of heathens."[20]

Within two decades, Sam would be doing his best to penetrate that same snob culture, and succeeding. Yet, once ensconced, he would immediately turn his yearnings back to Hannibal.

The Clemens family had begun to venture back into the life of Hannibal as the 1850s began. With Orion having sold a tiny sliver of the

Tennessee Land and opening up his little newspaper, some of the everyday pleasures of living seemed possible again.

In the summer of 1850 Sam joined the Cadets of Temperance, dazzled by the red merino sashes the Cadets got to wear and the parades they got to march in. (As it turned out, they didn't get to march in nearly enough.) He coaxed Henry along with him, but found he could not abide the organization's draconian rules—he had to give up smoking—and quit after three months. He was able, he recalled, to remain steadfast "until I had gathered the glory of two displays—May Day and the Fourth of July." After the second parade he forsook the sash, left the lodge, and dove for his first cigar of the summer. "I do not now know what the brand of the cigar was. It was probably not choice, or the previous smoker would not have thrown it away so soon. But I realized that it was the best cigar that was ever made."[21]

Tom Sawyer joins the Cadets too, "being attracted by the showy character of their 'regalia.'" He, too, swears off smoking, chewing, and profanity and is immediately tormented with a desire to indulge. He wants to quit the Cadets, but decides to hold out for a parade. He fixes his hopes on old Judge Frazier, who is on his deathbed and is sure to command a big public funeral. Annoyingly, the Judge appears to be on the mend. Tom resigns. That night the Judge dies. "Tom resolved that he would never trust a man like that again."[22]

Sallow Pamela married in October 1851, at the advanced bridal age of twenty-four. The groom was a former neighbor named Will Moffett. She had run into him during a visit to her Aunt Pamela in Kentucky. The two honeymooned at Niagara Falls and settled in St. Louis, where Moffett became a successful businessman. They would have two children, and Will, his commission business destroyed by the Civil War, would leave her a widow in 1865, after which she would rejoin her widowed mother.

Sam and Henry, the Good Boy, worked side by side during these years, but the depth of their relationship is unclear. From the sketchy evidence, they behaved toward one another like typical siblings, a little fractiously, each trying to get an edge. They would not make overtures of real friendship toward one another for another half-decade, toward the end of their adolescences.

It was just before this period, however—while Sam was still apprenticing at the *Courier*—that he attacked Henry with the dropped watermelon. It was a thing, he wrote in 1906 with fascinating ambiguity, "which I have been trying to regret for fifty-five years."[23]

The bombardment occurred on a beautiful summer holiday, when, for some unknown punishment, Sam was being held "prisoner" in Ament's third-story printing office, forbidden to go larking on the river with his friends. (Held prisoner by whom—Ament or his mother—he doesn't say.) His one consolation was a half of a ripe melon. Sam gouged out chunks of it and ate them with his knife; then, on impulse, he looked out the window and took on the notion to drop the shell on someone's head. He waited for the ideal victim. Henry soon appeared on the street, and for some reason, all of Sam's resentments against his younger brother's goodness welled up.

> He was the best boy in the whole region. He never did harm to anybody, he never offended anybody. He was exasperatingly good. He had an overflowing abundance of goodness—but not enough to save him this time. I watched his approach with eager interest.[24]

When Henry had drawn within six steps of being directly underneath his lurking brother, Sam let "that canoe" go. "The accuracy of the gunnery was beyond admiration . . . it was lovely to see those two bodies gradually closing in on each other." Here Mark Twain takes refuge in facetiousness. "(T)hat shell smashed down right on the top of his head and drove him into the earth up to the chin. . . . I wanted to go down and condole with him but it would not have been safe. He would have suspected me at once."[25]

The tale's denouement is that Henry waits a few days, saying nothing, until Sam's guard is down, then fires a cobblestone into the side of his head that raised a bump "so large that I had to wear two hats for a time."[26]

An amusing set-piece anecdote of exactly the kind that contributed to Mark Twain's enshrinement as the National Uncle. The only undercurrents are that cryptic "trying to regret for fifty-five years" and the brooding preoccupation with Henry's goodness.

The new American culture, brassy and gilded, continued to find its way into Hannibal in those dreamy prewar days, tempting a boy's thoughts to a world beyond the white town drowsing. It floated in mostly on the breezes of spring and summer, when the big alabaster showboats tied up at the levee and turned their uniformed brass bands loose and glinting on the deck; and when the Mississippi packets and the dirt roads into town from the south brought gaudy wonders: dustcovered circus trains and lion-menageries; traveling portraitists and orators and ventriloquists and phrenologists and scientific speechifiers on human magnetism and animal magnetism; and mind-readers, mountebanks, frauds, and spurious mystics of all sorts. Sam himself was considered quite the telepath by the locals now, after his dramatic triumph on the mesmerizer's stage. Jane certainly believed he was gifted with second sight; it seemed to give her pleasure to consider that she had an exceptional child.

He was exceptional, but in other ways. He relished every new phenomenon of the culture that moved through Hannibal, but he may have developed a special fondness for the mountebanks and frauds. As he had proved with the mesmerizer, Sam was quick to pick up on stagecraft and its possibilities for exploitation. This interest spread to other subtleties. "Church ain't shucks to a circus," says Tom to Becky, but as Sam matured into mid-adolescence, the circus might not have been shucks to the confidence man.

The confidence man figured in Sam's autumn 1852 takeover of Orion's pages. In the September 16 edition of the *Journal,* alongside his first strike at J. T. Hinton, Sam published three other pieces of light writing as "W. Epaminondas," changing the last name from "Perkins" to "Blab."

The most ambitious of these was a piece of some sixteen hundred words called "Historical Exhibition—A No. 1 Ruse." Written with labored grown-up facetiousness and cast as a "frame" story, it begins, "A young friend gives me the following yarn as fact." The sketch dealt with a supposed exhibition at Curts & Lockwood, an actual grocery and dry-goods establishment in Hannibal. The exhibition was called "Bonaparte crossing the Rhine"; the publicity announced that proprietor Curts was to deliver a lecture explaining the history of the "piece" at admission price of one dime, children half price. A swarm of boys soon swoops down on the store "like half a dozen telegraphs,"[27] and their leader, one Jim C—, plunks down his nickel and demands to see the show. What he sees is Mr. Curts passing a three-inch piece of hog-leg (the "bony part") across a dollar-sized strip of hog-skin (the "rind"). "You have now learned a valuable lesson," the proprietor tells the stricken boy.

"Historical Exhibition" lumbers along, reaches its thematic climax in the middle and continues uncertainly after that. Perhaps because it was based on an actual incident and involved identifiable people including a merchant, the boy grew self-conscious and wordy. But in this mannered little experiment can be seen the seeds of some of Mark Twain's great rogues and pretenders, including Huckleberry Finn's companions the Duke and the King.

Sam retired "W. Epaminondas Adrastus Blab" in the following week's edition, letting Blab announce that he was going to repair to Glasscock's Island in the Mississippi ("Jackson's Island" in the Tom and Huck books).

It was around this time that Sam must have been asking himself a version of the same thing. Three weeks shy of his seventeenth birthday, he could look back on three years of drudgery in various cramped printing offices, and forward to uncounted years more of the same. His own bachelor years had grown short on joyous freedom and discretion; he must have felt at times as though he were married to the printing life.

While other Hannibal men and boys were rushing westward for gold—the California mines would yield $65 million in the ensuing year—Sam was climbing the stairs every day to Orion's shop above Stover & Horr's Clothing Store on Main Street. Outside of Sam's own items, the *Journal* was a desolate, uninviting little sheet that made almost no money. And Orion himself seemed to attract buffoonish catastrophe, a new and unremarked strain of human magnetism.

On January 29, 1853, the *Journal* had scooped the competition on another town fire, this one in its own offices. Before the fire was doused with buckets, it ravaged the shop and destroyed the *Journal's* presses. The other papers in town pitched in, including the abused *Messenger,* which lent Orion its type case containing the market reports and delinquent tax files. There may have been some Hintonesque satisfaction here; the files reported $10 owed by one Orion Clemens against the assessed valuation of $200 on the Hill Street House.[28]

Orion collected $150 in fire-insurance payments and managed to restart his paper. He lugged his little collection of cast-iron equipment, temporarily, into the parlor of Jane's house, and promptly received another pie in the face: a cow wandered in one night, knocked over a type case and ate a few composition rollers.[29] All in all, this was not feeling like the foundation of a newspaper dynasty.

Twelve

"But I reckon I got to light out for the Territory
ahead of the rest, because Aunt Sally she's going
to adopt me and sivilize me and I can't stand it.
I been there before.

So endeth this chronicle," Mark Twain wrote in his Conclusion
to *Tom Sawyer*. "It being strictly the history of a *boy*, it must
stop here; the story could not go much further without becoming the
history of a *man*." By the end of 1852 Sam's own boyhood chronicle
had effectively ended. Six months later, in the eternal summer that was
the climate for his fictional boyhood adventures, Hannibal would be
behind him as well. He would be gone from the town, embarked on a
lifetime of wandering, largely over water, a citizen of the world and an
exile from his troubled Eden. His way of writing about his wanderings,
and the people he met in the course of them, would enshrine the sojourner as the representative speaker of American literature. "When I
find a well-drawn character in fiction or biography I generally take a
warm personal interest in him," Mark Twain would write, "for the reason that I have known him before—met him on the river,"[1] and Jack
Kerouac would answer back seventy-four years later, from the Road,
"But then they danced down the street like dingledodies, and I sham-

bled after as I've been doing all my life after people who interest me, because the only people for me are the mad ones . . . "[2]

Twain's original plot design was to set Huck off, not down the river, but out across Illinois—on the road.

Among his last gestures in Orion's newspaper would be a weird impulsive prank, an impudent parody of the all-too-frequent announcements of a Mississippi steamboat snagging or explosion. It took the form of a two-line item headlined: TERRIBLE ACCIDENT! 500 MEN KILLED AND MISSING!!!

This sickening claim was immediately followed by the deadpan announcement underneath: "We had set the above head up, expecting (of course) to use it, but as the accident hasn't happened yet, we'll say (To be Continued.)"

It was a real "terrible accident" that brought death at the turning of his final year in Hannibal. This one involved not water but fire. It killed a man. And Sam—at least in his own tortured imagination—was responsible.

Fires had flared in the town throughout his boyhood; fire terrified him; he hallucinated that he'd seen the infant Henry walking into fire; it was the fiery martyr's death of Joan of Arc that had annealed his interest in her. In the West, in a few years, he would accidentally set a mountain on fire and watch with detached fascination as it reached the remote ramparts with a tangled network of red lava streams.

But on this January night in 1853, Sam watched an accidental fire with no detachment at all. The horror that he saw would take its place in his lengthening list of guilts.

A tramp had been wandering the streets, pipe in his mouth, begging for matches. Sam's band of night-prowling boys had only made fun of him. But finally an attack of conscience moved Sam:

... some appeal which the wayfarer made for forbearance, accompanying it with a pathetic reference to his forlorn and friendless condition, touched such sense [sic] of shame and remnant of right feeling as were left in me, and I went away and got him some matches, then hied me home and to bed ... [3]

Not long after that the marshal tossed the tramp into the little brick jailhouse with its furnishings of dry timber, then went home to bed. Not long after that, Sam was awakened by the church bells.

The marshal with his key was five miles out of reach. Some citizens improvised a battering ram; it thundered against the cell door but did not break it. With about two hundred other onlookers, Sam watched the man's face as he gripped the bars, the firelight white and intense at his back. His nightmares began again that night.

I saw that face, so situated, every night for a long time afterward; and I believed myself as guilty of the man's death as if I had given him the matches purposely that he might burn himself up with them. I had no doubt that I should be hanged if my connection with this tragedy were found out. The happenings and the impressions of that time are burnt into my memory, and the study of them entertains me as much now as they themselves distressed me then.[4]

Orion's *Journal,* in its detached, professional January 27 coverage written probably by Orion himself, filled in some details that Mark Twain later forgot, or ignored. The victim was "an insane Irishman—made insane by liquor," and the precise reason for his incarceration was that he had broken down the door of a negro cabin with an ax and terrified the "inmates." The account added—oblivious of Sam's guilty memory, or perception—that "It is supposed he set his bed clothes on fire with matches, as he usually carried them in his pocket to light his pipe, and the fire . . . was in the corner occupied by his bed." In a passage at once understated and macabre, the article reported that "Before he was deprived of his intellect, he said his name was Dennis McDermid, and that he had a mother and brother living in Madison, Indiana." As for the death itself, ". . . he seemed to be shrieking and moaning, until, stifled by smoke and heated air, he fell to the floor." [5]

Sam almost certainly read the coverage in his brother's paper. Yet the ever-embellishing Mark Twain chose to draw upon his own inventory of details: "It was said that the man's death-grip still held fast to the bars after he was dead; and that in this position the fires wrapped about him and consumed him."[6]

The power that this hideous incident held over Twain is evident from the uses he made of it, in his fiction and in his fictionalized nonfiction. In *Tom Sawyer*, after Muff Potter is wrongfully jailed on suspicion of having stabbed Dr. Robinson, Tom and Huck smuggle him tobacco and matches through the grated window of the jailhouse (described as "a trifling little brick den that stood in a marsh at the edge of the village"). The murder itself, which Tom and Huck had witnessed from behind the three great elms, so traumatizes Tom that he talks in his sleep. When his younger brother Sid complains of it—"Tom, you pitch around and talk in your sleep so much that you keep me awake about half the time"[7]—Tom fears that he has divulged his knowledge of the murder and, under the pretext of a toothache, ties up his jaws every night.

In his reminiscence of the incident in *Life on the Mississippi*, the issue of guilt, divulgence, and the attentive, potentially implicating younger brother resurfaces. Twain unaccountably misremembers his age at the time of the fire as ten, not seventeen (the approximate age of Tom Sawyer) and then reproduces a long and suspiciously detailed nighttime conversation with Henry. It begins with Sam waking up one night after the accident and finding his younger brother contemplating him "by the light of the moon":

> "What is the matter?"
> "You talk so much I can't sleep."
> I came to a sitting posture in an instant, with my kidneys in my throat and my hair on end.
> "What did I say? Quick—out with it—what did I say?"
> "Nothing much."
> "It's a lie—you know everything."[8]

Only after a long, penetrating inquisition does Henry admit that he heard Sam "tell" who the "murderer" of the tramp in the calaboose was. The twist, though, is that Henry got it wrong: Hearing Sam mention Ben Coontz's name, along with "matches," he inferred that Coontz was the culprit. Over the course of this lengthy interchange, Mark Twain subtly, and perhaps unconsciously, converts horror to comedy:* when Henry asks him whether he is going to "give up" Ben Coontz to the law, Sam replies expansively that "it shall never be said that I betrayed him."

---

*Mark Twain made this conversion at least one other time in recalling an incident that involved fire. He told his biographer Albert Bigelow Paine of his opening pleasantries during a visit he once paid on some new neighbors: "My name is Clemens; we ought to have called on you before, and I beg your pardon for intruding now in this informal way, but your house is on fire."

"How good you are!"

"Well, I try to be. It is all a person can do in a world like this."[9]

Times were changing. The intense postwar American culture that Twain would dissect in his books and embody in his life was already forming itself in these final prewar years. The Crystal Palace went up in New York that year—Sam would visit and describe it before long. The first known coverage of a baseball game appeared that spring, in the New York Mercury. (Twain and Howells would attend ball games together.) People had begun to write and talk of a time when machinery would replace all human work. And already, four years before he began his cub-piloting on the Mississippi, the demise of the riverboat culture he would mythify was set in motion: In March, the U.S. Congress appropriated $150,000 for surveying work that would lead to the transcontinental railroad.

Times were changing in the Hannibal he would soon leave. Noisy, teeth-rattling plank roads were beginning to replace the mud sloughs stretching out of town to the west, and in the spring of that year town fathers held groundbreaking ceremonies for the Hannibal–St. Joseph Railroad, John Marshall's dream. People dug barbecue pits in a meadow, and a military drill team came up from St. Louis to run through its snappy routine.

The population was swelling. People gradually overtook pigs, from 2316 at the beginning of the decade toward 6324 at its end.[10] Shoppers and sellers were getting so frantic on the streets that the town erected a nineteenth-century version of a mall: a Market House on Market Street (later Broadway), to be run by a Market Master. The stalls on the north side sold meat, and the stalls on the south side sold vegetables and fish and fruit. No one else in town could sell these things during Market hours.[11] On the cultural front, somebody organized a brass band, thirteen members, and they practiced weeknights in a hall above a furniture store.

Floating as a backdrop to all this town activity, generating and defining much of it, were the accumulating steamboats. So many steamboats were docking at the riverfront—a thousand a year, now—that the town must have looked and felt at times like a miniature London, its skyline to the east festooned with smokestacks instead of mizzenmasts. In 1852 the City Council had found it necessary to appoint its first Wharfmaster to organize and direct things, such as "the landing and stationing of all steamboats, watercraft, lumber, logs, rafts and wood," and to make sure everybody paid a wharfage fee—$1.50 per steamboat. A firm soon developed an industry of building steamboat hulls, in a valley north of town.[12]

The steamboat culture seemed to cast a spell over a town already saturated in dreams, enchantments, and paranormal fantasies. The riverfront, which only a few years earlier had afforded idlers an open view to the episodic canoes and rafts and keelboats that scuttled past, heading south on the current, was now clogged with gaudy, majestic, many-tiered behemoths bobbing and jostling against one another as they took on freight and discharged passengers. Sam and his friends (most of them future pilots) took to hanging out on the levee in their free time, listening for the great blast that announced the next incoming sidewheeler or sternwheeler, watching the eruptions of black smoke from its tall stacks, gazing as it neared the levee, taking on shape and specificity, white-painted with brilliant-colored lettering that announced its name and owner; a creature at once terrifying and fragile—tragic, almost, in its oddly delicate bulk and sweep, given the many hazards on the river that it was prey to. (Most steamboats did not survive the river's rocks, snags, and shallows, nor their own explosive boilers, for more than five years.[13]) Its half-glimpsed inner environment, red-plush carpets and polished mahogany paneling, an intimation of prostitutes and gamblers—all just out of landlocked reach—must have seemed a dream-realm, a different order of reality entirely than the cramped interior of Orion's second-floor print shop.

The Mississippi River had begun its decisive pull at Sam, replacing the allure of his uncle's farm with its singing storytelling slaves, and of the cave, the embrasure of hills, the town itself. Now it took a steamboat, he saw, to bring "the dead town" alive and moving. The river was a daily *event,* a ticket to somewhere else in a visceral way that merely selling an essay to a newspaper could never be.

Mimetic, he dove inside the images of the levee, committed its shapes and colors and movement and human voices to memory with Dickensian fidelity. He ogled the high architecture of the riverboat—"long and sharp and trim and pretty" with its tall, fancy-topped chimneys. He enjoyed watching (and hated enjoying, and enjoyed hating) the privileged deckhands of his own age who strutted on the decks, coils of rope in hand, flaunting their connection to the river life. He admired the captain lounging by the big bell, calm, "the envy of all." He applauded the black smoke rolling out of the chimneys, even though he was shrewd enough to grasp that the blast was "a husbanded grandeur created with a bit of pitch pine just before arriving." He savored the absurdities of his fellow townspeople as a steamer approached: excitable John Stavely the saddler, tearing down the street and struggling with his fluttering coat twice each day at the blast of a whistle—"he liked to seem to himself to be expecting a hundred thousand tons of saddles by this boat, and so he went on all his life, enjoying being faithfully on hand to receive and receipt for those saddles, in case by any miracle they should come."[14]

At this moment, as with so many moments over the course of his long life, Sam Clemens had joined himself to a distinctly American moment: in this case, the brief golden age of the riverboats.

The moment could be redefined in another distinctly American way as well. As he moved into the summer of 1853, Sam Clemens was caught between two powerful calls: the call of place and the call of flight. Reconciling the two would become, in a sense, the work of his life.

It is conceivable that he never took a more acute, photographic accounting of Hannibal than in the months before he left it. His great lyric images of the "white town drowsing in the sunshine of a summer's morning," its sudden stir to life by the drayman's cry of "S-t-e-a-m-boat a-comin'!", the boys onshore dreaming of the exalted life of a deckhand or a cabin boy—these are among the few images of Twain that have worked their way into the nation's collective consciousness, that are still memorized by schoolchildren.

It is conceivable, too, that nothing became his life in Hannibal like the leaving of it; or at least, that nothing was as necessary to his crystalline memories of the town as his departure. Abandoning his native place when he did, virtually at the final moment of his boyhood, ensured that his memories of the town would forever be sealed off *as* a boy's memories: undiluted, safeguarded from the inevitable revisions of a grown man living on in the same place. Hannibal-as-St. Petersburg—as Eden—was, by the grace of his departure, preserved for literature.

His distinctive voice had been missing from the *Journal* during the first winter months of 1853. Orion had turned the paper into a daily in March. The timing was perfect, in an Orionean way of looking at things—people were already paying for their subscriptions in turnips and cordwood instead of cash, and a week earlier someone had spilled several columns of type, delaying publication of the weekly version. He was on a roll.

More space to fill meant more dependence on Sam, and this last blooming spring of his boyhood found Sam in a romantically humid (not to say a somewhat randy) frame of mind. He apparently had been moved by the hearts-and-flowers verse of Thomas Moore, Robert Burns, and others; on May 5, writing as "Rambler," he disgorged a lovesick ode loaded with "thou's," "wilts," "thines," and "mines" titled "The Heart's Lament," and addressed to one "Bettie W—E, of Tennessee." Derivative and sentimental, the poem was the first of two in that vein, published on successive days. The second, equally seasoned with striving hearts and restrained pride and a lonely life tortured—and called "Love Concealed"—was addressed "To Miss Katie of H—L."*

The poems are forgettable. The spree of self-mocking, identity-switching foolery they prompted him to unleash in the paper is less so. (Not entirely coincidentally, Orion was out of town again that week. He had left behind a notice in the *Journal* announcing his trip to St. Louis and adding, in his chronic myopia, "This must be our excuse if the paper is lacking interest."[15])

Orion's notice ran on May 6, the day the party began. Just below it, Sam slipped in his jokey "TERRIBLE ACCIDENT!" paragraph. A bit further down the column, "To Miss Katie of H—L" was placed.

---

*A third poem, titled "Separation" and also signed "Rambler," appeared in the rival *Missouri Courier* on May 12. As the editors of *Early Tales and Sketches* point out, its authorship cannot be conclusively attributed to Clemens; it may have been the work of an imitator.

The following day, readers of the *Journal* were confronted with a short, waspish letter to the editor expressing outrage at the poem's title: "Now, I've often seen pieces to 'Mary in Heaven,' or 'Lucy in Heaven,' or something of that sort, but 'Katie in *Hell*,' is carrying the matter too far." The letter was signed GRUMBLER.[16] There is no doubting who the real author was.

The day after that, RAMBLER shot back at GRUMBLER: "Are you so ignorant as not to be able to distinguish 'of' from 'in'? Read again—see if it is not 'of' H—L (Hannibal), instead of 'in' Hell. . . . Poor fellow, I much fear that some Lunatic Asylum will have to mourn the absence of a fit subject until you are placed in a straight [sic] jacket and sent there . . . "[17]

GRUMBLER was not about to take this lying down. Two days later, on May 9, he attacked again: "Must apologise. I merely glanced at your doggerel, and naturally supposing that you had friends in 'H—L,' (or *Hannibal*, as you are pleased to interpret it,) I . . . considered it my duty, in a friendly way, to tell you that you were going too far."[18]

Three days after that another voice joined the fray—this one the high, reedy know-it-all voice of "PETER PENCILCASE'S SON, JOHN SNOOKS." Snooks chose to ignore the vulgar dustup between RAMBLER and GRUMBLER, and instead offered RAMBLER some corrective advice on lovemaking: "It is really amusing to every intelligent and intellectual mind, to see how consequential some coxcombs are. The parlor is too remote a place, and not conspicuous enough to reveal the overflowing affections of the H-e-a-r-t. . . . I can assure Mr. 'Rambler,' that the above courses will never win the affections and admiration of the young Misses in this latitude . . . "[19]

RAMBLER was back in print the next day, getting the last, somewhat heavy-handed adolescent word: ". . . I find that I have attracted the notice of a—fool. . . . Here, now, comes poor pitiful 'Snooks' charging upon me. . . . He calls me a 'Cox-Comb.' I will not say that he belongs to that long eared race of animals that have more head and ears than brains . . . "[20]

This one-man repertory revue, which had overtones of a vaudeville turn or a puppet-show with one actor supplying all the personae, was Sam taking a final boyhood romp through his developing gift of "voice"—of tonal and syntactic mimicry.

The gift would never cease to entertain him. Fifty-three years later, in 1906, he could still supply his biographer Paine with a perfect rendition of the German shoemaker in Hannibal of that same era. He recalled how, in trying to teach Sam German, the fellow mangled his own attempts at English with outbursts such as, "De hain eet flee whoop in de hayer"— by which he meant, "The hen, it flies up in the air."[21] In the intervening years between boyhood and old age, his countless forays into voice and dialect ranged well beyond the celebrated recitations in *Huckleberry Finn*. They included the priceless catalogue of frontier-hipster slang as spewed by Scotty Briggs in arranging Buck Fanshaw's funeral: "Cheese it, pard; you've banked your ball clean outside the string. What I was drivin' at, was, that he never *throwed off* on his mother—don't you see?"[22] And in "The American Claimant," Twain took care to assure his readers that "the Honourable Kirkcudbright Llanover Marjoribanks Sellers Viscount Berkeley, of Cholmondeley Castle, Warwickshire," would be ground down by the British into "K'koobry Thlanover Marshbanks Sellers Vycount Barkly, of Chumly Castle, Warrikshr."

Orion had returned to Hannibal in time to witness the winding-down stages of Sam's latest romp through his *Journal*. (In addition to the Rambler-Grumbler put-on, Sam had laced nearly everything in the paper with his madcap wit—proposing in one news item, for instance, that a newly enacted whiskey tax made it a patriotic duty to drink. In another item he proposed a mind-teaser: "If eight men dig twelve days and find nothing, how long must twenty-two men dig to find just double this amount?"[23])

With ponderous good humor, Orion made a stab at acknowledging the frivolities without quite approving them. "'Rambler' and his enemies must stop their 'stuff,'" he wrote under the masthead of May 13. "It is a great bore to us, and doubtless to the public generally."[24] Then he drew attention to an unsigned piece that would prove to be Sam's final essay of any length in the *Journal,* a sunny homage called "Oh, She Has a Red Head!" Ornate and mock-epic, it claimed that redheads (such as Sam and his mother Jane) could claim affinities with Thomas Jefferson, Jesus Christ, and Adam and Eve, who were already emerging as objects of Sam's seriocomic preoccupation. He signed his piece, "A Son of Adam." Ten days later his darker, vengeful side surfaced again with a venom-tipped poem called "The Burial of Sir Abner Gilstrap, Editor of the Bloomington Republican." (The poem frankly acknowledged its debt to Charles Wolfe's "The Burial of Sir John Moore.") Gilstrap was in fact not dead, but as J. T. Hinton could have told him, he was the next best thing: the initiator of a feud with the *Journal.* Gilstrap had picked the fight when Hannibal was chosen over Bloomington as the terminus of the Hannibal–St. Joseph Railroad, and in six stanzas Sam metaphorically and tartly put him deep in his place:

> *The "Iron Horse" will snort o'er his head,*
> *And the notes of its whistle upbraid him;*
> *But nothing he'll care if they let him sleep on,*
> *In the grave where his nonsense hath laid him.*[25]

By this time a little light had begun to glow in the labyrinthine consciousness of the editor and publisher of the Hannibal *Daily Journal*. Prodded incrementally by several months of incandescent evidence, Orion Clemens was at last starting to perceive that in his younger brother he might be harboring a resource useful in ways that extended beyond setting type without pay.

Envisioning perhaps a newspaper so provocative that its subscribers actually paid to read it, Orion moved to reward and showcase his newly identified treasure. The Abner Gilstrap poem of May 23 ran within the inaugural appearance of "Our Assistant's Column," a potpourri of topical items, gossip, feuds, and the general discharge of Sam's rocketing mind.

"Our Assistant's Column" might have become one of the early sensations of Missouri Journalism, had it run for more than three editions. Orion's timing, then as always, was misbegotten. Sam was bored, he was broke, and he was benumbed by the heavy, aching futility of drudge-work in his brother's office, his daily diet at Jane's table of bacon, butter, bread, and coffee. Mentally, he was doubtless out the door before Orion approached him—committed to floating outward on the late-spring breezes. It did not help that he had asked Orion for money to buy a secondhand gun and Orion had refused him. It did not help that Sam was coming to suspect, in the absence of any demonstrated gratitude, that Orion hated him.

His three columns were a hint at what might have been—including what might have been his gradual surrender to the crude orthodoxies of adult life in a small town. Among the items he churned out was a nod to the approach of summer weather, in which "niggers begin to sweat and look greasy."[26] It would in fact be several years before the young admirer of slave spirituals could fully separate himself from the received bigotries of his native place.

His last Assistant's Column contained a strong and specific indication of where he would rather be: an item reporting that "from fifteen to twenty thousand persons are continually congregated around the new Crystal Palace in New York City, and drunkenness and debauchery are carried on to their fullest extent."[27]

On May 27, 1853, a Notice appeared in the *Hannibal Journal*: "*Wanted!* An Apprentice of the Printing Business. Apply soon." A few days earlier, Sam had told Jane he was leaving. His destination, he said, was St. Louis, where he would put up at the home of Pamela and her husband, get a printing job maybe, and plan his next moves. Already Sam had set his sights on destinations far beyond St. Louis, but he did not let Jane in on these. She was already forty-nine, thin and beset. He was not inclined to add to her anxieties.

Mark Twain in fact allowed a picturesque legend to be built around the moment of leavetaking from his mother, one that rivaled the scene at John Marshall's deathbed. It had Jane holding up a Testament, demanding that Sam take hold of the other end, and extracting a promise from him: "I do solemnly swear that I will not throw a card or drink a drop of liquor while I am gone." In that legend, Sam repeats the oath and receives his mother's kiss.[28]

Whatever the truth of this, Sam's departure had a quantifiable effect on Orion: It nearly felled him. Shocked, distraught, and immediately self-lacerating, he sank into a depression so paralyzing that he was unable to get an edition of the *Journal* out for an entire month.

Early in June, Sam took a night packet down the Mississippi. The date is lost in the mists; as an old man he simply recalled that "I disappeared one night and fled to St. Louis."[29] There are no accounts of his farewells to anyone besides Jane; what he said to Orion or to his younger brother Henry is likewise lost. His itinerary would take him south, then east, then west, then halfway around the world. Eventually he would circle the globe. He would travel, mostly over water, or reside in some form of exile for most of the rest of his life. He would never again be as integrated with a holy place as he had been with Hannibal. He would return to the town just six more times in his life, and he would never live there again, never be a boy again, except in his literature and in his dreams.

Thirteen

"Travel has no longer any charm for me.
I have seen all the foreign countries I want to see
except heaven and hell, and I have only
a vague curiosity as concerns one of those."

A round the first of September, 1853, Jane Clemens opened a letter from Sam bearing an unanticipated postmark, written and mailed not from St. Louis but New York City, nearly a thousand miles east. It was dated Wednesday, August 24. Sam's salutation anticipated his mother's shock and tried to jolly her into a forgiving frame of mind:

My Dear Mother:

You will doubtless be a little surprised, and somewhat angry when you receive this, and find me so far from home; but you must bear a little with me, for you know I was always the best boy you had, and perhaps you remember the people used to say to their children—"Now don't do like Orion and Henry Clemens but take Sam for your guide!"[1]

Sam's lifetime of wandering had begun, as had his lifetime of describing it in irreverent, insouciant prose. Over the next six or seven months he would, in effect, perform a dress rehearsal for his half century of forays into unknown territory, as well as the great linkages of journeying and narrative that resulted. The letters he wrote during this period, to his mother, his sister and brothers, and to Orion's newspapers, amount to the first rough drafts of the meta-saga called Mark Twain.

These letters are exhilarating to read even though they do not—could not—show the Twain genius fully formed. The architecture of that formation would take years, oceans, continents, and the motivating irritants of grief and failure to complete. Most conspicuously absent is Twain's humor. At seventeen and eighteen Sam tended to report his new frontiers as he saw and felt them. Self-absorbed, as anyone of that age would be, preoccupied with freedom, strutting the strut of the boy rampant in the world, he was no more prepared for discipline and technique than Huck for an evening of Moses and the Bulrushers with the Widow Douglas. Moreover, as Mark Twain liked to say, "The secret source of humor is not joy but sorrow." Sam was having too much joy just now to be funny. He'd had more than his share of sorrow, and in the years ahead, the humor would start to flow like tears.

At their worst, the letters betray a streak of nativist bigotry and self-righteousness. This streak can shock the reader familiar only with Twain the social democrat. Sam's prejudices, one suspects, were received and mostly rhetorical; they would famously be modified over time. Yet they are exposed on this sojourn, where many races and degrees of apostasy mingled in a more or less egalitarian way, as they were seldom exposed in Puritan, white-supremacist Hannibal.

What the letters reveal of irreducible value is the early maturity of Sam Clemens's mastery over language, a maturity that he had achieved largely on his own. All those immersions in John Marshall's little library; the romances of Scott, Byron, Cooper; his reading and memorizing *The Arabian Nights, Robin Hood, Ivanhoe, Robinson Crusoe, Gulliver's Travels.* All those dreary years of setting type in Orion's office, reading the texts of what he was assembling; all those newspapers and journals drifting in. And all the imagery and passion and structure of the slave stories, and their nighttime singing. Now the reader, the hearer, was ready to write a bold harvest of words.

The letters reveal one other singular gift, this one extra-literary, yet indispensable, at least to the distinctive American literature that Mark Twain himself largely enshrined. This is the gift for simply plunging into the world, for crossing the threshhold that separates the familiar from the exotic, and for converting the terror and the ecstasy of that plunge into indelible observation. Whatever American writing that flowered from "the cult of experience" (in Philip Rahv's phrase) can trace some little part of its root system to Sam Clemens's eastern vacation in 1853–54. His writing during this time developed the literary model for such protean writers of wandering experience as Thomas Wolfe, who perhaps most closely replicated Twain's twin obsessions for outward journeying and safe return; that emissary from Terre Haute to the fleshpots of metropolis, Theodore Dreiser; and the Chicago-born, European "hotel-child" and constant traveler John Dos Passos with his "camera-eye" model of prose in constant motion. In 1957 John Steinbeck, who traveled to write and who wrote of travelers, built a six-sided study for his work overlooking the ocean in Sag Harbor because he'd read somewhere that Mark Twain had written in such surroundings.[2]

In the first installment of his lifelong journey, Sam had made it to St. Louis as promised. He'd stayed for a while in the rented Pine Street house of Pamela, her husband, and their year-old daughter Annie, with whom Mark Twain would later correspond. He had found work as a typesetter for the St. Louis *Evening News* and also for some weekly papers around town, hoarding his money (maybe $8 or $9 a week) and struggling to bring his work up to adult, urban standards of speed and cleanliness. But by July he was bored again. The summer's big national event, the World's Fair inside the Crystal Palace in New York, had captured his imagination. On August 19, he'd packed his belongings and left the known universe of Missouri behind. He began a five-day odyssey east by stage, boat, and train, a seventeen-year-old provincial boy who had never before set foot in a railroad car. He wrote his first letter home on the day of his arrival.

The letter—which Orion had the wit to publish in the *Journal* on September 5—recounted the journey with the studied deadpan of the staunchly unimpressed Southwesterner. It was "an awful trip, taking five days, where it should have been only three." Sam had negotiated his way by steamboat to Alton, Ill.; then by train and stage to Springfield (where the former Congressman Abe Lincoln was practicing law and reading Euclid at night in his house at Eighth and Jackson). From there, he'd taken a stage to Bloomington; then a train to Chicago, where he'd endured a twenty-six-hour layover; then several train connections and a steamboat to Buffalo, New York; then on to Albany via the New York "Lightning Express," then down the Hudson River to the city as a passenger on the steamer *Isaac Newton*, arriving at 5 in the morning.

On this first sojourn he was pure tourist, an innocent aboard. His rustic wonder at the paranormal showed through, however, and he wore his received bigotries like a protective homespun coat. As his train passed through Rochester he thought at once of the famous "Spirit Rappings"* reported there some years before. At a stopover in Syracuse he glimpsed the Court House and remembered news accounts of it being surrounded with chains and soldiers "to prevent the rescue of McReynolds' nigger,† by the infernal abolitionists. I reckon I had better black my face," he blustered, "for in these Eastern States niggers are considerably better than white people."

Yet his eye for the telling detail was already far in advance of most larking travelers. So were his survival instincts. New York City was not yet the great dark Babylon of world finance and capital that Herman Melville would find it in the postwar decades, but it was tending in that direction. A lowslung metropolis of shipyards, mills, and dry-goods merchants, it had already approached 1 million in population, an immigrant-swollen density that was fully capable of swallowing up a small-boned boy from frontier Missouri.

But Sam watched his back. Almost instantly he adapted and took charge, as he would always adapt and take charge of exotic surroundings. Sauntering along Broadway on the day he hit town, he happened upon an exhibition of the humanoids whom P. T. Barnum would make famous years later as "the Wild Men of Borneo," and his scrutiny of them showed a cool, professional aplomb. They were about the size

---

*Two young teenaged sisters, Margaret and Kate Fox, had triggered the national "spiritualist" fad there in 1848 by inviting visitors to listen in on mysterious sharp sounds in their darkened house. Nearly half a century later Margaret owned up that the noise was produced by the sisters cracking the joints of their toes.

†A fugitive slave, whose name was Jerry McHenry. He had been tracked down and arrested in Syracuse in 1851, but freed by an abolitionist crowd that stormed the courthouse. The incident received national attention.

"of Harvel Jordan's oldest boy," he told his mother, then dropped the homey pose for a precise evocation of the surreal: The creatures had "small lips and full breast, with a constant uneasy, fidgeting motion, bright, intelligent eyes, that seems [sic] as if they would look through you."[3] The beings had no apple in their throats, he noted, and could therefore scarcely make a sound; and no memory, either. "Their faces and eyes are those of the beast, and when they fix their glittering orbs on you with a steady, unflinching gaze, you instinctively draw back a step, and a very unpleasant sensation steals through your veins."[4]

All in all, a quite different letter than one that Jane Clemens might have expected from Sam—one dealing with the diapering adventures of little Annie Moffett, say.

The provincial from squatter country showed an uncanny knack for making out in the land of dandies. He negotiated a room in a boarding house in Duane Street on what is now the Lower East Side of Manhattan, near what would be the approach to the Brooklyn Bridge. (The food offended him, especially the stale "light-bread" that for some reason was served in place of good Southern biscuits.)

More impressively still, he found work. A week after his arrival he reported to Jane that he'd landed a job as a printer, even though—to hear him tell it at least—there were already thirty to fifty printers in the city who were unemployed. He'd been hired by John A. Gray's compositor shop in Cliff Street about ten blocks south, on the East River, a concern that set type for books and nearly a dozen periodicals including *Choral Advocate, Jewish Chronicle,* and *Littell's Living Age.* His pay, the bottom of the scale among the forty or so compositors in the shop, was twenty-three cents per one thousand ems, an "em" being a unit of type. He was living in the general neighborhood that would become Melville's dreary haunt during his postwar decades as a custom's inspector. The two writers would never meet, but they shared a legacy as wanderers over the watery portions of the world, and as moral prophets of their country. A month after Sam's arrival, the thirty-four-year-old Melville, living then among the literati in the Massachusetts Berkshires, published the first installment of "Bartleby the Scrivener" in *Putnam's Monthly:* a gloomy forecasting of the dehumanization of work by the mechanization of jobs. The future investor in the Paige typesetter might have done well to read it.

But Sam was up to his elbows in skilled work just then, and relishing it. He seemed at great pains to assure his mother that he was living the Model Boy's life and taking his work seriously—perhaps there had been some oath-taking at the House on Hill Street after all. "Even if I do not make much money, I will learn a great deal," he wrote, and, after detailing the exactitude of his job, "I expected this, and worked accordingly from the beginning; and out of all the proofs I saw, without boasting, I can say mine was by far the cleanest. . . . I believe I *do* set a clean proof." [5] As for his leisure hours, "Last night I was in what is known as one of *the* finest fruit salons in the world. The gas lamps hang in clusters of half a dozen together—representing grapes, I suppose—all over the hall." And once the excitement of that scene had gotten a little heady, he could always taper off at the library. The printers supported two of these in the city, admission free to the brotherhood. "[I]n these I can spend my evenings most pleasantly. If books are not good company, where will I find it?"[6]

The nocturnal pub-crawling, opium den-frequenting, brothel-visiting, rooftop-traipsing, moon-howling Sam Clemens of Virginia City, Nevada, a decade in the future, could have supplied several answers to that pious question. But just now the boy, embarked on his biggest truancy ever, was establishing his bona fides. Let it go.

Like Walt Whitman across the East River in Brooklyn, like Thomas Wolfe eighty years in the future, and like the ten thousand young journalist-writers who were his heirs, he bestrode the million-footed city, was caught up in the manswarm, heard the blab of the pave, sensed the souls moving along, listened to the living and buried speech that was always vibrating there. His letters home, unselfconscious and marveling, contained passages that anticipated Whitman's meters. Crossing Broadway, he wrote, he got into the crowd, "and when I get in, I am borne, and rubbed, and crowded along, and need scarcely trouble myself about using my own legs." (Somewhat less transcendently, he aimed a snarl at the "brats" in his way—"Niggers, mulattoes, quadroons, Chinese . . . to wade through this mass of human vermin, would raise the ire of the most patient person that ever lived.")

Squeezed finally inside the Crystal Palace, he noted from the second-floor gallery "the flags of the different countries represented, the lofty dome, glittering jewelry, gaudy tapestry, &c., with the busy crowd passing to and fro . . ." The ensuing observation was vintage, house-counting Clemens: "The visitors to the Palace average 6,000 daily—double the population of Hannibal. The price of admission being 50 cents, they take in about $3,000." (In fact, the Exposition proved a financial failure.)

He discoursed learnedly on the Latting Observatory and the Croton Aqueduct, "the greatest wonder yet." If necessary, he told his wan sister, it could easily supply every family in New York "with *one hundred barrels of water per day!*" He bought himself a ticket to a Broadway play, this future Broadway impresario;* he watched the famous

---

*In 1874 Mark Twain bought and revised an earlier stage adaptation of *The American Claimant* for a successful Broadway run and national tour under the title *Colonel Sellers*. Two years later he formed a partnership with Bret Harte and Charles T. Parloe to stage a Broadway production of his comic collaboration with Harte, *Ah Sin*.

Edwin Forrest star in *The Gladiator,* and reviewed it for the home folks with the slightly labored pose of a lifelong drama critic:

> I did not like parts of it much, but other portions were really splendid. In the latter part of the last act, where the "Gladiator" (Forrest) dies at his brother's feet, (in all the fierce pleasure of gratified revenge,) . . . the man's whole soul seems absorbed in the part he is playing; and it is really startling to see him. I am sorry I did not see him play "Damon and Pythias"—the former character being his greatest.[7]

Back home, life had changed a little, as he learned by return mail from Pamela. His little brother Henry had taken ill, a development that alarmed Sam: "He ought to go to the country and take exercise; for he is not half so healthy as Ma thinks he is. If he had my walking to do, he would be another boy entirely." Will Bowen's father, the Captain, was failing. By December he would be dead.

Most significant to the family was the news regarding Sam's older brother. ("Where is it Orion is going to?" Sam queried Pamela.[8]) Orion had never really recovered from Sam's departure; the *Journal* never made any real money, and now Orion was preparing to rid himself of the whole dreary enterprise.

This meant in turn that the Clemens family epoch in Hannibal had reached its end. In late September Orion unloaded the paper to a local buyer, sold the house on Hill Street, and moved north to the Mississippi rivertown of Muscatine, Iowa, with Jane and young Henry in tow.

Pathetically, one of his final editions of the *Journal* carried the text of Sam's August 31 letter announcing his position with John A. Gray—introduced, by Orion, in tones of button-busting pride:

The following letter is some encouragement to apprentices in country printing offices, as it shows that it is practicable to acquire enough knowledge of the business in a Western country office, to command the best situations, West or East. There are a great many who suppose that no mechanical business can be learned well in the West.[9]

While his family was struggling through its bleak destinies, Sam was restless, insurgent, ready for new cities to conquer. By early October he was spoiling to leave New York. A week or so later he was gone—bound for Philadelphia. On October 26 he fired off a letter to Orion and Henry from that city, where he was "subbing" at the Pennsylvania *Inquirer and National Gazette.* He was waspish about the lack of correspondence from home, which might have been a cover for his own homesickness.

I have been writing to Pamela, till I am tired of it, and have received no answer. I have been wanting for the last two or three weeks to send Ma some money, but devil take me if I knew where she was, and so the money has slipped out of my pocket somehow or other, but I have a dollar left. . . . I know it's a small amount, but then it will buy her a handkerchief . . . [10]

He bragged about the money he was making, rattled on about the omnibus tours of the city he'd taken, clucked about the peculiar etiquette in force on Philadelphia 'buses.

A gentleman is always expected to hand up a lady's money for her. Yesterday, I sat in the front end of the 'bus, directly under the driver's box—a lady sat opposite me. She handed me her money, which was right. But, Lord! A St.

Louis lady would think herself ruined, if she should be so familiar with a stranger.[11]

As for his general mood, Sam was never better. In fact the only thing that ticked him off was being constantly encouraged by the other printers not to be "downhearted."

> "Downhearted," the devil! I have not had a particle of such feeling since I left Hannibal, more than four months ago. I fancy they'll have to wait some time till they see me downhearted or afraid of starving. . . . When I was in Hannibal, before I had scarcely stepped out of the town limits, nothing could have convinced me than [sic] I would starve as soon as I got a little way from home.[12]

As for the city itself—why, Philadelphia was "one of the healthiest places in the Union," an opinion he mentioned twice.

The intended audience for this bravado may have been Jane, whom Sam, despite his bluster, had constantly on his mind. "Tell Ma my promises are faithfully kept," he'd instructed Pamela in an earlier letter. Jane was a good candidate for filial concern: six years a widow, separated from two of her surviving children in the space of two years, then hauled off to a strange town in the dubious care of her incompetent, penniless eldest son. A handkerchief, to say the least. But Sam was also attentive of Jane's yearning to visit her family homegrounds in Kentucky in the spring; he told Pamela that he intended to take her there "if I have my health."

Orion showed some stirrings of enterprise in Muscatine. He had agreed on a partnership with one John Mahin to start up a *Journal* there, and on September 30 he published his first edition. He sent a copy to Sam, apparently, in lieu of a letter. He promptly began printing chunks of Sam's correspondence in it, under such portentous headings as "extract from a private letter to the senior editor."[13]

Sam, meanwhile, appeared to be experimenting with various versions of his new grown-up persona—or, conceivably, with protective coloration to mask his new adult habits. In November, two days before his eighteenth birthday, he wrote to Orion from Philadelphia in what was almost a caricature of the Western Puritan squarehead; he railed against "abominable foreigners" and "whisky-swilling, God-despising heathens," and let it slip that "I believe I am the only person in the Inquirer office that does not drink." He said he would "like amazingly to see a good, old-fashioned negro," promised to try to write for Orion's new paper and repeated his intention of taking Jane to Kentucky in the spring. A few days later he mailed off his first submission, a kind of portrait of Philadelphia whose opening sentence may have burlesqued Orion's leaden approach to journalism: "There is very little news of consequence stirring just now." (Orion dutifully ran this intelligence as written.) Later in the dispatch, Sam, the self-advertised teetotaler, revealed a suspicious intimacy with the city's fleshpots:

> It is hard to get tired of Philadelphia, for amusements are not scarce. We have what is called a "free-and-easy," at the saloons on Saturday nights. At a free-and-easy, a chairman is appointed, who calls on any of the assembled company for a song or a recitation, and as there are plenty of singers and spouters, one may laugh himself into fits at a very small expense.[14]

Through the late fall of 1853 and the early winter of 1854, Sam wrote a few more travelogue letters for his brother's paper. He took a Dickensian interest in the bustling Christmas shoppers crowding the shops—"Turkeys and fowls of all kinds, are vanishing from the markets as if by magic." He gave the good Iowans a taste of urban gothic by describing a fire that left a policeman buried in the rubble, his feet burned off, "his face burnt to a crisp, and his head crushed in."[15] The dedicated scourge of Hannibal schoolrooms displayed an informed interest in Philadelphia's Revolutionary arcana. He pointed with pride to Carpenter's Hall, where the first Congress of the United States had assembled—"a fact which should entitle it to a place in the heart of every true lover of his country." And he noted, in its present use, a desecration of the sort that would be widely lamented a century and a half later: "It is now occupied by an auction mart. Alas! That these old buildings, so intimately connected with the principal scenes in the history of our country, should thus be so profaned."[16]

He happened on the "queer looking old house occupied by the heroic Lydia Darrah," he told his readers. He recounted from memory the mythic tale of how the woman set off from the house and its occupying British officer, her empty flourbag on her back,* to inform Washington of a planned British attack on his camp: "her heroic conduct defeated the plans of the red-coats, and saved the Americans. Well does she deserve a monument; but no such monument is hers." And then the inevitable deflating aside: "As one might almost guess, her old mansion is now occupied by a Jew, as a clothing store."[17]

---

*In folklore, her pretext for crossing British lines was that she needed to buy flour.

His final dispatch from Philadelphia, dated February 3, 1854, showed a proprietary interest in the city's municipal government. A Consolidation Bill, which had kept "our" citizens in a state of excitement, had passed the Legislature, making Philadelphia the largest city—in sheer area—in the nation. He told the Iowa homefolks about the increased wages of the city's journeymen rope-makers.

A week or so after that, he was gone—on the move again. His next letter home was datelined Washington, D.C.

Sam never did get around to escorting Jane back to Kentucky. That plan evaporated as the boy's eastern odyssey ran out of momentum— or money—in the spring of 1854. The Washington letter to the *Journal* was his last from the east, and in certain ways the high-water mark of his journalistic audacity to date. In the nation's capital he took on several reportorial roles. As architecture critic he allowed as how the public buildings of Washington were all fine specimens of architecture, "and would add greatly to . . . such a city as New York—but here they are sadly out of place looking like so many palaces in a Hottentot village." The clusters of poor houses "look as though they might have been emptied out of a sack by some Brobdingnagian [sic] gentleman, and when falling, been scattered about by the winds." The Capitol, he opined, was a very fine building, as advertised; the art critic in him found the many large paintings in the Congressional Chambers to be fresh, natural, noble.

When he slid into the Senate Chamber, he tried on the persona of political pundit. "The Senate is now composed of a different material from what it once was," he began this section of the letter, in a promisingly world-weary way. "Its glory hath departed. Its halls no longer echo the words of a Clay, or Webster, or Calhoun." But as he tried to assess the merits and performance of their replacements, Sam's deeper analytical skills failed him: "Mr. Cass is a fine looking old man; Mr. Douglas, or 'Young America,' looks like a lawyer's clerk, and Mr. Seward is a slim, dark, bony individual, and looks like a respectable wind would blow him out of the country."[18] There was in fact a bit more to the three than that. Lewis Cass was soon to become Secretary of State under President Buchanan. Stephen A. Douglas was to enter American history as Abraham Lincoln's rival for the Senate and the Presidency, as well as in the Lincoln-Douglas debates. William H. Seward would also oppose Lincoln for the Presidency and then serve as his Secretary of State before purchasing Alaska in 1867.

Sam Clemens himself was destined to penetrate the Washington political culture a good deal more deeply and to convert his experience into satiric art. He returned there in 1867 as the private secretary to W. M. Stewart, the Senator from Nevada, and shrewdly studied its characters and its currents of political intrigue. His fictive embodiment of all the sham and demented ambition, Col. Sellers, gave *The Gilded Age* (his collaboration with Charles Dudley Warner) its few moments of greatness.

But all of that was for another time. The adolescent Sam concluded his letter to the *Journal* with a favorable review of the Washington Monument, then under construction (it was "as yet but a plain white marble obelisk 150 feet high. It will no doubt be very beautiful when finished"); he caught Mr. Forrest on the stage again, this time playing Othello at the National Theatre ("This is a very large theatre . . . ").

And then, for historic purposes at least, Sam Clemens dropped out of sight. His letters ceased for the ensuing twelve months—or were lost—as did his sources for revenue. The invincible boy who had scoffed about being downhearted found himself now unemployed. He wandered about the cities of the east for a while, and finally, sometime in the spring, he bought a train ticket west to Missouri, sitting upright in a smoking car for three days and nights. When he boarded an up-river steamboat in St. Louis, he fell asleep and did not awaken for thirty-six hours. When he awoke he was not in his familiar Hannibal, but in a strange Iowa village named Muscatine. In the mid–nineteenth century, Sam Clemens was undergoing another formative experience that anticipated the twentieth: displacement from his native place. Like many American wanderer-artists after him, Sam had come back home, to find that "home" was already removed to the province of memory.

Fourteen

"I have no desire for riches.
Honest poverty and a conscience torpid through
virtuous inaction are more to me than
corner lots and praise."

Sam arrived at Orion's house in Muscatine at breakfast-time brandishing a gun. Jane and the others rose from the table watching him. Sam spelled it out, holding the weapon in front of him: Orion had once denied him a loan to buy a secondhand gun back in Hannibal; now he'd bought one on his own, "and I'm going to use it, now, in self-defense."[1]

It was a joke, a visual tall tale. Sam's way of making an entrance. Once again, he was foreshadowing twentieth-century American idioms.

Orion had established himself, Jane, and Henry in a small cottage on tree-lined Walnut Street in the graceful little redbricked Iowa city, at the crest of a hill overlooking the Mississippi. Reprising its presence in Hannibal throughout his boyhood, the river reemerged as a daily event in his consciousness, its southward flow channeling his thoughts. Before very long, he was imagining himself in South America.

Meanwhile, the new editor of the Muscatine *Journal* was managing his life with his customary finesse. Orion had discovered women. He had perhaps discovered women too emphatically; at the very least, he had discovered too many women. He was courting two of them at the same time. Each was under the impression, in fact, that she was engaged to Orion. One of his sweethearts hailed from Quincy, Illinois, just across the river from Hannibal—"a winning and pretty girl,"[2] as Sam recalled her. The other Orion had met during a visit to Keokuk, another Iowa rivertown about eighty miles to the south. This one was somewhat harder to look at; she was nineteen, and her principal agenda was to get herself married off.

Orion had blundered into a situation even more compromising than the one in Dr. Meredith's maiden sister's bed. "He didn't know whether to marry the Keokuk one or the Quincy one," Twain dryly observed, "or whether to try to marry both of them and suit everyone concerned."[3] The Keokuk girl, one Mary Eleanor (Mollie) Stotts, was gracious enough to relieve Orion of the decision-making burden. She browbeat him into writing a letter to her attractive rival breaking off that particular engagement. Orion and triumphant Mollie were wedded in December 1854 at the Stotts home in their town.[4] It could not have been a gala occasion. Only Henry was there to represent the Clemens clan. Sam had long since left town, but more curiously, Jane Clemens missed the ceremony as well. Perhaps she had had her fill of marriages made somewhere other than in heaven. She contrived the eminently plausible excuse of having to visit her daughter Pamela, more than two hundred miles downriver in St. Louis, at the time.

Her absence may not have had much impact on Orion, who himself seemed hardly to notice that he had gotten hitched. He later recalled an episode that suggested a certain detachment from the afterglow of the happy event:

At sunrise on the next morning after the wedding we left in a stage for Muscatine. We halted for dinner at Burlington. After dispatching that meal we stood on the pavement when the stage drove up, ready for departure. I climbed in, gathered the buffalo robe around me, and leaned back unconscious that I had anything further to do. A gentleman standing on the pavement said to my wife, "Miss, do you go by this stage?" I said, "Oh, I forgot!" and sprang out and helped her in. A wife was a new kind of possession to which I had not yet become accustomed; I had forgotten her.[5]

Sam had stayed around Muscatine for the summer and perhaps into the early fall. By the time of Orion's wedding, he was back in St. Louis and his old place as a typesetter on the *Evening News.* In his absence, Mollie cajoled Orion into folding his operation in Muscatine and setting up housekeeping in her hometown of Keokuk. There, in June 1855, Orion started all over yet again, as his father John Marshall had started over so many times. He was no longer a newspaper publisher, but just a job-printer now, having bought the bootstrap Ben Franklin Book and Job office on the third floor of a Main Street storefront (a music school and then a bookstore were below). His consignments were city directories, odd-job pamphlets. He conscripted the ever-trusty Henry, seventeen now, as his assistant. In midsummer he sent a plea downriver for Sam to come north again and join the operation at a salary of $5 a week. Perhaps to Orion's surprise, Sam accepted the offer.

It wasn't as though Sam lacked ambition. His river dreams, in fact, were at full tide. Before he'd resumed his compositing job, he had been agitating his wealthy cousin James Clemens, Jr., in St. Louis to help him get a position as a riverboat pilot. Clemens pleaded illness, and later wrote to Orion that he believed "your brother should stick to his present trade or art."[6] Sam's own visits to the magisterial captains on their boats produced no offers. So in late June, Sam boarded an upriver packet as a passenger en route to rejoin his brother, who was now a prospective father in the fall. He stopped off briefly at Hannibal to gather up some of Orion's possessions for shipment north. Then he traveled inland to revisit the old beloved Quarles farm, now sold, and his uncle John, who lived on in the Florida area. Finally, Keokuk.

These last couple of years in Iowa before he began his life on the Mississippi were languid, amber-tinted times for Sam. As the northern Mississippi Valley's prewar innocence reached its sunset years, his adolescence was fading in a similar golden haze. He worked happily, fatalistically for his brother—as if he took for granted that something larger would blow his way. He and Henry shared a bed in the printing office, Sam often reading into the night after his brother had dropped off, while puffing on a complicated Oriental water-bubble pipe. When another boarder in the building looked in on him one night and asked him what he was reading, Sam replied that it was a "so-called funny-book." He muttered absently that one of these days he would write a funnier book himself. The boarder expressed doubts: Sam was too lazy. And when the inevitable money crisis struck the business and Orion was forced to suspend pay, Sam shrugged that off; he had free board; he didn't need money just then.

There would be few times in his life when he was indifferent to money, but this was one of them. He seemed distracted by more elemental satisfactions. His renewed friendship with his younger brother was one of them. Sam and Henry had begun to outgrow their boyish fractiousness and discover one another as young adults. Sam sensed that Henry—and perhaps Henry alone—understood him deeply.* As Sam's closest sibling in age, and quite likely in intellect as well, Henry may have been a kind of alter ego to Sam; in certain ways, even, a kind of twin.

Another good reason for Sam's indolence may have been that he too had discovered, or rediscovered, women. He sang along with them in the music studio downstairs from Orion's shop and strummed for them on the guitar and banjo; the young women laughed at his dreamy affect and affectionately called him a fool.[7]

Flirting made him buoyant, and silly with wordplay. He met a rather spectacular new friend named Ann Elizabeth Taylor, a bookish but witty student at Iowa Wesleyan College in Mt. Pleasant. The Victorian gentleman in him—the eventual source of *Personal Recollections of Joan of Arc*—treated her with eminent respectful gentleness and modesty. He romanced her; encouraged her writing aspirations: "Ah, Annie, I have a slight horror of writing essays myself; and if I were to write one I should be afraid to do it, knowing that you could do it so much better if you would only get industrious once and try."[8] When she returned to school he wrote her wild giddy letters of ardent nonsense:

> . . . Bugs! Yes, B-U-G-S! What of the bugs? Why, perdition take the bugs! That is all. Night before last I stood at the little press until nearly 2 o'clock, and the flaring gas light over my head attracted all the varieties of bugs which

---

*In 1869 (as Justin Kaplan has noted), trying to ingratiate himself to the parents of his beloved Olivia Langdon, Clemens proclaimed that only five people had ever known him well, and that he had felt sympathy with only two of them: his dead brother Henry and Livy.

are to be found in natural history. . . . They at first came in
little social crowds of a dozen or so, but soon . . . a religious mass meeting of several millions was assembled on
the board before me, presided over by a venerable beetle
[!], who occupied the most prominent lock of my hair as
his chair of state . . .

The big "president" beetle (who, when he frowned,
closely resembled Isbell* when the pupils are out of time)
rose and ducked his head and, crossing his arms over his
shoulders, stroked them down to the tip of his nose several
times, and after thus disposing of the perspiration, stuck
his hands under his wings, propped his back against a lock
of hair, and then, bobbing his head at the congregation, remarked, "B-u-z-z!" To which the congregation devoutly
responded, "B-u-z-z!" Satisfied with this promptness on
the part of his flock, he took a more imposing perpendic-
ular against another lock of hair . . . [9]

He gave what almost surely was his first after-dinner speech in January 1856, at a printer's banquet at the Ivins House in Keokuk com-
memorating Franklin's 150th birthday. Orion was chairman of the
event and seized the opportunity to deliver one of his patented incomprehensible orations; but it was his brother who was "loudly and
repeatedly called for."[10] Clearly Sam's reputation as a wag had gotten
around. The young man arose with no preparation and began speaking in a slow, uncertain drawl. But once on his feet, he managed to im-
provise a speech that was at once touching and hilarious. Accounts of

---

*Oliver C. Isbell, the music school proprietor.

the evening indicate that he "convulsed his hearers," who interrupted with "loud and continued bursts of applause."[11] A lifetime of such responses would follow.

It was around this time, in the early months of 1856, that Sam started to burn for South America. Rumors of fortunes to be made by harvesting a certain bit of vegetation called the coca leaf along the Amazon were trickling back to the American Interior. Mark Twain would write[12] of how he'd been intrigued by a book that "told an astonishing tale about *coca*, a vegetable product of miraculous powers . . . so nourishing and so strength-giving that the native of the mountains of the Madeira region would tramp up-hill and down all day on a pinch of powdered coca and require no other substance."[13] Indeed. The "product" that had Sam so intrigued, of course, was cocaine; once again he seemed astrally connected to the predilections of the century to come.

Here was whiteness of a different aura entirely. Its exploitation a hundred-odd years later would sustain criminal/business empires of incredible wealth and power. Sam (and for that matter, certain of his relatives) may not have anticipated the criminality of the drug, but they certainly understood its profitability. His cousin Jeremiah Clemens had published a plan to establish "a mighty Anglo-Saxon empire" on the banks of the Amazon.[14] No doubt influenced by this, Sam longed, he wrote, "to open up a trade in coca with all the world."[15]

Schemes for getting rich quick, at any rate, would overwhelm his passions throughout his life—"in all that time my temperament has not changed by even a shade," he acknowledged as an old man to his biographer Paine. "When I am reflecting on these occasions, even deaf persons can hear me think."

Suddenly typesetting was hateful and dangerous work. He got his hand caught in the rolling press one day; it was severely pinched but he managed to pull it back before it was maimed. Orion's business was slowly going bust—an especial inconvenience given that he and Mollie had a baby now, Jennie, born in September 1855. His prospects seemed to spiral downward toward failure and struggle. Meanwhile, other typesetters' work ended up unfinished on Sam's tray. His irascibility seared through in his letters. "I don't like to work too many things at once," he wrote to Jane and Pamela in June. "I am not getting along well with the job-work. I can't work blindly—without system."[16]

He kept the South America dream a secret from Orion but broached it to his mother. And in an August letter to Henry, who was visiting in St. Louis, he revealed that his Brazilian itinerary had formed. He was going to embark in six weeks with Joseph S. Martin, a Keokuk doctor and "Lecturer on Chemistry and Toxicology,"[17] and someone named Ward. They planned to travel by way of New York. Sam relayed to Henry the mordant wisecrack that this information had drawn from Jane: "She says I can treat [Orion] as I did her when I started to St. Louis and went to New York—I can start to New York and go to South America!"[18]

That letter to Henry featured some piquant brotherly asides: several goading references, like so many elbow-jabs to the ribs, regarding the health of Ann Taylor: "Annie is well"; "(by the way, I forgot to mention that *Annie* is well)" "(This reminds me that—Annie *is* well)"; "(I must not forget to say that Annie is *well)*"; "I may as well remark that *Annie is well.*"; and the postscript, "I will just add that *Annie* is WELL."[19] Just possibly, a bit of a rivalry had sprung up between the brothers for Miss Taylor's attentions and Sam, not quite so Victorian when he had a competitive advantage, was rubbing it in.

As summer gave way to autumn, the high hopes for a South American odyssey evaporated. Apparently neither Ward, nor the Lecturer on Toxicology, nor Clemens could scrape up the money. He would get no kick from cocaine. Sam seethed, and labored on for nothing in the third-story shop.

But one day he struck it rich in the most hackneyed, banal, cartoon-strip manner imaginable.

He was trudging along the main street in Keokuk one bitter morning in October, fighting an early swirl of dry snow, when a rectangular scrap of paper fluttered past his eyes and flattened against the wall of a house. Sam peeled it off and examined it. It was a fifty-dollar bill— "the only one I had ever seen, and the largest assemblage of money I had ever seen in one spot." To be sure, it was more than triple the $16 that the Campbellites had brought into the Hannibal shop.

Astonishingly enough, Sam advertised his literal windfall in the local newspapers. (Not everything he did foretold the twentieth century.) Perhaps even more astonishingly still, after four days, not a solitary Iowa soul had responded to claim the money. On the fifth day, it struck Sam that virtue had its limits. ("Truth is the most valuable thing we have," he later wrote. "Let us economize it."[20]) He bought a ticket to St. Louis, and South America suddenly seemed possible after all.

His plan was to work his way down the Mississippi, making money where he could, and then, vaguely, to board a ship headed for Brazil. (He had only the foggiest notions about the location and nature of Brazil, and none at all about the lethal complexities of the Amazon.) Before he left town—and left Orion, once again, in the lurch—he struck a deal to write some humorous travel sketches back to the Keokuk *Daily Post*, for $5 each.

The first letter was postmarked October 18, 1856, from St. Louis, and it introduced the last pen name, and alter ego, that Sam would try out before he unveiled Mark Twain in Nevada in February 1863. This was the bumptious Iowa rustic Thomas Jefferson Snodgrass, just a little bit higher on the evolutionary scale than Simon Suggs. Heavily imitative of the old Southwestern traditions, his comic appeal depending on misspellings and grossly exaggerated ignorance, Snodgrass was not an especially clever creation in himself. As portrayed in Sam's first letter, Snodgrass and a companion go to the theater to see an actor named Nealy play *Julius Caesar*. Out of his element, Snodgrass decides to compete with the house orchestra by whipping out an old pocket comb and playing on it, taking "them one-hoss fiddlers down a peg and bring down the house, too."[21] The audience laughs, which gets Snodgrass riled:

> Darn my skin if I wasn't mad. I jerked off my coat and jumped at the little man and, says I, "You nasty, sneakin' degenerate great grandson of a ring-tailed monkey, I kin jest lam . . . "[22]

Snodgrass's summary of the plotline is as follows:

> At last it come time to remove Mr. Cesar from office . . . so all the conspirators got around the throne, and directly Cesar come steppin in, putting on as many airs as if he was mayor of Alexandria. Arter he had sot on the throne awhile they all jumped on him at once like a batch of Irish on a sick nigger.[23]

What was most useful about this and the two* other Snodgrass letters Sam wrote, perhaps, is that they earned him $5 apiece—his first fees for freelance writing.

That, and the fact that Snodgrass, however crude, is the literary "missing link" between Simon Suggs and Huckleberry Finn. As his skills deepened in the Nevada years and beyond, Mark Twain would keep writing in assumed human voices. But gradually he shed the arch misspellings and the clownish faked ignorance, and based his vernacular writing more and more on authentic figures of speech and the natural rhythms of spoken dialect. Thus when Huckleberry Finn finally emerged in 1884, he emerged with the capacities of the ironist and even the poet, without breaking the consistency of his character— qualities to which Suggs and his generation could never aspire.

Sam was restless. St. Louis could not hold him. Suddenly the need to make money and head off for the unknown overwhelmed him. He stayed only about a week, boarding with Jane and Pamela's family. In mid-October he threw himself into the slow journey upriver to Keokuk again, for the sole purpose of looking in on the editor at the *Post* and bargaining for more money for further Snodgrass letters. The next day he was heading back downstream, to Quincy. There he boarded a train for the two hundred-mile trip to Chicago. He made connections south to Indianapolis, and finally, around October 24, he arrived in Cincinnati. He landed a printing job there, at T. Wrightson & Co., where he worked through the spring of 1857.

---

*The scholar Minnie Brashear discovered four additional Snodgrass letters in the *New Orleans Crescent* beginning January 21, 1861, but their authorship by Clemens is doubtful. This character is called Quintus Curtius Snodgrass, and his voice is not vernacular, but pretentious and literary.

Mark Twain never wrote much about those months in Cincinnati. By all inferences they were lonely and fitful: boardinghouses and drudgework through a long winter. Hoarding his pay. Two more Snodgrass letters issued from there to be printed in the Keokuk paper.

Finally, on April 15, 1857, Sam Clemens made the break from his landlocked life. More decisively, in the short run at least, than leaving Hannibal, he left the world of safe employment, the world of dry ground, and hit the river for adventure. At age twenty-one, he booked passage on the steamboat *Paul Jones,* out of Cincinnati, bound westward on the Ohio and then down the Mississippi for New Orleans. His plan, manifestly, was to find a seagoing ship that would get him to South America. Unfortunately for his Amazon dreams and Henry Clemens, and fortunately for American literature, the pilot of the *Paul Jones* had a sore foot and a malleable turn of mind. By the time the boat docked at New Orleans eleven days later, Sam had talked his way onto the texas deck, had taken over most of the steering, and had become convinced that his real destiny was to steer riverboats for a living.

The pilot's name was Horace Bixby. A small sturdy man of thirty-one when Sam Clemens made his intrusion, he had a prominent nose, a firmly set mouth, and hair brushed all the way across his head from a low part. He would survive a steamboat explosion near New Madrid, Missouri in 1858, pilot heroically for the Union flotilla during the Civil War, achieve greatness in his trade, and outlive Mark Twain by two years, dying a few months after the *Titanic* sank in 1912, in a St. Louis suburb. Thus he lived to see the full effusion and even share the celebrityhood unleashed by his indulgence of the small, drawling young man suddenly at his elbow on the Ohio River, where the young man was now for the second time being conceived.

In Mark Twain's semifictionalized remembrance of his first encounter with Bixby, he retained the affect of a boy, rather than a twenty-one-year-old man. Once the "ancient tub" is under way downriver, for instance, he was overcome with a boy's exultant sense of being a king, "bound for mysterious lands and distant climes."

> . . . when we stopped at villages and wood-yards, I could not help lolling carelessly upon the railings of the boiler-deck to enjoy the envy of the country boys on the bank. If they did not seem to discover me, I presently sneezed to attract their attention, or moved to a position where they could not help seeing me. And as soon as I knew they saw me I gaped and stretched, and gave other signs of being mightily bored with travelling.[24]

A good deal more revealing than that set-piece bit of cuteness, perhaps, is his revelation a few paragraphs later of his delight in the *language* that washed over him on board—the rich, profane vernacular of the rivermen:

> "Here, now, start that gang-plank for'ard! Lively, now! *What*'re you about! Snatch it! *Snatch* it! There! There! Aft again! aft again! Don't you hear me? Dash it to dash! Are you going to *sleep* over it! '*Vast* heaving. 'Vast heaving, I tell you! Going to heave it clear astern? WHERE're you going with that barrel! *For'ard* with it 'fore I make you swallow it, you dash-dash-dash-*dashed* split between a tired mud-turtle and a crippled hearse-horse!"
>
> I wished I could talk like that.[25]

He could, of course, and did; ultimately such a passage is mimetic Twain, talking. The passage, and many others like it in *Life on the Mississippi*, suggest that Sam Clemens's attraction to the river derived as much from the human language peculiar to the river culture as from the river itself. (Indisputably, he heard money talking as well: river-pilots' "princely" salaries, up to $250 a month, were legendary in the country then, and Sam would forever be drawn to the prospect of the big payday.) River and language, in any case, would soon be conjoined in his creative consciousness. His language would flow like a river; his books, never tightly plotted, would seem instead to follow some mysterious course of their own making—shifting channels, eroding certain boundaries, flooding at times, running nearly dry at others, spilling over capriciously onto the high ground. As for the river itself, he learned to "read" it, and the river became a wonderful book, "a book that was a dead language to the uneducated . . . but which told its mind to me without reserve, delivering its most cherished secrets as clearly as if it had uttered them with a voice."[26]

Twain even seems to drop a prophetic reprimand, a paragraph later, to the literary clinicians of the century to come. An overemphasis of the river as text, he warns, has hazards of its own to give:

> Now when I had mastered the language of this water and had come to know every trifling feature that bordered the great river as familiarly as I knew the letters of the alphabet, I had made a valuable acquisition. But I had lost something, too. I had lost something which could never be restored to me while I lived. All the grace, the beauty, the poetry had gone out of the majestic river![27]

But all that mastery, and all that loss, were yet to come. His first agenda aboard the *Paul Jones* was to somehow meet the pilot and get control of the wheel.

Horace Bixby himself recalled to the biographer Paine that his first awareness of Sam Clemens was as a voice—a "slow, pleasant voice" that spoke up one sunlit day from behind his shoulder as he steered the boat along toward St. Louis. The voice wanted to know whether Bixby would like to teach a young man the river. Bixby thought he wouldn't like it at all. But the voice itself caught his attention. "What makes you pull your words that way?" he remembered asking; and the answer came back, more slowly still and in some way irresistibly comic, "You'll have to ask my mother. She pulls hers, too."[28]

Then the owner of the voice—"a rather slender, loose-limbed young fellow with a fair, girlish complexion and a great tangle of auburn hair"[29]—took a seat on the visitors bench a few feet from the wheel and asked Bixby whether he knew the Bowen brothers. Bixby said he did; he'd supervised Will Bowen's first steering. "A mighty good boy, too. Had a Testament in his pocket when he came aboard; in a week's time he had it swapped for a deck of cards."[30] The auburn-haired youth replied that Will, Sam, and Bart had been schoolmates of his in Hannibal. Bixby asked him whether he drank, gambled, swore, or chewed. The young man replied that he did not. Well, qualify that: in terms of swearing, "Not for amusement; only under pressure."[31] It occurred to Bixby that he could use a little relief for his sore foot. He sat down and let the young man take the wheel. "Keep her as she is—toward that lower cottonwood snag."[32] The Amazon receded; the Mississippi swelled.

It was in New Orleans that Sam launched his plea to Bixby for a position as an apprentice, or cub pilot. Before he did that, he apparently made some last inquiries around town about whether it would be possible to make a boat connection to the Amazon. (It wasn't.) He and Bixby agreed on terms: $500, of which $100 must be paid in advance. (In *Life on the Mississippi*, Mark Twain suggests that the bargaining occurred during a "three-day seige" en route downriver from Cincinnati.) The *Paul Jones* left New Orleans for St. Louis on April 30, where Sam set about rounding up the money. He called on his wealthy distant cousin James Clemens again, and again left without satisfaction: "Before I got to the subject he was wailing about having to pay $25,000 taxes in N.Y. City—said it makes a man poor! So I didn't ask him."[33] Sam was luckier with William A. Moffett, Pamela's husband. He secured a loan, presented it as the deposit, closed the agreement with Bixby, and on May 22, he and his mentor were steaming back down to New Orleans aboard the *Crescent City*, his career as a riverboat pilot contractually underway.

The river distance between St. Louis and New Orleans—Bixby's essential territory—was thirteen hundred miles. Every mile bore its distinct feature: river width, river depth, location of the channel, the presence of underwater snags, rocks, shoals, and previously sunken watercraft, including giant steamers. Sam's first revelation regarding the immensity of his chosen trade was that he would have to memorize the river. Mile by mile. His second revelation was that his education had begun before he knew it—Bixby's habit of mentioning landmarks to him on that first downriver passage had not been a matter of idle chitchat. Mark Twain made great semifictional sport of this—James Cox has likened the episodes to a series of vaudeville acts—in his reminiscences:

> Presently he turned on me and said:—
>
> "What's the name of the first point above New Orleans?"

I was gratified to be able to answer promptly, and I did.
I said I didn't know.[34]

But it wasn't a matter of sport at the time. Sam's third revelation was that he had to memorize the river in both directions: memorize twenty-six hundred miles of river, that is; or, more accurately, memorize two separate rivers, given not only that the visual prospect was utterly different, but also that a boat behaved quite differently with the flow behind it than it did breasting the current.

His fourth revelation was that he had to retain a mental image of the *shape* of the river, the river entire, for there were times when the river's particularized contours could not matter. As Bixby explained: "It is all there is left to steer by on a very dark night. Everything else is blotted out and gone." That was the easy part. "But mind you, it has n't the same shape in the night that it has in the daytime."[35]

The fifth and final revelation, following quickly on the fourth, was that the imprinted shape of the river entire did not matter ultimately anyway, given that the river entire never sustained itself, as Heraclitus saw, from one second to the next. The river's banks were constantly caving in, new channels constantly spilling across dry land, new islands constantly being formed and obliterated, and land that had been Missouri property one day reemerging as a part of Illinois the next.

These revelations may well have been fictionalized compressions of more subtle and complex processes by which Sam Clemens learned the pilot's trade. But to the extent that they are true—and their irreducible truth has not been contradicted by scholarship—they suggest an elemental conversion in Sam's lifelong comprehension of the river.

The river, it was turning out, was never exactly what it appeared to be. The river was a chimera, a memory.

The river that he had known since childhood—the greatest constant in his oft-disrupted life, more enduring even than his family—this river, the Father of Waters—did not, in certain ways of thinking of it, exist. Certainly it did not flow into or out of a world that could be understood in terms of the rational, the predictable, the sunlit. The river was a dream, dark and mystical, forever evanescent, yet forever in terrible control of the lives of mortal men. The dream was dangerous—dangerous water; that's what the leadsman's cry of "mark twain" essentially meant: two marks, two fathoms, twelve feet, the bottom rushing up from the depths to scrape and threaten and capsize the craft. The danger of running aground was his most searing association with the cry of "*Mark* twain":

Then came the leadsman's sepulchral cry:—
  "D-e-e-p four!"
  Deep four in a bottomless crossing! The terror of it took my breath away.
  "M-a-r-k three! . . . M-a-r-k three . . . Quarter less three! . . . Half twain!"
  This was frightful! I seized the bell-ropes and stopped the engines.
  "Quarter twain! Quarter twain! *Mark* twain!"
  I was helpless. I did not know what in the world to do. I was quaking from head to foot, and I could have hung my hat on my eyes, they stuck out so far.
  "Quarter *less* twain! Nine and a *half!*"
  . . . My hands were in a nervous flutter. I could not ring a bell intelligibly with them. I flew to the speaking-tube and shouted to the engineer,—

"Oh, Ben, if you love me, *back* her! Quick, Ben! Oh,
back the immortal *soul* out of her!"[36]

The consummating irony here is that Sam's peril is itself an illusion,
his terror a construct of Horace Bixby's mentoring strategies. The
"crossing"* in this incident was not shallow at all, a fact that Sam had
already committed to memory. Bixby had instructed the leadsman to
call out false depths as a way of testing Sam's courage and his confidence in his own knowledge of the river.

What it may have done, in some incremental way (along with a
thousand other episodes of unreliable perception), is reinforce an
abiding metaphor in Mark Twain's life and work: that things are seldom what they seem, reality and illusion being deeply intertwined.
The river was awash in dualities; it ceaselessly reinvented itself; it
switched identities; it was its own twin, upstream and down. Its deceptively sweet currents masked deeply encoded messages. Its many
interconnected stretches, running fast and slow, straight and curved,
were dialects that needed close attention. Wreckage lay strewn below
the surface. Danger was the only constant of life on the phantasmal
Mississippi; that is to say, of life. And the only question to be asked, in
retrospect, was: *Which Was the Dream?*

---

*A "crossing" was a lateral movement by a pilot seeking to maneuver his boat from
one side of the river to the other in search of the deepest water. Crossings were frequent, and called forth the pilot's greatest navigational skills and most intimate knowledge of the river's varying depths.

Fifteen

"I think a pilot's memory is about
the most wonderful thing in the world."

The dangers of the river are curiously muted in Mark Twain's writings. The man who would come, enraged, to forage through the dark side of nearly everything else of value in his life—his friends, his work, his nation, his god, his faith in man, even (in "The Mysterious Stranger" and "The Man That Corrupted Hadleyburg") his edenic hometown—this same embittered man would never profane the sanctity of the Mississippi. In *Huckleberry Finn,* most of the perils that confront Huck and Jim are the perils of dry land: the feuding Shepardsons/Grangerfords, the murderous Colonel Sherburn, the predatory con artists who come aboard the raft. On the river, they are safe. Even in the latter chapters of *Life on the Mississippi*, the "unnerved terror" and the "miasma of negativity" noticed by critics such as Richard Bridgman[1] have as their referents not the river so much as the America and the world that surround it.

In fact, something like the reverse was the case. While inland America was anything but a peaceable kingdom, its rivers seemed to attract its roughest, most predatory citizens. From Mike Fink and his fellow flatboatmen onward, riverways and their shores were conduits for crime, carnality, and confidence men. All the reckless and violent impulses of the frontier coalesced on the river, where the action was.

Twain's wish for a myth of the river as semi-divine obliged him to avert his gaze from these impulses. (This wish bears intriguing parallels to the prophylactic wishes his daughter, close friends, and biographer nursed for his own posthumous reputation.) His blindered ardency is nowhere more concisely expressed than in the four-paragraph chapter 21 of *Life on the Mississippi*, the one entitled "A Section of My Biography." This is the transitional chapter that conjoins the earlier sections, most of them previously published in *The Atlantic Monthly* in 1875, with the new material that Twain gathered upon his return to the river in 1882.

"I supposed—and hoped—that I was going to follow the river the rest of my days, and die at the wheel when my mission was ended," he writes. "But by and by the war came, commerce was suspended, my occupation was gone."[2] He disposes of the intervening twenty-one "slow-drifting" years of his life in seventy-four words:

> I had to seek another livelihood. So I became a silver miner in Nevada; next, a newspaper reporter; next, a gold miner, in California; next, a reporter in San Francisco; next, a special correspondent in the Sandwich Islands; next, a roving correspondent in Europe and the East; next, an instructional torch-bearer on the lecture platform; and, finally, I became a scribbler of books, and an immovable fixture among the other rocks of New England.[3]

"Let us," he writes at the end of this, "resume now."

But resume what? The four years (April 1857 to May 1861) that Sam spent as a pilot on the Mississippi, by implication the happiest of his life, are also among his least revealed. Only fourteen of his letters are preserved from that time, including four written during his apprentice-pilot period, and two of his notebooks, largely devoted to river minutiae but also containing a little melancholy poetry and some exercises in the French language. Inferential evidence suggests that he became a highly skilled pilot (contrary to the self-lampooning persona that he created in memoirs). But the evidence also suggests that the river culture he cherished was far from the elegant, bucolic, and light-hearted realm that Mark Twain immortalized in his books.

In fact the evidence suggests that in steamboating Sam Clemens descended into a dark demimonde indeed: a substrata of American materialism, greed, vice, and corruption that rivaled and foreshadowed any measure of commercial mendacity the late twentieth century had to offer.

"An economic reality hideous with cut-throat tactics," the historian Bernard DeVoto has called it—"an American commerce without conscience, responsibility or control."[4] The great alabastrine sidewheelers and sternwheelers that crowded the river in that thirty-five-year era have been enshrined in the country's souvenir-ashtray art and in popular memory as "floating palaces," "multi-tiered wedding cakes," "Turkish minarets." In fact they were gilding, as false and mannered as the fantasy architecture coating a twentieth-century shopping mall. As false, and far more dangerous. What the gilding obfuscated was an ongoing tournament of rapacious profiteering, bribery, unenforced standards of safety, and, all too frequently, abrupt, fiery mass death.

The steamboats, owned by wealthy individuals and small companies, were all going after a lucrative but finite universe of commercial freight: cotton, livestock, hay, corn, turpentine, dry goods, light machinery, imported European wines and perfumes, and other luxuries from the docks at New Orleans. Chockablock with the commodities was the human cargo: merchants, touring folk, immigrants, farmers, poor laborers who slept on the main deck; slaves and their masters en route from one condition of bondage to another; gamblers, swindlers, pimps, and prostitutes. "Floating brothels" was a common description that never quite made it to the souvenir ashtrays. "Floating casinos" would have served just as well, and the perfumed, broad-hatted "riverboat gambler" indeed became enshrined in the nation's folklore.

There were few rules, and the owners, who did not themselves typically travel by riverboat, were not especially ardent to play by those few. Often, the captains, pilots, and crew either matched this cynicism or were, at crucial moments, too drunk or absorbed in racing another craft to care. And yet a rough law-and-order system prevailed. Thieves, rapists, brawlers, whores, card-sharks, and other familiar troublemakers could find themselves hauled up before a makeshift jury of their fellow passengers; if "convicted," they faced flogging, being tossed onto the wilderness shore, or running the gauntlet. The ultimate jurist on a riverboat was the captain, and the captain's dispensation could be primitive and terrifying.

These scabrous facts of steamboat life were camouflaged, to some extent, by surface packaging. Superficially, the great boats could be as ornate and rococo as a theme restaurant; their grace-notes wowed the rubes and the paying customers. Sam Clemens of Hill Street in Hannibal was plausibly dazzled by the *Crescent City's* long, gilded saloon, its oil paintings, its prism-fringed chandeliers. He was understandably in awe of another big New Orleans boat's "bright, fanciful 'cuspadores'"[sic], the sumptuous glass temple of its pilot house, and its white-aproned black servant who brought tarts, ices, and coffee to the lounging pilots during mid-watch. But Mark Twain is effectively silent about the pervasive, lethal cost-cutting and the often pitiless attitudes that these showy appointments concealed.

The overall construction of the boats, for example, was often shockingly slapdash. Steamers of up to 350 feet in length—the distance from home plate to the outfield wall in a typical baseball stadium—were made of thin, resinous, dry timber and whitened with turpentine-rich paint that responded incandescently to sparks. This was the experience of the *Ben Sherrod* in 1837, among many others. Headed upriver to Louisville, her captain and crew firing the furnaces in an effort to outrace another boat, the *Ben Sherrod*'s superstructure received one enflamed ember too many. Oblivious to the safety of the two hundred passengers, the captain ordered the ignited boat to continue its upriver surge. By the time the tiller ropes had burned, making steering impossible, the engineer had fled his post and the boat was out of control. Soon the flames had reached the cargo, which included several casks of brandy and several others of gunpowder. When these exploded, the boilers went up. Survivors recalled

> [t]he screams of men, women and children [that] pierced
> the air for miles around while in the bright light that went
> up from the waters the hanging forms of the poor wretches
> as they clung convulsively to the burning sides of the boat
> struck the deepest anguish into the hearts of spectators.[5]

Another steamboat, the *Alton,* churned upriver past the stricken boat, but the pilot was in a hurry and did not stop. In fact an investigating committee found that his craft had run over many people flailing about in the water, and drowned still others with its waves. In all, about 150 of the 200 were lost.

RON POWERS

The boats' similarly thin flat bottoms offered little resistance to
snags, rocks, or the jutting structures of their sunken counterparts. In
1851 the *John Adams*, headed upriver, struck a snag about 200 miles
below Memphis. The impact split the boat's hull in two; it sank almost
instantly, drowning 113 of the 230 people on board.[6]

Bursting boilers were perhaps the major source of catastrophe. The
Moselle, for example, paid a dear price in 1838 for its captain's thought
to put on a splendid show of dashing past the Cincinnati waterfront.
He overheated the fires a bit and made the regrettable mistake of loading down the safety valve. The resulting explosion afforded Cincinna-
tians the spectacle of a steam-and-smoke cloud that rose several
hundred feet in the air, along with debris and fragments of many
human bodies.[7]

The thing about the boilers was that no one could figure out for the
longest time—decades, in fact—just what it was that made them
explode.

In all, some 995 accidents were reported on the Western rivers in
the years 1811–51 alone—the heyday of such occurrences. The average lifespan of a riverboat was four to five years.

The conflagrations, explosions, and snaggings were hardly secret; the
newspapers covered them lavishly. Yet virtually no depiction of the
causative aggression, the cynicism, or the resulting horror appears in
Mark Twain's writings about the river, in fiction or memoir. ("Racing
was royal fun," he wrote fatuously in a chapter devoted to that deadly
pastime.[8]) His typic Victorian reticence might explain the silence regarding the prostitution that flourished there. But sexuality aside, he
was never hesitant to limn human avarice and cruelty in his other
books and essays: the trigger-happy psychopaths and the opium dens

of the West, the macabre dueling societies of Heidelberg, the savagery of King Leopold of the Congo, the greed of the plutocratic robber barons, the iniquities of the Christian God, a thousand other examples. It is the river alone that he held, for the most part, sacrosanct.

It was not a matter of a faulty memory. To be sure, Twain's memory was, in many human ways, flawed. As he aged, he developed an absentmindedness about names, dates, and events. Much of this, however, was less a fading of his faculties than a kind of psychic editing; he was forever revising his life to make it even more interesting and melodramatic than it had been. In most important ways, his recall was extraordinary. His reproduction of human speech, while nearly always revised by his poetic instincts for what the speaker *should have* said, was one of the wonders of the nineteenth century's artistic universe; it prefigured and enabled the great stream of American Southern dialecticians to come, including Faulkner, O'Connor, Welty, and Wolfe, and perhaps even such Yankees as Fitzgerald, O'Hara, and Salinger.

His memory was trained on the river, by Bixby's constant goadings. "To know the Old and New Testaments by heart . . . is no extravagant mass of knowledge," he liked to claim, "compared to a pilot's massed knowledge of the Mississippi and his marvellous [sic] facility in the handling of it."[9]

One possible explanation for this great vacuum in his critical attention is that Mark Twain was complicit in the corruptions of the river as he was complicit in no other topic for his moral satire. (The Wall Street plutocracy, which helped rescue him from bankruptcy in his old age, may be the exception.) The Mississippi River steamboat trade was about money and what money would buy, and Clemens spent his life following money. Along with his fellow pilots, he well appreciated the connection between money and memory: "At the time that wages soared so high on the Missouri River, my chief, Mr. Bixby, went up there and learned more than a thousand miles of that stream with an ease and rapidity that were astonishing."[10] Among the first things he noticed about the grand pilots (as an envious cub) were their polished silk hats, their elaborate shirt fronts, their diamond breastpins, their kid gloves, and their patent-leather boots. Before long, he was showing up on deck in patent-leather boots, blue serge coats, white duck trousers and boldly striped shirts, a French reader or a copy of Tom Paine's *Common Sense* tucked under his arm. And he was "dissipating" with his master Bixby on ten-dollar New Orleans dinners of sheepshead fish, oysters, birds, and mushrooms,[11] washed down presumably with something other than Mississippi ice-water.

As an apprentice and later as a pilot, he found himself at the epicenter of the entire system of money, goods, power, pleasure; he and his skilled, memory-saturated peers at the big spiked wheels were literally what made it all run.

To criticize (or even to feel critical of) the steamboat culture from that vantage point would have been virtually self-negating. It would have been comparable to a truck driver of a later time speaking out against the highway lobby or the moral outrages of driving cross-country on amphetamines. Truck drivers typically sentimentalize their calling, encoding their attitude toward it in the self-lionizing verses of country-western songs. "Old Times on the Mississippi," Twain's series of reminiscences in the Atlantic that form the first half of his 1883 book, are to some limited extent the extended-prose ancestors of the Flying Burrito Brothers hit "Six Days on the Road (And I'm Gonna Make It Home Tonight)."

He reaped another substantial dividend from his river-years, one that he did not hesitate to describe in terms of capital gain:

I am to this day profiting somewhat by that experience; for in that brief, sharp schooling, I got personally and familiarly acquainted with about all the different types of human nature that are to be found in fiction, biography, or history. . . . When I find a well-drawn character in fiction or biography, I generally take a warm personal interest in him, for the reason that I have known him before—known him on the river.[12]

He found there, in other words, the mother-lode of human character: character even more diverse and abject and vivid than he was to encounter in Nevada, the land of the mother lode itself. On the river he found characters who (as has been said of the characters in *The Great Gatsby,* who share subtle affinities) were constantly in the act of self-revelation. Illusion always existed in tension with the hard facts. River characters were blunt prolific talkers, for the most part, giving to Twain's ear the stripped-down, high-velocity pitch that he hurled into the thick upholstery of American letters. River characters talked in jargon, in a thousand jargons: pilots, roustabouts, officers, hustlers, slaves, refined women, unrefined women, Europeans, mystics, soldiers, killers, the clergy. Collectively they offered up a constant bonanza of language and predicament.

Sam may or may not have written it all down—there is little evidence that he did—but he invested it somehow, and when the time came to draw interest, it was all there, waiting. The effect of those years, as DeVoto said, is visible in Mark Twain's perception of the human animal. He imported those effects off the river and into his books. *Tom Sawyer* may have been possible without the river years, but certainly not *Huckleberry Finn, Pudd'nhead Wilson, The Gilded*

Age, The American Claimant, any number of his essays and sketches—
to say nothing of the vast and enigmatic *Life on the Mississippi.* T. S.
Eliot was right in calling him a servant of the river-god.

Little wonder, then, that Mark Twain might have wished to spare
the river the revelations of its sweet sinfulness—or his own sweet sinfulness—on the printed page.

But there is a final reason why Mark Twain might have wanted to
leave the darker reaches of the Mississippi River undisturbed in his
many literary revisitings, a reason connected to the final sorrow of his
youth, a sorrow spawned of fire and water, fire and water out of kilter,
fire and water bringing death.

Sixteen

"... my darling, my pride, my glory, my all ..."

Ripe New Orleans put him in mind of death. It seemed to belong to some other order of things, a city at the end of the river, where the vital current dissipated finally into the infinite vastness. A city of masks and funerals and above-ground cemeteries, "cities of the dead"; of Catholic symbols and bawdy celebrations; a place where Europeans and Africans, slave and free, commingled and made a dense compost of mysticism—New Orleans was a hive of voodoo priests and fortune-tellers, of conjure women who got in touch with the other side.

He prowled the teeming precincts each time his boat docked there, the end of the line. The cemeteries, with their exposed vaults,[1] caught his imagination above everything else. He marveled at them in a letter to Annie Taylor on June 1, after he and Bixby had disembarked the town's namesake boat, the *Crescent City*. He pouted a little about her lack of correspondence, then described his visit to the lushly vegetative French market, with its "pretty pyramids of fresh fruit." Finally, he dwelt on his visit to one of the many distinctive cemeteries in the heart of town: "a veritable little city, for they *bury* everybody *above* ground here." He told Annie about the tiered vaults, twelve feet high and laid off in straight streets, each tier containing several marble tombs where the coffins were inserted endways. "I noticed one beautiful white marble tomb, with a white lace curtain in front of it, under which, on a little shelf, were vases of fresh flowers, several little statuettes, and cups of water. . . . It looked so pretty."* He spent half an hour absorbed in the chameleons that scurried along the tombs, "strange animals, to change their clothes so often!" He teased and prodded one of them under a fresh leaf, "and he turned the brightest green color you ever saw!"

Twenty-five years later, revisiting New Orleans for the composition of his great river book, Mark Twain would not find the cemeteries quite so enchanting. The chameleons were merely reptilian little fly-catchers; their changes of color "are not up to the creature's reputation." He curled his lip at the "immortelles," or black-linen wreaths, that "pious hands" had placed on the tombs of their beloved: "you just hang it up, and there you are; just leave it alone, it will take care of your grief for you, and keep it in mind better than you can; stands weather first-rate, and lasts like boiler-iron."[2] As for the corpses themselves, they gave off unhealthy gases and ought to have been cremated; one could burn a person for four or five dollars and get soap enough out of his ashes to foot the bill. The entire subject of graveyards he found "grotesque, ghastly, horrible."[3]

No letters from Sam survive, beyond the Annie Taylor one, for the next nine months. This was the most intensive period of his cub-piloting experience; he doubtless had little time for correspondence. He continued up and down the Mississippi under Bixby until July,

---

*Underground cemeteries in New Orleans were impossible, given the city ground's high-water table and frequent flooding, which guaranteed that coffins would be waterlogged. The forty-odd "cities of the dead" that still exist there, with their marbled facades and wrought-iron gatings, are world-famous tourist attractions.

then was assigned to a series of other pilots after Bixby decided to try the Missouri River. In his old age his reminiscences of this period call back happy times: moonlight dancing on the boiler-deck, daylight frolics, shipmates who were good-hearted and convivial.

Bixby returned in the fall for a couple of trips with Sam, and then, in November, reassigned him again, this time to a sumptuous boat named the *Pennsylvania*, piloted by a team that included a man named Brown. Each entity proved something other than it might at first have seemed.

The *Pennsylvania* was an elegant behemoth, a 486-ton sidewheeler built in 1854 to carry passengers and mail. River-trade reportage of the time praised its "beautiful proportions" and "magnificent style."[4] Yet for all its harmonious facade, the boat was, in terms of its relationship to its host economy, a predator; a kind of death's-head in disguise. It was owned not by an independent rogue-businessman of the classic antebellum stripe, but by a newer, more extractive sort of corporatized master: the St. Louis, Cairo, and New Orleans Railroad Line. Its function was to provide a river link to an emerging, competitive system of transportation. That system would, in the post–Civil War years, usurp the steamboat economy, vitiate its gaudy, sordid culture, and introduce the nation to a new form of rapacious capitalism. "The unholy train," Mark Twain would call it upon his 1882 return to the river, that ultimately made havoc with his beloved era.

Brown, too, was a figure apart—apart, even, from the hardheaded, cocky run of Mississippi riverboat pilots. It is interesting that "Brown" became a favored fictive name in Mark Twain's travel writings of the 1860s. In his newspaper letters from Hawaii, in his subsequent dispatches en route from California to New York, and in the essays from the *Quaker City* that formed the first draft of *The Innocents Abroad*,

"Brown" is an all-purpose dark-comic foil, a know-it-all evil twin who voices the less palatable of Twain's observations. In his first appearance in *Life on the Mississippi,* it is hard to tell William Brown from Twain's fictionalized device: He is a garrulous windbag who can remember absolutely everything, but understand virtually nothing.

But William Brown of the *Pennsylvania* emerges from stereotype in good time. He becomes as genuine an article as a bolt of lightning on a summer night over Hannibal, foreshadowing God's dark judgment. An "ignorant, stingy, malicious, snarling, fault-finding, mote-magnifying tyrant," as Twain excoriated him. On the evidence, a sadist, if not a psychopath.

Sam's first memorable experience aboard the *Pennsylvania* was a near-catastrophe. The boat collided with the *Vicksburg* a few miles above New Orleans within a couple of weeks after he came onboard. Its starboard wheelhouse knocked askew, it was placed in drydock for repairs that stretched over eleven weeks. Sam spent part of that time as a night watchman on the New Orleans levee. He may have traveled up to St. Louis for the Christmas holidays.

He was aboard the *Pennsylvania* when it left drydock and headed back upriver in February 1858. Again, he flirted with disaster, as he described in a letter to Orion and Mollie Clemens up in Iowa.[5] The Mississippi was clogged with ice. The *Pennsylvania* inched upriver, stopping frequently so the captain could send small sounding boats out to locate the shifting channel. Sam saw duty on several of these expeditions. He struggled along with his mates in the frigid waters, was nearly run over by the parent boat on one occasion; on another, was forced ashore on an island in rain and sleet; on another, labored in the yawl from 4 in the morning until 9:30 at night without benefit of a warming fire. "There was a thick coating of ice over men, yawl, ropes, and everything else," he told Orion and Mollie, "and we looked like rock-candy statuary."[6]

In the very next sentence he reported that he had drawn his younger brother Henry into employment on the *Pennsylvania*.

> Henry was doing little or nothing here [St. Louis], and I sent him to our clerk to work his way for a trip, by measuring woodpiles, counting coal boxes, and other clerkly duties, which he performed satisfactorily. He may go down with us again, for I expect he likes our bill of fare better than that of his boarding house.[7]

Henry was nineteen then. His life is mostly a closed book to history, save through his brother's observations. A photograph made probably in 1858, when he was nearing twenty, shows him ovalfaced, clean-shaven, and pompadoured, with perhaps a trace of baby-fat still in his cheeks. (Beside him, bearded haunted Orion looks positively soignee.) His mouth, not so wide as Sam's rather shapely and sensuous one, is faintly pursed, and his eyes, fixed and serious as they gaze past the camera, have caught the glint of the flash-powder. He is wearing a wide-lapeled coat and a badly knotted bow tie that is too large for his starched whitecollar.

He never traveled on his own; he stuck close to the family. Intelligent, inward, he seems content to have haunted libraries, met obligations, behaved responsibly. What external definition his life had seems mostly to have been supplied by Orion and Sam. Orion could always count on Henry for employment in his ragtag printshop enterprises; Sam, when he was around, would provide companionship, teasing, and the occasional well-aimed watermelon shell.

In the spring of 1858, Sam saw the chance to deepen the newfound friendship with Henry that had begun in Keokuk. Orion and Mollie had left Iowa for Tennessee with their daughter; Orion would study law and try (without luck) to unload the Tennessee land. Henry was more or less stranded in St. Louis, working odd jobs, living at a boarding house, keeping in touch with his sister and mother, who were living in the city.

Getting Henry a position on the *Pennsylvania* was Sam's way of offering the boy an entree to his own exotic world. It was the kind of goodwill gesture that Mark Twain would curse in his old age—or more precisely, the kind of gesture that he would come to behold as cursed.

Henry and Sam made six trips together, in all, aboard the *Pennsylvania*. While Sam continued his pilot's training under Brown, intellectual Henry labored as an unpaid "mud-clerk," hopping off the boat at obscure stops to receive freight, hoping for a promotion up the line of status, to chief clerk, perhaps, or purser.

That spring was at once a demonic and a romantic time for Sam. The despot Brown had worked up a hatred for him, a frothing, hysterical torrent of sarcasm and abuse that seemed to serve as a perverse hobby of his at the wheel. (Apparently Brown sensed a class difference between himself and this son of a slave-owner who had been to school.) His constant hazing and fault-finding etched its way into Sam's nighttime reveries: "I killed Brown every night for months; not in old, stale, commonplace ways, but in new and picturesque ones,— ways that were sometimes surprising for freshness of design and ghastliness of situation and environment."[8]

As if to compensate for this torture, Sam spent that spring and summer in love, and loving what vanished. He sent pressed orange leaves with his letters to Annie Taylor. He searched for Keokuk girls in the French market. Blue-serge'd, white-duck'd, he strutted constantly, on the lookout. And then, as if summoned by a conjure spell, on the New Orleans waterfront, "floating upon my enchanted vision," there was Laura Wright.

Or, perhaps, there was, in Mark Twain's overheated memory of that catastrophic season, simply a dream of Laura Wright.

His memoirs have him encountering this vision one summer night as he invited himself aboard the *John J. Roe,* whose fo'castle the *Pennsylvania's* stern lapped upon putting in at the docks. Sam had been a steersman aboard the *Roe.* He knew its easygoing, jolly crew; a kind of sprawling family, really, of well-off Indiana hayseeds who always had an entourage of larking friends aboard. Joining this circle "was like arriving home at the farmhouse after a long absence."[9]

Laura Wright was among the guests, a judge's daughter. His first glimpse of her staggered Sam, as had his first glimpse of Laura Hawkins/Becky Thatcher in Hannibal. Not quite fifteen, on her first visit away from Missouri, this Laura overwhelmed him with some redolence of home, of purity in this decadent demimonde, of his own fast-receding boyhood. She "had brought with her to these distant regions the freshness and the fragrance of her own prairies."[10] He seems to have sanctified her on the spot—she became his "instantly elected sweetheart"—and forty-eight years later spoke of her with undiminished lyric passion: He could see her still with perfect distinctness "in the unfaded bloom of her youth, with her plaited tails dangling from her young head and her white summer frock puffing about in the wind of that ancient Mississippi time."[11] The passion must have been dangerously real to him; no hint of Laura Wright appears in *Life on the Mississippi,* written while Olivia was still alive.

Sam made some time for her. "I was not four inches from that girl's elbow during our waking hours for the next three days." In his dreamy recall he turned the parting into a theatrical *grand jete*, worthy of Sir Walter Scott (or Erroll Flynn): "Then there came a sudden interruption. Zeb Leavenworth came flying aft shouting, 'The *Pennsylvania* is backing out.' I fled at my best speed . . . made a flying leap and just did manage to make the connection, and nothing to spare. My toes found room on the guard; my finger-ends hooked themselves upon the guard-rail, and a quartermaster made a snatch for me and hauled me aboard."[12] In the dream, it became the last time he ever saw her.

Scholars have kept a wary distance between themselves and Mark Twain's salving dream. They have sensed the writer's famous mythifying imagination at work. That leap from boat to boat has struck the scholarly mind as awfully . . . convenient. The biographer John Lauber has stated categorically that the *Roe* and the *Pennsylvania* did not tie up together on the New Orleans waterfront that spring,[13] although his footnotes provide no substantiation of that.

And yet a Laura Wright there most assuredly was. And if Sam was guilty of falsely placing her aboard the *Roe,* Laura suffered under the same delusion. In a letter to him nearly half a century on, she described a frightening episode on the *Roe's* subsequent upriver journey: The boat struck a snag; an evacuation was ordered; one of the pilots discovered that Laura was not among the passengers massed for rescue. Knocking on her stateroom door, Laura's uncle and a mate heard her reply "quite calmly" that something was the matter with her hoop skirt and she would not come out until she had repaired it. "She kept her word and came ashore at her leisure, completely dressed."[14]

An entry in Sam's own notebook, dated May 6, reads: "This date, 1858, parted from L. Who said 'We shall meet again 30 years from now.'"[15] But they never did. Sam wrote to her; her mother probably intercepted the letters. A New Orleans fortune-teller described Laura to him with amazing accuracy in 1861. He wrote to Orion about that encounter, but added that even though Laura would always fault him for the impasse, he would not be the first to speak. Hurt pride prevented him from closing the gap between them, as hurt pride had prevented Jane Lampton from coming forward to her true love.

Two aftershocks renewed the pain of Laura. The first occurred in 1880 when he received a worshipful letter from a schoolboy in Dallas named Wattie Bowser, who wrote that "Mr. Twain" was the great man with whom he would most like to change places—would Mr. Twain be willing to trade off with him and become a boy again? Wattie's postscript jolted Twain: "Our principal used to know you, when you were a little boy and she was a little girl, but I expect you have forgotten her, it was so long ago." The principal's name was Laura Dake—the former Laura Wright. The great author's response was passionate and torrential. Yes, he would change places, if he could "emerge from boyhood as a 'cub pilot' on a Mississippi boat and become a pilot, and remain one." He would stipulate an eternal summer, with the oleanders in bloom and the sugar cane green, and a crew that would never change . . . and never die.[16]

The second aftershock hit twenty-six years later, during his *Autobiography* dictations. Within a few days after Mark Twain had found himself thinking and talking about Laura once more, he was stunned to receive a letter from her—a "world-worn and trouble-worn widow of sixty-two."[17] She needed money; money for herself and for her disabled son, who was thirty-seven. He sent her a thousand dollars, and wailed at the fiendishness of the world.

It was in her return letter of thanks that Laura told Twain about the *Roe's* snagging and her hoop-skirt crisis.

Within a few weeks after his initial discovery of Laura, death reasserted itself in young Sam Clemens's thoughts, with a dream of Henry inside a metal coffin.

At least he remembered that he did. Once again, the mythmaking habits of the aging writer seem a likely explanation for this fantasy of foreshadowing—as do the tendencies of traumatized people to transpose images of a tragedy to a time before the event. But here again, evidence disallows easy rationalizing: Annie Moffett, Pamela's young daughter, later recalled that Sam had spoken of the dream the morning after it supposedly occurred.

The dream, if it happened, probably happened around the first of June. The two brothers were in St. Louis for a three-day layover—Sam lodging at the Moffett household, Henry sleeping onboard the boat so as to be ready for his early-morning duties. Mark Twain's reconstruction of the dream did not lack for particulars.

> . . . I had seen Henry a corpse. He lay in a metallic burial case. He was dressed in a suit of my clothing and on his breast lay a great bouquet of flowers, mainly white roses, with a red rose in the center. The casket stood upon a couple of chairs.

The dream was so real to Sam that he had finished dressing and walked toward the door of the sitting room where he thought the coffin to be before changing his mind about entering: "I thought I could not yet bear to meet my mother. I thought I would wait awhile and make some preparation for that ordeal."[18] Not until he had left the Moffett house and walked a full block outdoors did he comprehend that the image of the coffin had been a dream. "I can still feel something of the grateful upheaval of joy of that moment."[19] But he also felt a lingering doubt, so he dashed back to the house, bounded up the stairs and into the sitting room, "and was made glad again, for there was no casket there."[20]

Later that day the *Pennsylvania* left the port at St. Louis and steamed south for New Orleans.

It was on this voyage that the pilot William Brown turned his sadistic attentions from Sam to Henry Clemens.

The seeds of the confrontation were planted sometime in the morning of June 3. It would have been the beginning of high summer on the river; of hot days, long lingering twilights; of lightning-bugs and mosquitoes thickening the shoreline at night, and the river itself heavy with scent. On this morning the boat was passing along the bluffs of the state of Mississippi to the east, the grassy swamplands of Louisiana to the west. Brown was at the wheel. Sam was in the pilothouse with him. Henry stepped into view on the hurricane deck to relay an order from the boat's captain, John S. Klinefelter, to stop at a plantation a short distance downstream. A stiff wind was blowing and Brown, whom Twain recalled as being deaf but unwilling to acknowledge it, gave no indication that he had heard the boy's message. Sam, who had heard it, elected not to speak.

As the boat steamed past its requested stop, Klinefelter swung out on deck and gave the order to come about, adding, in Twain's recollection, "Did n't Henry tell you to land here?" Brown snapped that

Henry had appeared, but "He never said anything." The captain turned to Sam: "Did n't *you* hear him?"

Here was a horrifying dilemma for Sam. To contradict Brown would be to invite retribution from a dangerous enemy. In the compacted universe of the western riverboat of the 1850s, the pilot enjoyed a sovereignty as absolute, in proportion, as any person of power in America. Tradition held that not even a boat's captain, not even the owner himself, could preempt a pilot's authority once the boat was under steam and the pilot had control of the wheel. On the other hand, to deny that he had heard Henry's message would be a bald betrayal of his brother. In a moment as fraught with moral significance as Huck Finn's decision to lie about Jim and "go to hell," Sam opted for the truth—and consigned himself, over the torments of his lifetime, to the same hot place. He said: "Yes, sir."

Brown's instant retort was: "Shut your mouth! You never heard anything of the kind."[21]

The inevitable payback came an hour later. Mark Twain put the location at a stretch on the Mississippi called Eagle Bend, near Pawpaw Island, about eighteen miles upriver from Vicksburg.[22] Henry entered the pilothouse, oblivious to the tension that had been building. Brown pounced on him.

> "Here! Why did n't you tell me we'd got to land at that plantation?"
> "I did tell you, Mr. Brown."
> "It's a lie!"
> I said:—
> "You lie yourself. He did tell you."[23]

This outburst of Sam's—his second direct challenge of Brown—un-hinged the pilot. He stared at Sam, then turned to Henry and ordered him out of the pilothouse. Mark Twain recalled that as the boy started to leave, Brown snatched a heavy lump of coal and made as if to hit him with it; "but I was between, with a heavy stool, and I hit Brown a good honest blow which stretched him out."[24] Then Sam fell upon his tormentor and pounded him with his fists—the only act of physical violence for which Samuel Clemens was ever known. The struggle on the floor lasted perhaps five minutes. A crowd gathered on the hurricane deck to watch it. While all this was happening, the 486-ton *Pennsylvania* wafted along in the current, fifteen miles an hour, with no one at the wheel to control its rudders.

William Brown eventually struggled out from beneath the pummeling Sam and grabbed the wheel. Luckily, the steamboat was drifting down the middle of a deep channel in a full river. After he had stabilized the boat, Brown raged at Sam to leave the pilothouse, brandishing a spyglass. Sam elected to stay awhile, mocking the man he had just humiliated. This moment irresistibly calls Charlie Chaplin to mind; the Tramp, having gained the edge over some bullying authority-figure, sticking around to rub it in a little before hotfooting it to safety. ("I tarried, and criticised [sic] his grammar; I reformed his ferocious speeches for him, and put them into good English, calling his attention to the advantage of pure English over the bastard dialect of the Pennsylvanian collieries whence he was extracted . . . "[25])

Captain Klinefelter was waiting for him beside the door. He led Sam into a small parlor and grilled him about the brawl. Mark Twain recalled that after he had confessed to flattening Brown and then pummeling him ("I supposed I was booked for the penitentiary sure"), the captain surprised him by announcing his sympathy for the attack.

> I'm deuced glad of it! Hark ye, never mention that I said that. You have been guilty of a great crime; and don't you ever be guilty of it again, on this boat. *But*—lay for him ashore! Give him a good sound thrashing, do you hear? I'll pay the expenses. Now go—[26]

In the end it was Sam and Henry who paid the expenses. With the inevitability of Greek drama, the consequences of Sam's fight with William Brown—and of Sam's two outbursts of truth-telling on Henry's behalf, which guaranteed the confrontation—began to spread themselves through the brothers' destinies, like pent-up water rushing through a sluice-gate that has been opened.

Brown, coming off his watch, confronted Klinefelter and demanded that "*one* of us—either himself or Sam—be put ashore immediately. (Obviously, he assumed that Sam would be the one removed from the boat.) "Very well," Klinefelter replied, "Let it be yourself."[27] His bluff called, Brown stalked back to the pilothouse. If any faint hope had existed for repairing the standoff between himself and Sam, none existed now.

In New Orleans, Klinefelter searched for a pilot to replace Brown on the return voyage upriver. After three days he had not succeeded. Brown made it clear that he would not set foot aboard a boat that included Sam Clemens. The *Pennsylvania*'s captain offered another solution: He would arrange passage to St. Louis for Sam aboard another boat, the *A. T. Lacey*. Once in St. Louis, Klinefelter would replace Brown and restore Sam to his position as steersman. Henry, unobtrusive as always, would remain on board the *Pennsylvania.* All concerned parties agreed.

The last night that Sam and Henry were to spend together was a languorous evening of intimate conversation on a freight pile on the riverfront in ripe New Orleans. Whatever passed between them on that night became enfolded, along with the Laura Wright encounter and the dream of Henry in the metallic burial case, into the operatic remembrance that Mark Twain reconstructed, episodically, over the remainder of his life, most conspicuously in *Life on the Mississippi* and in his autobiographical dictations. Like other elements in this intensely braided and textured libretto of the early river summer of 1858, the objective truth of it can never be fully known. Twain himself never conjoined all the remarkable, highly suggestive subplots of those fateful weeks into a unified narrative; the elements of his foredoomed romance with Laura and of his struggle with Brown, as sub-verses in the great threnody for his brother, remain sequestered in two separate texts, their resonating metaphors never integrated by him into the whole.

As to that final evening together on the freight pile:

> The subject of the chat, mainly, was one which I think we had not exploited before—steamboat disasters. One was then on its way to us, little as we suspected it; the water which was to make the steam which should cause it, was washing past some point fifteen hundred miles up the river while we talked;—but it would arrive at the right time and the right place . . . we decided that if a disaster ever fell within our experience we would at least stick to the boat, and give such minor service as chance might throw in the

way. Henry remembered this, afterward, when the disaster came, and acted accordingly.[28]

Henry left New Orleans on the *Pennsylvania* the next morning. The *A.T. Lacey* pulled out two days later, on June 11, with Sam aboard. Among its pilots was Barton Bowen, Will's brother.

It was at Greenville, Mississippi, two days afterward, that Sam received the first intimation of tragedy. A stranger on the levee was shouting: "The *Pennsylvania* is blown up at Ship Island, and a hundred fifty lives lost!"[29] The date was June 13, Henry Clemens's twentieth birthday.

At Napoleon, Arkansas, the *Lacey* crew found copies of a Memphis newspaper, an "extra" edition that reported some details. Henry Clemens's name was listed; he was described as unhurt.

Farther along, another extra surfaced. This one reported, as Mark Twain recalled, that Henry was "hurt beyond help."[30]

The *Lacey* steamed on, upriver. Within a hundred miles of Memphis its crew began to see more direct evidence of catastrophe: debris from the *Pennsylvania*'s superstructure, and human corpses carried along in the current.

The explosion had occurred about four miles upriver from Ship Island, some seventy miles below Memphis, at around 6 a.m. on Sunday the thirteenth. Apparently the *Pennsylvania* had engaged in a race with a rival steamboat, and had just taken on a load of wood for fuel-burning in preparation for another race: The firemen on board were tossing pine-knots and coal into the furnace—despite knowledge that at least one of the ship's boilers suffered a bad leak.

Four boilers went up in the initial outburst, splintering the forward third of the boat, including the pilothouse. The sudden nebula of steam killed the firemen and many of the passengers on deck. No one who breathed the scalding vapor survived. Most of the deaths* occurred in this opening instant. The pilot William Brown went flying into the Mississippi on a trajectory of steam. He was seized by a coal-boat pilot named Reed Young, who had hold of a life preserver, but he died in Young's arms, muttering, "My poor wife and children."[31]

Captain Klinefelter was sitting in a barber's chair when the boilers blew, waiting for a shave. He was unhurt, but the released energy tore a gigantic hole in the floor directly behind his chair; in front of it the barber stood for several seconds after the impact, "still stirring his lather unconsciously, and saying not a word."[32] A priest was impaled with a crowbar and died horribly. The fifteen-year-old son of a French admiral, wrote Twain, "was fearfully scalded, but bore his tortures manfully."[33]

Many people were killed, hurt, or trapped by the debris launched into the air by the explosion as it fell back on the boat. Another pilot, a gentle Shakespeare-reading friend of Sam's named George Ealer, escaped serious injury when the boat's heavy pilot-wheel landed near him. In shock, Ealer collected the pieces to his chess set and the joints of his flute before disembarking the stricken boat.

Henry Clemens had been sleeping in a stateroom directly above the boilers. Like Brown, he was propelled into the river by the blast. Unlike Brown, he did not die right away.

---

*No one knows how many people were killed in this explosion; the loss of the ship's register and the many immigrants traveling on "deck passage" have made a precise tabulation impossible. Mark Twain himself, perhaps going on the early newspaper estimates, reported three hundred lives lost. Captain Klinefelter put the number at thirty-eight. Other estimates ranged between twenty and one hundred-sixty. The editors of *Mark Twain's Letters, Vol. 1,* have suggested that "eighty to one hundred deaths seems a reasonable estimate," although they acknowledge that the total could have been much higher.

Exactly what happened to Henry, and to the *Pennsylvania,* after those first concussive moments are matters of confusion, conflicting testimony, and, perhaps, Mark Twain's compulsive search for meaning within patterns, howsoever those patterns needed to be invented. The onset of the fire, for instance: Twain wrote that fire broke out on what remained of the boat "after a little." At least one other contemporary report had the conflagration starting within a minute after the boilers exploded. But George C. Harrison, the son of the owner of the wood-yard landing where the steamboat had just taken on fuel, told a newspaper that the fire did not take hold "for some thirty or forty minutes (perhaps longer) after the explosion,"[34] which allowed the Harrisons and others time to evacuate a number of passengers and crew—nearly two hundred onto the Harrison wood-boat alone.

Everyone agreed, though, that when the fire began, it spread—in Harrison's words—"with the greatest rapidity."[35] Soon the super-structure was a burning mass, intensely heated. Twain wrote of a "striker" unhurt but imprisoned in the debris: "when he saw that the fire was likely to drive away the workers, he begged that some one would shoot him, and thus save him from the more dreadful death . . . [rescuers] had to listen to this poor fellow's supplications till the flames ended his miseries."[36] The image of the Tramp imprisoned in the burning Hannibal jail could not have been far from Twain's mind as he wrote these lines.

Then there was the uncertain matter of Henry's fate once he hit the water. In a letter written from Memphis, Sam told his relatives, some-what ambiguously, that Henry had first fallen back on the hot boilers, then was bombarded by falling rubbish, and that finally he "got into the water and swam to shore, and got into the flatboat with the other survivors."[37] (Why Henry would have climbed into the flatboat after reaching shore was not explained.) In a tribute to Henry published a few weeks after the disaster, Sam repeated the image of Henry falling back on the boilers, then "extricating himself" and escaping on a mattress or raft to an open rescue boat, "where he lay exposed . . . to the wind and the scorching rays of a Southern sun, for eight hours . . . "[38]

By the time of *Life on the Mississippi,* written mostly in 1882, Mark Twain had finally distilled his version, or vision, of Henry's fate:

> When Mr. Wood [another clerk] and Henry fell in the water, they struck out for shore, which was only a few hundred yards away; but Henry presently said he believed he was unhurt (what an unaccountable error!) and therefore would swim back to the boat and help save the wounded. So they parted, and Henry returned.

Thus Twain consummated, in his art, the conversation Henry and Sam had had on the freight pile in New Orleans the night before the *Pennsylvania* disembarked.

Whatever his actions, Henry was eventually loaded with other survivors onto the steamer *Kate Frisbee* and transported the sixty miles to Memphis. There, nearly a full day after the explosion, they were placed on mattresses in a vast makeshift hospital inside the Memphis Exchange and attended by volunteer doctors and nurses. This is how Sam found Henry when he arrived at Memphis on Tuesday, June 15. After viewing his brother, Sam sent a terse telegraph—in which his last name was misspelled—to the Moffett household in St. Louis:

> Henrys recovery is very doubtful [signed] Sam Clements[39]

A local newspaper reporter was present when Sam rushed into the Memphis Exchange. His account of Sam's reaction told of the depths of agony beneath that terse information:

> We witnessed one of the most affecting scenes at the Exchange yesterday that has ever been seen. The brother of Mr. Henry Clemens, second clerk of the *Pennsylvania*, who now lies dangerously ill from the injuries received by the explosion of that boat, arrived in the city yesterday afternoon, on the steamer *A. T. Lacy* [sic]. He hurried to the Exchange to see his brother, and on approaching the bedside of the wounded man, his feelings so much overcame him, at the scalded and emaciated form before him, that he sunk to the floor overpowered. There was scarcely a dry eye in the house; the poor sufferers shed tears at the sight. This brother had been pilot on the *Pennsylvania*, but fortunately for him, had remained in New Orleans when the boat started up.[40]

That phrase, "fortunately for him," and its variants would enflame Sam Clemens/Mark Twain's torture in the years to come. Beginning while he was still watching over his brother, and continuing upon his return to the river several weeks later, Sam found himself festooned with a new nickname in honor of his evasion of the catastrophe: "Lucky."

Lucky? Lucky that he would have to live on with the memory of coaxing his younger brother out of his libraries and onto the *Pennsylvania?* Lucky to live with the twisted consequences of his fight with Brown—his own saving removal from the doomed boat while Henry, whom he'd sought to save, churned upriver to his oblivion? No, Sam was not lucky. Sam was responsible. He was as responsible for Henry's death as he had been for the death of his brother Ben in his enigmatic "treachery" to him; as responsible as he had been for the drownings of Dutchy and "Lem Hackett" as revealed in the prophetic lightning over Hannibal; as responsible as he had been for the incineration of the tramp. Among all the American national tendencies that Mark Twain embodied, or became enmeshed in, perhaps none was more gothically emblematic than this one: the tendency to run afoul of the law of unintended consequences, to see one's innocent magnanimous impulses converted bewilderingly to flaming devastation.

No, "luck" was not the point of his survival. The point was culpability, the annealing of his guilty conscience and the beginning of a lifelong flight from incarceration inside his damned human self.

Luck? Luck—or envy—was the privilege of the dead, as he pointed out in a torrent of dark aphorisms late in his life. "Whoever has lived long enough to find out what life is, knows how deep a debt of gratitude we owe to Adam, the first benefactor of our race. He brought death into the world," Mark Twain would write, and: "Why is it that we rejoice at a birth and grieve at a funeral? It is because we are not involved," and: "All say, 'How hard it is that we have to die'—a strange complaint to come from the mouths of people who have had to live."[41]

He unleashed a strong foretaste of this anguished self-recrimination in a letter from Memphis to Mollie Clemens on Friday, June 18, while Henry still lay critically ill:

Long before this reaches you, my poor Henry,—my darling, my pride, my glory, my all, will have finished his blameless career, and the light of my life will have gone out in utter darkness.

*O, God! This is hard to bear. Hardened, hopeless,—aye, lost—
lost—lost and ruined sinner as I am—I, even I, have humbled myself to the ground and prayed as never man prayed before, that the
great God might let this cup pass from me—that he would strike
me to the earth, but spare my brother—that he would pour out the
fulness [sic] of his just wrath upon my wicked head, but have
mercy, mercy, mercy upon that unoffending boy . . . poor wretched
me, that was once so proud, was humbled to the very dust—lower
than dust—for the vilest beggar in the streets of St. Louis could
never conceive a humiliation like mine. Men take me by the hand
and congratulate me, and call me "**lucky**" because I was not on
the Pennsylvania when she blew up! May God forgive them, for
they know not what they say!*[42]

Henry died at about dawn on June 21. Sam, nearly out of his mind
with grief, rested a few hours at a private home, then accompanied his
brother's body to St. Louis via steamer. A young man from Memphis
went along to look after Sam. Orion hurried home from Jamestown,
Tennessee. Jane Clemens and the Moffetts joined the cortege that
bore the body to Hannibal, where he was buried on June 25 in the
Baptist cemetery on the top of the hill, next to John Marshall. In 1876
both bodies were transferred to the new Mount Olivet cemetery south
of town, above the river.

In his old age, Mark Twain recalled (or, more probably, invented) yet
another layer of pathos surrounding the loss, another reason for self-
flagellation and guilt. Henry had not died from his scalding wounds,
but from a misdosage of medication; and the bumbler who commanded that misdosage was Sam Clemens. The sequence, in Twain's

mind, was as follows: A Memphis doctor named Thomas F. Peyton had paid special attention to Henry through the week of his suffering. Though Sam's letters at the time mention nothing of it, his reverie convinced him that Dr. Peyton, "a fine and large-hearted old physician of great reputation in the community," had succeeded in bringing Henry out of danger. Peyton then suggested that, in order to assure Henry's peaceful sleep, Sam ask the physician on watch to administer an eighth of a grain of morphine to the boy. The physicians, "young fellows hardly out of college," botched the dosage, giving Henry "a vast quantity heaped on a knife-blade." This proved to be the fatal stroke. If only Sam had not insisted on that morphine . . . [43]

There was the final matter of the consummation of the dream.

While Sam slept off his fatigue in the private home (as he recalled it in his memoirs) something was happening at the Memphis Exchange. Most of the dead victims had been placed in unpainted coffins of white pine, but Henry had been a favorite with the women volunteers, and they had made up a fund of sixty dollars and bought a metallic case. When Sam returned to the Exchange and saw Henry, he recognized his dream, reproduced. Henry was even wearing Sam's clothes.

> And I think I missed one detail; but that one was immediately supplied, for just then an elderly lady entered the place with a large bouquet consisting mainly of white roses, and in the centre of it was a red rose, and she laid it on his breast.[44]

Sam Clemens's youth ended with the consummation of that dream. His boyhood was buried in the coffin with Henry. Nothing of his correspondence survived the ensuing nine months. He returned to the river about a month after the funeral and remained on it until the Civil War interrupted steamboat traffic there. He piloted with various of the Bowen brothers; haunted New Orleans and immersed himself in Mardi Gras; applied for membership in the Masons and was accepted; saw a fortuneteller regarding Laura Wright. He departed the riverlife in St. Louis in May 1861, stepping off the *Nebraska*, the last boat to enjoy free passage upriver through the Union blockade at Memphis. He hid out at the Moffett home, fearing arrest by Union agents; joined the Confederate volunteer group, the Marion Rangers, in mid-June; lasted two weeks; then lit out west with Orion, who had been appointed secretary of the Nevada Territory in a document signed by Abraham Lincoln. There he prospected for silver and gold, found none, set a mountain on fire, drank heavily, never spoke of the War nor of Henry, took up with a proto-countercultural enclave of wild and gifted journalists in Virginia City, and became the central figure in their improvisation of a surreal, fabricating, fabulating new form of newspapering that received attention and reproduction back East.

In the Territory, on February 3, 1863, a month after Lincoln announced the Emancipation Proclamation, Sam Clemens found emancipation from his own enslavement of the soul. At age twenty-eight he discovered and entered into his immortal pseudonym, Mark Twain. Something in this name released him from himself; the alias took the function of a magical mask, or a gorgeous puppet, through which he could address the world in voices not identifiably his own. As "Mark Twain," he would invent a new literature borne on the currents of dialect, but in its deepest fathoms concerned with a kind of resurrection: the resurrection of humor from the abyss of pathos, hostility, tragedy, and loss. Sweet Henry, so silent in life, would speak forever through his brother's pen. Among Mark Twain's most recurrent themes would be twinning—the diverging but inextricable fates of brothers; the perverse fortunes of switched identity; the unstable boundaries between dream and reality; the dialectic between innocence and fallen man. The first sentence of the first essay he published under his new pen name read: "I feel very much as if I had just awakened out of a long sleep." He had indeed awakened, emerged as from a dream into his genius. In "Mark Twain" he had found his frame; in his lifelong flight from the melancholy of Henry's flowered metal casket, and from his childhood, and from the nighttime terrors of Hannibal's embrace, he had become his own tall tale.

Seventeen

"I . . . bid you farewell."

On May 29, 1902, a year and a half after his return to America, Mark Twain reentered the long dark dream of his boyhood and visited Hannibal for the last time.

He was sixty-six. At the height of his public celebrity, he was likewise at the height of his private ruminations on the pain of existence. He had been working on the baleful "Extracts from Adam's Diary" and "The Death Disk"; the outlines of "The Mysterious Stranger" had entered his fantasies; "Amended Obituaries" and "Was It Heaven? Or Hell?" would see print before the year's end.

On this last week of May 1902, Mark Twain was ascendant as few men in history, and no literary figure, had ever been ascendant. He was a known figure throughout the world. Before the gaze of the nations, he had circled the globe and raised a fortune with his lectures to pay his creditors and erase his stupendous bankruptcy. He had been translated into all the important languages. He had met Freud in Vienna and had a private audience with the Austrian emperor Franz-Joseph. He had been compared to Cervantes, Shakespeare. Prestigious Howells had called him "sole, incomparable . . . the Lincoln of our literature." Oxford waited to drape him in its robes. People wanted his autograph. The dukes and dauphins of the world made risky fortunes claiming his identity.

In his native land, which he had mythified for a previously skeptical world, it had been even more intense. He had become the first public man to cause frenzy on the streets, to trigger the release of an American obsession that, once released, would renew its energies again and again, like a rage against the absence of the numinous in a democracy. This was the obsessive need to worship a secular god.

His world and his new century were still sunlit. Marchese Marconi was working toward the transmission of the first transatlantic radio signal. The Wright Brothers were working toward liftoff at Kitty Hawk. Halley's Comet was hurtling toward the solar neighborhood. The first World Series was a little more than a year away.

He had been invited to receive an honorary degree from the University of Missouri at Columbia on June 4. Still, his preliminary detour to Hannibal was unannounced; he wrote to no one there in advance of his coming.

In 1902 Hannibal was a far more ambitious burg than the white town drowsing in the sunshine of a summer's morning that Sam Clemens had languished through in the 1840s. It was a railroad center—John Marshall's dream, consummated—and stout red brick had replaced most of the white clapboard. Its population had reached 12,500 and was climbing. It was a city of merchants and manufacturers; cement; shoes; the Bluff City (a boosterish salute to the embrasure of hills). A city quite proud, thank you, to trumpet Mark Twain as its foremost native son. Perhaps that is why he did not communicate in advance.

He slipped into town on a late-afternoon weekday train from St. Louis, accompanied by an awed book reviewer from the *Post-Dispatch* named Robertus Love. The newspaper had given Love the assignment of following Twain around Hannibal and writing up the "color" of the visit; and Love filed dispatches reporting virtually his every movement and inflating every nuance.

> Hannibal had no idea that Mark Twain was coming when he did. . . . "If we had known he was aboard that train," remarked a citizen, "the Union Depot platform would not have been big enough to hold the chairmen of committees."[1]

Twain walked the single block from the train station to the Windsor Hotel,* where he had booked a room. Love trailed along, alert for comic byplay, which the great man indulgently provided:

Will Sutton, the hotel clerk, remarked:

> "Mr. Clemens, I was born close to your birthplace at Florida, and have been in the house where you were born, often."
>
> "I was not born often—only once," responded the humorist; "but I'm glad to see you, all the same."[2]

The next morning he presented himself before the house at 206 Hill Street and certified its landmark status by proclaiming it his boyhood residence. He posed for a photographer in its front door in a

---

*The Windsor stood at 125 South Main, just a block from where the Mark Twain Hotel would rise three years later. It lasted until 1962, when it was torn down for a parking lot.

light gray suit, hands thrust into his jacket-pockets; the resulting image would continue to be reproduced on postcards throughout the century. Then he entered a carriage in the company of a wealthy widow named Helen Garth and was driven to Mt. Olivet Cemetery overlooking the Mississippi, where he viewed the gravesites of Jane, who had died in 1890, and John Marshall, and Orion, and Henry.

"It is very beautifully situated, that cemetery," he told Robertus Love upon returning to the hotel. "If I had the time I should look for the boys out there." He meant the boys of his youth. "That is where they are . . . most of them are out there in that cemetery. I could pick them out if I had the time to walk about and read their names."[3]

By this time an entourage had gathered. Old men crowded into the hotel office to announce their names to him and make their claims of boyhood friendship. Some of these, he recognized.

"How are you doing, Eddie?" he inquired of Mr. Pierce.

"Like yourself, Sam," replied the schoolmate, "like a cow's tail going down."[4]

A mob was waiting for him at the Farmers and Merchants Bank, where a reception had been arranged. More old chums pled for recognition.

"Hello, Sam," said one old man; "I'm Lippincott, and used to play marbles with you, but probably you remember my brother, Dave Lippincott." Mr. Clemens could not recall the Lippincotts.

"You and Dave and I and Charley Buchanan used to—"

"Ah, Charley Buchanan," said the humorist. "Yes, indeed. I remember Charley."[5]

He told everyone he would make a speech if he could think of a topic. And then he went off to a ceremony at Jane's old Presbyterian church. That evening he distributed some diplomas to the Hannibal High School graduating class of 1902.

The town had quickly worked itself into a frenzy over his presence. By Friday afternoon the populace had begun to costume itself in his honor—as it would continue to do episodically for the next hundred years. Robertus Love took it all in.

> Today Hannibal is full of Huck Finns, Tom Sawyers and Beckys.
>
> There are more "originals" of Huck, Tom and Becky in this town since Mark Twain arrived than one would expect to meet in a staid old town with 23 respectable Sunday schools and a Salvation Army.
>
> You don't need to bait your hook if you go fishing for a Huck. Just make a cast anywhere around town, and there's your Huckleberry.

Love encountered the obligatory citizen who didn't get it.

> "I've lived in this town 71 years," remarked one reputable native, "and forever was accused of being Huck Finn until last night. I submit that my reputation has been good, and if I ever was Huckleberry Finn, I can't recall it. It's a base slander to put upon a man in his old age."[6]

On Friday evening, Hannibal's jamboree of costumery and role-playing in its native son's honor reached a surreal apogee. In a staged encounter of multiple identities, the kind of stroke that would have sealed a publicist's career nine or ten decades in the future, Mark Twain/Samuel Clemens/Tom Sawyer sat down to dinner with Laura Frazier/Laura Hawkins/Becky Thatcher.

In describing the event, the *Post-Dispatch* reporter fell into a moist swoon of rhetoric—of "showing off."

> Sam Clemens and Laura Hawkins, both aged 15, ate dinner together Friday evening. They were guests of Mrs. Helen Garth, at her costly mansion on South Fifth Street.
>
> Sam, who in the future is destined to be one Mark Twain, genial humorist and one of the most famous men in the world, and Laura Hawkins, whose star of fortune reads that she will become the Widow Frazier and serve as matron for the Home of the Friendless in Hannibal—these two, playmates in 1840, schoolmates in 1845, and pledged sweethearts in this present year of 1850—met Friday evening at dinner, with Mrs. Garth as chaperone.
>
> Strange to say, Sam was staying at the Windsor Hotel on Main street instead of at his mother's house on Hill street. This Hannibal boy of 15 was reveling in the splendors of two connecting rooms, with a whole bed to himself and also a wardrobe for his clothes.
>
> Just why he left home the Hannibal people—the whole 700 of them—are not quite sure, but it is hinted at Brittingham's drug store, around the corner from the Widow Clemens' house, that Sam has found at last a large quantity of the buried treasure in Loop Hollow, north of Holliday's hill, and is enjoying the luxuries . . . [7]

. . . And so on. Twain, ever the trouper, entered the spirit of the moment, played out the role. Upon his first glimpse of his former playmate, he cried out, "Gee whiz—it seems like I ain't seen you in 50 years, Laura."

Later, Twain received a delegation from the high school graduating class in the parlors of the Windsor Hotel; they presented him with a souvenir spoon that bore an engraving of the house on Hill Street. As he looked at the image of the house on the spoon, Twain was moved for some reason to remember his boyhood attempt to contract measles from Will Bowen. He recounted for the young people, who were conceivably unprepared for such a story, how he had jumped from the upper window of his bedroom into a pile of sand, and from there had run to the infected Bowen house.

"I was very near to death," he told the group, "and I have never had such a good opportunity to die. Sometimes I think I should have embraced the opportunity, thereby escaping many unpleasant things. But I have survived to enjoy some pleasant things, and this occasion is one of them. So it is worth while that I was cured of the measles."[8]

That flash of morbidity was but a prelude that foreshadowed a seizure of lamentation during a speech on the following night, his last ever in the town. The past spilled down upon him and he gave out a cry of anguish that shocked Robertus Love, shocked the five hundred men and women in attendance before him, shocked Laura Frazier who had come to watch and listen; shocked himself, probably: the shock of a man confronted with ghosts. Or rather, the shock of a man confronted with a recessional of ghosts: the ghosts of Margaret and Benjamin and John Marshall and Henry and Jane and Suzy and Orion; the ghosts of all the boys up in the graveyard; the ghost of his own boyhood self. All exiting the stage before his eyes.

His cry was of a man either emerging from or sinking helplessly into a dream.

The occasion was a speech at a women's charitable group called the Labinnah Club—Labinnah being "Hannibal" spelled backwards. Until the moment of his anguished cry, Mark Twain had been stunning, debonair, at the top of his form. "A moment before," wrote Love, "the scores of beautiful girls and matrons, handsomely gowned, and the clubmen and their friends had been laughing heartily at the flashes of Mark Twain's characteristic wit." He had been introduced to the gathering by a local minister, "in flattering terms," and quipped in response that it was hard to reply to such an introduction because all the good things said of him were true. He said some other funny things. He said something that had everyone helpless with mirth.

"His audience roared," Love wrote. "It was said so humorously that laughter exploded like a volcano. Everybody was saying to himself: 'He is the funniest man on earth.'"

Then came the stunning moment. Twain abruptly bowed his head, and his shoulders shook. Love thought that he appeared to be groping for words. "He mumbled something that was not understood, and at last he looked up into the now tense, sympathetic faces of his auditors."

And then Mark Twain became Sam Clemens once again.

"I realize that this must be my last visit to Hannibal," he said to the people who were looking at him, "and in bidding you hail I also bid you farewell."

His voice was choked, his utterance was broken. It was the almost wailing voice of an old man who realized that the

years are behind him and that he is bidding farewell forever and ever to the haunts and comrades of his childhood
days, leaving home never to return.

Mark Twain apparently had forgotten all save his early
life and the consciousness of increasing age. He had forgotten his world-wide fame, the plaudits of princes, the
friendship of emperors, the adulation of the multitudes of
many lands.

He had forgotten his books and his splendid home in
the East.

Nothing remained to him save the past of half a century
ago and the insistent clamor of that inward voice crying
across the years: "Farewell, farewell."

By the next day—Sunday, the first of June, departure day—he had
recovered his aplomb and his sense of humor. He asked a Baptist minister, the Rev. Everett Gill, to walk across town with him to his hotel,
where his luggage awaited him. "It will give me a better standing in
Hannibal," he pronounced, "to be seen on the street with a preacher."

At the railroad station, waiting for his connection to Columbia, he
stood with a spray of flowers in his fist and posed for photographers
one more time. Deaf Tom Nash, wraithlike, stepped from the crowd
then, and called out, "Same damned fools, Sam!"

And then, as it had been on the June day of forty-nine years ago, it
was time to go. A train took him away from his youth this time, instead
of a river packet. In leaving Hannibal for the last time, he was saying
farewell to the ghost of a national past, of an American Arcadia, of an
American concept of "the past," a concept he had largely created and
placed in his boyhood books for preservation. Evaporating now, that

ghost, in the substantial glare of electricity, in the metal hum of the telephone, in Marconi's waves and Einstein's curvatures, and in the gathering thunder of munitions the likes of which the Connecticut Yankee himself could not have imagined.

Times had changed, and water was giving way to fire.

SELECTED
BIBLIOGRAPHY

Books

Blair, Walter, *Mark Twain's Hannibal, Huck & Tom,* Berkeley: University of California Press, 1969.

Bloom, Harold, ed., *Mark Twain: Modern Critical Views,* New York: Chelsea House, 1986.

Bridgman, Edgar M., *Traveling in Mark Twain,* Berkeley: University of California Press, 1987.

Brooks, Van Wyck, *The Ordeal of Mark Twain,* New York: Dutton, 1920.

Cox, James M., *Mark Twain: The Fate of Humor,* Princeton, N.J.: Princeton University Press, 1966.

DeVoto, Bernard, *Mark Twain's America,* Boston: Little, Brown, 1932.

_____, *Mark Twain at Work,* Cambridge, Mass.: Harvard University Press, 1942.

Dunlop, M. H., *Sixty Miles from Contentment,* New York: Basic Books, 1995.

Emerson, Everett, *The Authentic Mark Twain,* Philadelphia: University of Pennsylvania Press, 1984.

Fatout, Paul, *Mark Twain in Virginia City,* Bloomington: Indiana University Press, 1960.

Ferguson, DeLancy, *Mark Twain: Man and Legend,* New York: Charter Books, 1963.

Fishkin, Shelly Fisher, *Lighting Out for the Territory: Reflections on Mark Twain and American Culture,* New York: Oxford University Press, 1997.

Gribben, Alan, *Mark Twain's Library: A Reconstruction,* Boston: G. K. Hall, 1980.

Hagood, J. Hurley and Roberta, *The Story of Hannibal: A Bicentennial History, 1976,* Hannibal: The Hannibal Free Public Library/Standard Printing Co., 1976.

Hecht, Ben, *A Child of the Century,* New York: Primus/Donald I. Fine, 1985.

Holcombe, R. I., *History of Marion County Missouri 1884,* reprinted for the Marion County Historical Society, Marceline, Mo.: Walsworth, 1979.

Howells, William Dean, *My Mark Twain: Reminiscences and Criticisms,* New York: Harper & Bros., 1910.

Hunter, Louis C., *Steamboats on the Western Rivers,* Boston: Harvard University Press, 1949.

Kaplan, Justin, *Mark Twain and His World: America's Greatest Writer and Wit,* New York: Crescent Books, 1974.

_____, *Mr. Clemens and Mark Twain: A Biography,* New York: Simon & Schuster, 1966.

Kerouac, Jack, *On the Road* (40th Anniversary Edition), New York: Viking, 1997.

Kruse, Horst, *Mark Twain and Life on the Mississippi,* Boston: University of Massachusetts Press, 1981.

Lauber, John, *The Making of Mark Twain,* New York: American Heritage, 1985.

Lewisohn, Ludwig, *Expression in America,* New York: Harper & Bros., 1932.

Lynn, Kenneth, *Mark Twain and Southwestern Humor,* Boston: Atlantic Monthly Press, 1959.

Macnaughton, William R., *Mark Twain's Last Years as a Writer,* Columbia: University of Missouri Press, 1979.

Mark Twain–Howells Letters, edited by William M. Gibson and Henry Nash Smith, Cambridge, Mass.: Harvard University Press, 1960.

Mark Twain: Tales, Speeches, Essays, and Sketches, edited by Tom Quirk, New York: Penguin Classics, 1994.

Mark Twain's Letters, Volume 1: 1853–1866, edited by Edgar Marquess Branch, Michael B. Frank, and Kenneth M. Sanderson, Berkeley: University of California Press, 1988.

Mark Twain's Notebooks and Journals, Volume 1: 1855–1873, edited by Frederick Anderson, Michael B. Frank, and Kenneth M. Sanderson, *The Mark Twain Papers,* Berkeley: University of California Press, 1975.

Mark Twain's Satires and Burlesques, edited by Franklin R. Rogers, Berkeley: University of California Press, 1967.

Michelson, Bruce, *Mark Twain on the Loose: A Comic Writer and the American Self,* Amherst: University of Massachusetts Press, 1995.

Paine, Albert Bigelow, *The Adventures of Mark Twain,* New York: Grosset & Dunlap, 1915.

———, *Mark Twain: A Biography: The Personal and Literary Life of Samuel Langhorne Clemens,* New York: Harper & Bros., 1912.

Parini, Jay, *John Steinbeck: A Biography,* New York: Holt, 1995.

Perelman, S. J., *The Road to Milltown, or Under the Spreading Atrophy,* New York: Simon & Schuster, 1957.

Rasmussen, R. Kent, *Mark Twain A to Z: The Essential Reference to His Life and Writings,* New York: Facts on File, 1995.

Sanborn, Margaret, *Mark Twain: The Bachelor Years,* New York: Doubleday, 1990.

Schudson, Michael, *Discovering the News,* New York: Basic Books, 1978.

Tocqueville, Alexis de, *Democracy in America,* New York: Harper & Row, 1966.

Twain, Mark, *The Adventures of Huckleberry Finn: The Only Comprehensive Edition,* Foreword and Addendum by Victor Doyno, New York: Random House, 1996.

———, *The Adventures of Tom Sawyer,* New York: Oxford University Press, 1996.

———, *The Autobiography of Mark Twain,* edited by Charles Neider, New York: Harper & Row, 1959.

———, *The Celebrated Jumping Frog of Calaveras County, and Other Sketches,* edited by Shelly Fisher Fishkin, New York and Oxford: Oxford University Press, 1996.

———, *The Complete Humorous Sketches* and *Tales of Mark Twain,* Garden City, N.Y.: Hanover House, 1961.

———, *A Connecticut Yankee in King Arthur's Court,* New York: Oxford University Press, 1996.

———, *Following the Equator* and *Anti-Imperialist Essays,* New York: Oxford University Press, 1996.

———, *The Innocents Abroad,* New York: Oxford University Press, 1996.

_____, *Letters from the Earth,* edited by Bernard DeVoto, New York: Perennial Library, 1974.

_____, *Life on the Mississippi,* New York: Oxford University Press, 1996.

_____, *Pudd'nhead Wilson,* New York: Penguin Classics, 1986.

_____, *Roughing It,* New York: Oxford University Press, 1996.

_____, *The Works of Mark Twain: Early Tales and Sketches, Volume 1, 1851–1864,* edited by Edgar Marquess Branch and Robert H. Hirst, with the assistance of Harriet Elinor Smith, Berkeley: University of California Press, 1979.

_____, and Charles Dudley Warner, *The Gilded Age: A Tale of Today,* New York: Meridian, 1994.

Wecter, Dixon, *Sam Clemens of Hannibal,* Boston: Houghton Mifflin, 1952.

Whitman, Walt, *Leaves of Grass,* New York: Penguin Books, 1975.

Wonham, Henry B., *Mark Twain and the Art of the Tall Tale,* New York: Oxford University Press, 1993.

Periodicals

The Hannibal *Courier-Post,* April 21, 1910.

The *New York Times,* October 16, 1900.

The *North American Review,* March and April 1907.

The St. Louis *Post-Dispatch,* May 30, 1902.

NOTES

Chapter 1

1. Cited by Justin Kaplan, *Mr. Clemens and Mark Twain: A Biography* (New York: Simon & Schuster, 1966).

2. Twain's dockside comments are quoted from the October 16, 1900, edition of the *New York Times*.

3. Ibid.

4. "Chapters from My Autobiography," *The North American Review* (April 5, 1907); dictated October 1906.

5. Kaplan, op. cit.

6. From the clippings file of the Mark Twain Papers, Bancroft Library, the University of California, Berkeley; quoted by William R. Macnaughton in *Mark Twain's Last Years as a Writer* (Columbia: University of Missouri Press, 1979).

7. Quoted in *The Autobiography of Mark Twain*, edited by Charles Neider (New York: Harper & Row, 1959).

8. Ibid.

9. 1910 essay reprinted in G. K. Chesterton, *A Handful of Authors: Essays on Books and Writers*, edited by Dorothy Collins (New York: Sheed & Ward, 1953).

10. William Dean Howells, *My Mark Twain: Reminiscences and Criticisms* (New York: Harper & Bros., 1910).

11. *Mark Twain–Howells Letters*, edited by William M. Gibson and Henry Nash Smith (Cambridge, Mass.: Harvard University Press, 1960); quoted by Macnaughton.

12. *Letters from the Earth*, edited by Bernard DeVoto (New York: Perennial Library, 1974).

13. Justin Kaplan, *Mark Twain and His World: America's Greatest Writer and Wit* (New York: Crescent Books, 1974).

14. *Mark Twain–Howells Letters,* quoted by Kaplan, *Mr. Clemens and Mark Twain.*

15. *Mark Twain–Howells Letters,* quoted by Macnaughton, op. cit.

16. Mark Twain's notebooks.

Chapter 2

1. Alexis de Tocqueville, *Democracy in America,* part I, ch. 3 (New York: Harper & Row, 1966).

2. Ibid.

3. Dixon Wecter, *Sam Clemens of Hannibal* (Boston: Houghton Mifflin, 1952).

4. Quoted by Walter Blair, op. cit. Walter Blair, *Mark Twain's Hannibal, Huck & Tom,* Berkeley: University of California Press, 1969.

5. Ibid.

6. Ibid.

7. Ibid.

8. Ibid.

9. *The Adventures of Tom Sawyer* (New York: Oxford University Press, 1996).

10. *Pudd'nhead Wilson* (New York: Penguin Classics, 1986).

11. Ibid.

12. Ibid.

13. R. I. Holcombe, *History of Marion County Missouri 1884,* reprinted for the Marion County Historical Society (Marceline, Mo.: Walsworth, 1979).

14. *Autobiography.*

15. "The Facts Concerning the Recent Carnival of Crime in Connecticut," in *The Complete Humorous Sketches and Tales of Mark Twain,* edited by Charles Neider (Garden City, N.Y.: Hanover House, 1961).

16. Wecter, op. cit.

17. "Jane Lampton Clemens," included by Paine in *Autobiography.*

18. *Autobiography.*

19. Ibid.

20. *Mark Twain–Howells Letters* (this letter was written May 19, 1886).

21. See footnote p.568 in *Mark Twain–Howells Letters.*

22. Details of these Kentucky and Tennessee years, and of the Clemens family's migration from Tennessee to Florida, Mo., are taken principally from Wecter, op. cit.

23. Mark Twain and Charles Dudley Warner, *The Gilded Age: A Tale of Today* (New York and Oxford, UK: Oxford University Press, 1996).

Chapter 3

1. From a description of a massacre in Minnesota retold by Satan in *Letters from the Earth.*

2. Wecter, op. cit.

3. Ibid.

4. *Autobiography.*

5. Ibid.

6. Ibid.

7. "Chapters from My Autobiography," *The North American Review* (March 1907).

8. In the preface to "Sociable Jimmy," in *Mark Twain: Tales, Speeches, Essays, and Sketches,* edited by Tom Quirk (New York: Penguin, 1994).

9. Ibid.

10. Bernard DeVoto, *Mark Twain's America* (Boston: Little, Brown, 1932).

11. Wecter, op. cit.

12. Ibid.

13. Ibid.

14. DeVoto, *Mark Twain's America.*

15. Ibid.

16. Probably Mrs. T. B. Aldrich in "Crowding Memories," cited by Kaplan, *Mr. Clemens and Mark Twain.*

17. Ibid.

18. Bernard DeVoto, *Mark Twain at Work* (Cambridge, Mass.: Harvard University Press, 1942).

19. Wecter, op. cit.

Chapter 4

1. Wecter, op. cit.

2. Ibid.

3. *Courier-Post* interview.

4. Autobiographical sketch, Berg Collection, New York Public Library; cited by Wecter, op. cit.

5. *The Gilded Age.*

6. *The Galaxy,* quoted by Wecter, op. cit.

7. Van Wyck Brooks, *The Ordeal of Mark Twain* (New York: Dutton, 1920).

8. Letter to the *Philadelphia American Courier,* cited by Everett Emerson, *The Authentic Mark Twain* (Philadelphia: University of Pennsylvania Press, 1984).

9. *Autobiography.*

10. Ibid.

Chapter 5

1. DeVoto, *Mark Twain's America.*

2. Ludwig Lewisohn, *Expression in America* (New York: Harper & Bros., 1932).

3. *Autobiography.*

4. Ibid.

5. *Adventures of Huckleberry Finn* (New York: Random House, 1996).

6. *Autobiography.*

7. Ibid.

8. Ibid.

9. Ibid.

10. Ibid.

11. Letter to the British psychologist John Adams, cited by Kaplan, *Mr. Clemens and Mark Twain.*

12. *Autobiography.*

13. Albert Bigelow Paine, *Mark Twain: A Biography* (New York: Harper & Bros., 1912).

14. *Autobiography.*

15. Ibid.

16. Ibid.

17. Ibid.

18. Ibid.

19. *The Adventures of Tom Sawyer.*

20. Ibid.

21. Ibid.

22. Ibid.

23. Ibid.

24. Notebook entry, cited by Horst H. Kruse in *Mark Twain and Life on the Mississippi* (Boston: University of Massachusetts Press, 1981).

Chapter 6

1. Blair, op. cit.

2. Paine, *Mark Twain: A Biography.*

3. *The Innocents Abroad.*

4. Wecter, op. cit.

5. *Autobiography.*

6. Ibid.

7. Ibid.

8. Ibid.

9. Ibid.

10. Ibid.

11. Ibid.

12. Ibid.

13. Theodore Hornberger, ed., *Mark Twain's Letters to Will Bowen* (Austin: University of Texas, 1941); cited by Kaplan, *Mr. Clemens and Mark Twain.*

14. James M. Cox, *Mark Twain: The Fate of Humor* (Princeton: Princeton University Press, 1966).

15. Mark Twain's letters to Bowen, cited by Wecter, op. cit.; and by Kaplan, *Mr. Clemens and Mark Twain*. Twain revised and softened this draft of a letter he eventually sent to Bowen.

16. Twain's Notebook No. 16, cited by Blair, op. cit.

17. Wecter, op. cit.

18. *Autobiography*.

19. Ibid.

20. Ibid.

21. Interview in the Hannibal *Courier-Post,* April 21, 1910; cited by Wecter, op. cit.

22. Alan Gribben, *Mark Twain's Library: A Reconstruction* (Boston: G. K. Hall, 1980).

23. *Letters from the Earth.*

24. Newspaper clipping; cited by Wecter, op. cit.

25. Letter in the Keokuk *Gate City* in 1862; cited by Emerson, op. cit.

26. Cited by Kaplan, *Mr. Clemens and Mark Twain.*

27. Cited by Emerson, op. cit.

Chapter 7

1. In "The Adventures of Tom Sawyer: A Nightmare Vision of American Boyhood," *Massachusetts Review* (Winter 1980); reprinted in Harold Bloom, ed., *Mark Twain: Modern Critical Views* (New York: Chelsea House, 1986).

2. *Adventures of Huckleberry Finn.*

3. *Autobiography.*

4. Ibid.

5. *The Innocents Abroad.*

6. Ibid.

7. Ibid.

8. *Autobiography.*

9. *Autobiography.*

10. Walt Whitman, *Leaves of Grass* (New York: Penguin Books, 1975).

11. Ben Hecht, *A Child of the Century* (New York: Primus/Donald I. Fine, 1985).

12. *Autobiography.*

13. Paine, *Mark Twain: A Biography.*

14. Wecter, op. cit.

15. *Adventures of Huckleberry Finn: The Only Comprehensive Edition,* Foreword and Addendum by Victor Doyno (New York: Random House, 1996).

16. Ibid.

17. Ibid.

18. Robert Penn Warren, "Mark Twain," *The Southern Review* (July 1972); reprinted in Bloom, op cit.

19. *Adventures of Huckleberry Finn.*

Chapter 8

1. Wecter, op. cit.

2. Paine, *Mark Twain: A Biography.*

3. "Villagers of 1840–3," printed in *Mark Twain's Hannibal, Huck & Tom.*

4. From his afterword to *The Tragedy of Pudd'nhead Wilson* in *The Oxford Mark Twain* (Oxford, UK: Oxford University Press, 1996).

5. *Autobiography.*

6. Wecter, op. cit.

7. Mark Twain papers; cited by Wecter, op cit.

8. Ibid.

9. Wecter, op. cit.

10. Ibid.

11. Kaplan, *Mr. Clemens and Mark Twain.*

12. "Villagers."

13. Ibid.

14. Paine, *Mark Twain: A Biography.*

15. Ibid.

16. Ibid.

17. Brooks, op. cit.

18. Ibid.

29. Ibid.

20. "Life in Letters of William Dean Howells"; cited by Wecter, op. cit.

Chapter 9

1. DeVoto, *Mark Twain's America.*

2. *Life on the Mississippi.*

3. Kenneth S. Lynn, *Mark Twain and Southwestern Humor* (Boston: Atlantic Monthly Press, 1959).

4. Charles William Janson, quoted by Elliott J. Gorn in *American Historical Review,* 90:1 (February 1985).

5. Quoted by Gorn, op cit.

6. Ibid.

7. As heard in the documentary film, *When We Were Kings,* directed by Leon Gast, released in 1996.

8. *Life on the Mississippi.*

9. Lynn, op. cit.

10. Henry B. Wonham, *Mark Twain and the Art of the Tall Tale* (New York: Oxford University Press, 1993).

11. Ibid.

12. Lynn, op. cit.

13. M. H. Dunlop, *Sixty Miles from Contentment* (New York: Basic Books, 1995).

14. Harriet Martineau, quoted by Dunlop, op cit.

15. Timothy Flint, in a letter cited by Gorn, op. cit.

16. Ibid.

17. Lynn, op. cit.

18. Ibid.

19. Ibid.

20. *Life on the Mississippi.*

21. Ibid.

22. From A. B. Longstreet's "Georgia Theatrics," cited by Lynn, op. cit.

23. Lynn, op cit.

24. DeVoto, *Mark Twain's America.*

25. Richard Bucci, "Afterword" to *The Celebrated Jumping Frog of Calaveras County, and Other Sketches,* in *The Oxford Mark Twain.*

26. Cited by Lynn, op. cit.

Chapter 10

1. Michael Schudson, *Discovering the News* (New York: Basic Books, 1978).

2. J. Hurley and Roberta Hagood, *The Story of Hannibal: A Bicentennial History, 1976* (Hannibal, Mo.: The Hannibal Free Public Library [Standard Printing Co.], 1976).

3. *Autobiography.*

4. Cited by Wecter, op. cit.

5. Ibid.

6. *Autobiography.*

7. "William Dean Howells," in *Mark Twain: Tales, Speeches, Essays, and Sketches.*

8. "The Art of Composition," in *Mark Twain: Tales, Speeches, Essays, and Sketches.*

9. Notebook.

10. "The Last Words of Great Men," in *The Curious Republic of Gondour and Other Whimsical Sketches* (New York: Boni & Liveright, 1919).

11. Introduction, in Albert Bigelow Paine, ed., *Mark Twain's Speeches* (New York: Harper, 1910).

12. *Autobiography.*

13. Ibid.

14. Ibid.

15. Ibid.

16. Ibid.

17. Ibid.

18. Ibid.

19. Ibid.

20. Paine, *Mark Twain: A Biography.*

Chapter 11

1. As reprinted in *The Works of Mark Twain: Early Tales & Sketches, Volume 1, 1851–1864,* edited by Edgar Marquess Branch and Robert H. Hirst, with the assistance of Harriet Elinor Smith (Berkeley: University of California Press, 1979).

2. Ibid.

3. Ibid.

4. Jane Clemens letter printed in Samuel C. Webster, ed., *Mark Twain, Business Man* (Boston: Little, Brown, 1946); cited by Wecter, op. cit.

5. *Autobiography.*

6. Ibid.

7. Mark Twain letter to Howells; cited by Kaplan, *Mr. Clemens and Mark Twain.*

8. Twain, "My First Literary Venture," in Neider, ed., *The Complete Humorous Sketches and Tales.*

9. As recounted in "My First Literary Venture."

10. *Early Tales & Sketches.*

11. Ibid.

12. Ibid.

13. "My First Literary Venture."

14. Quoted by Paul Fatout, *Mark Twain in Virginia City* (Bloomington: University of Indiana Press, 1960).

15. *Autobiography.*

16. *Early Tales & Sketches.*

17. Ibid.

18. S. J. Perelman, "And Thou Beside Me, Yacketing in the Wilderness," from *The Road to Milltown, or Under the Spreading Atrophy* (New York: Simon & Schuster, 1957).

19. Ibid.

20. Ibid.

21. *Autobiography.*

22. *The Adventures of Tom Sawyer.*

23. *Autobiography.*

24. Ibid.

25. Ibid.

26. Ibid.

27. *Early Tales & Sketches.*

28. Wecter, op. cit.

29. Ibid.

Chapter 12

1. *Life on the Mississippi.*

2. Kerouac, *On the Road* (New York: Viking, the 40th Anniversary Edition, 1997).

3. *Life on the Mississippi.*

4. Ibid.

5. Hannibal *Journal;* cited by Wecter, op. cit.

6. *Life on the Mississippi.*

7. *The Adventures of Tom Sawyer.*

8. *Life on the Mississippi.*

9. Ibid.

10. Hagood and Hagood, op. cit.

11. Ibid.

12. Ibid.

13. R. Kent Rasmussen, *Mark Twain A to Z: The Essential Reference to his Life and Writings* (New York: Facts on File, 1995).

14. *Life on the Mississippi.*

15. Cited by Wecter, op. cit.

16. *Early Tales & Sketches.*

17. Ibid.

18. Ibid.

19. Ibid.

20. Ibid.

21. Paine, *Mark Twain: A Biography.*

22. *Roughing It.*

23. Wecter, op. cit.

24. *Early Tales & Sketches.*

25. Ibid.

26. Wecter., op. cit.

27. DeLancy Ferguson, *Mark Twain: Man and Legend* (New York Charter Books, 1963).

28. Paine, *Mark Twain: A Biography*.

29. *Autobiography*.

Chapter 13

1. *Mark Twain's Letters, Volume 1: 1853–1866,* edited by Edgar Marquess Branch, Michael B. Frank, and Kenneth M. Sanderson (Berkeley: University of California Press, 1988).

2. Jay Parini, *John Steinbeck: A Biography* (New York: Holt, 1995).

3. *Mark Twain's Letters, Vol. 1.*

4. Ibid.

5. Ibid.

6. Ibid.

7. Ibid.

8. Ibid.

9. Ibid.

10. Ibid.

11. Ibid.

12. Ibid.

13. Ibid.

14. Ibid.

15. Ibid.

16. Ibid.

17. Ibid.

18. Ibid.

Chapter 14

1. Paine, *Mark Twain: A Biography*.

2. *Autobiography*.

3. Ibid.

4. Margaret Sanborn, *Mark Twain: The Bachelor Years* (New York: Doubleday, 1990).

5. From Orion Clemens's unpublished autobiography, cited by Paine, *Mark Twain: A Biography.*

6. Cited in *Mark Twain's Letters, Vol. 1.*

7. Paine, *Mark Twain: A Biography.*

8. Sanborn, op. cit.

9. Cited in *Mark Twain's Letters, Vol. 1.*

10. Sanborn, op. cit.

11. Ibid.

12. In "The Turning Point of My Life," *Harper's Bazaar* (February 1910).

13. From William Lewis Herndon and Lardner Gibbon, *Exploration of the Valley of the Amazon, Made Under Direction of the Navy Department* (1853–54); cited in *Mark Twain's Letters, Vol. 1.*

14. "Another Grand Filibuster Scheme!" *Daily St. Louis Intelligencer,* March 15, 1855; cited by Edgar Marquess Branch, Mark Twain's Letters, vol. 1, 1853–1866 (Berkeley: University of California Press, 1988).

15. Ibid.

16. Cited by Paine, *Mark Twain: A Biography.*

17. *Mark Twain's Letters, Vol. 1.*

18. Ibid.

19. Ibid.

20. From "Puddn'head Wilson's New Calendar" in "Following the Equator." New York: Oxford University Press, 1996.

21. Cited in Sanborn, op. cit.

22. Ibid.

23. Ibid.

24. *Life on the Mississippi.*

25. Ibid.

26. Ibid.

27. Ibid.

28. Paine, *Mark Twain: A Biography.*

29. Ibid.

30. Ibid.

31. Ibid.

32. Ibid.

33. Mark Twain's autobiographical notes, cited in *Mark Twain's Letters, Vol. 1.*

34. *Life on the Mississippi.*
35. Ibid.
36. Ibid.

Chapter 15

1. Richard Bridgman, *Traveling in Mark Twain* (Berkeley: University of California Press, 1987).
2. *Life on the Mississippi.*
3. Ibid.
4. DeVoto, *Mark Twain's America.*
5. From the New Orleans *True American,* May 11, 1837; cited in Louis C. Hunter, *Steamboats on the Western Rivers* (Boston: Harvard University Press, 1949).
6. Ibid.
7. Ibid.
8. *Life on the Mississippi.*
9. Ibid.
10. Ibid.
11. Paine, *Mark Twain: A Biography.*
12. *Life on the Mississippi.*

Chapter 16

1. *Mark Twain's Letters, Vol. 1.*
2. *Life on the Mississippi.*
3. Ibid.
4. "River News," the Pittsburgh *Gazette,* February 15, 1854; cited in *Mark Twain's Letters, Vol. 1.*
5. Information regarding Clemens's activities in this period is summarized in *Mark Twain's Letters, Vol. 1.*
6. Ibid.
7. Ibid.
8. *Life on the Mississippi.*
9. *Autobiography.*

10. Ibid.

11. Ibid.

12. Ibid.

13. John Lauber, *The Making of Mark Twain* (New York: American Heritage, 1985).

14. *Autobiography.*

15. Ibid.

16. From Pascal Covici, Jr., "Dear Master Wattie: The Mark Twain–David Watt Bowser Letters," *The Southwest Review* (Spring 1960); cited in Kaplan, *Mr. Clemens and Mark Twain.*

17. *Autobiography.*

18. Ibid.

19. Ibid.

20. Ibid.

21. *Life on the Mississippi.*

22. *Mark Twain's Notebooks and Journals, Volume 1 (1855–1873)*, edited by Frederick Anderson, Michael B. Frank, and Kenneth M. Sanderson; *The Mark Twain Papers* (Berkeley: University of California Press, 1975).

23. *Life on the Mississippi.*

24. Ibid.

25. Ibid.

26. Ibid.

27. Ibid.

28. Ibid.

29. Ibid.

30. Ibid.

31. *Mark Twain's Letters, Vol. 1.*

32. *Life on the Mississippi.*

33. Ibid.

34. "The Disaster to the Steamer Pennsylvania: Statement of an Eyewitness," in the Memphis *Morning Bulletin*, June 22, 1858; cited in *Mark Twain's Letters, Vol. 1.*

35. Ibid.

36. *Life on the Mississippi.*

37. Letter to Mollie Clemens, June 18, 1858; cited in *Mark Twain's Letters, Vol. 1.*

38. Fragment of an undated newspaper article; cited in *Mark Twain's Letters, Vol. 1.*

39. *Mark Twain's Letters, Vol. 1.*

40. Ibid.

41. From "Pudd'nhead Wilson's Calendar" in *Pudd'nhead Wilson,* written in 1894.

42. *Mark Twain's Letters, Vol. 1.*

43. *Autobiography.*

44. Ibid.

Chapter 17

1. St. Louis *Post-Dispatch,* May 30, 1902.

2. Ibid.

3. Ibid.

4. Ibid.

5. Ibid.

6. Ibid.

7. Ibid.

8. Ibid.

INDEX